RENEWALS 458-4574

WITHDRAWN
UTSA LIBRARIES

African Parliaments

African Parliaments
Between Governance and Government

Edited by

M.A. Mohamed Salih

AFRICAN PARLIAMENTS
© M.A. Mohamed Salih, 2005.

All rights reserved. No part of this book may be used or reproduced in any manner whatsoever without written permission except in the case of brief quotations embodied in critical articles or reviews.

First published in 2005 by
PALGRAVE MACMILLAN™
175 Fifth Avenue, New York, N.Y. 10010 and
Houndmills, Basingstoke, Hampshire, England RG21 6XS
Companies and representatives throughout the world.

PALGRAVE MACMILLAN is the global academic imprint of the Palgrave Macmillan division of St. Martin's Press, LLC and of Palgrave Macmillan Ltd. Macmillan® is a registered trademark in the United States, United Kingdom and other countries. Palgrave is a registered trademark in the European Union and other countries.

ISBN 1-4039-7122-6

Library of Congress Cataloging-in-Publication Data is available from the Library of Congress.

A catalogue record for this book is available from the British Library.

Design by Newgen Imaging Systems (P) Ltd., Chennai, India.

First edition: December 2005

10 9 8 7 6 5 4 3 2 1

Printed in the United States of America.

Library
University of Texas
at San Antonio

Contents

List of Figures and Tables — vii
List of Abbreviations and Acronyms — ix
Notes on Contributors — xiii
Preface — xvii

PART I

1. Introduction: The Changing Governance Role of African Parliaments — 3
   M.A. Mohamed Salih

2. Parliaments, Politics, and Governance: African Democracies in Comparative Perspective — 25
   Wil Hout

3. Legislative Quotas for Women: Implications for Governance in Africa — 48
   Aili Mari Tripp

4. Local Assemblies and Local Democracy in sub-Saharan Africa — 61
   Dele Olowu

5. Citizen's Support for Legislature and Democratic Consolidation: A Comparative Study with Special Focus on Mali — 79
   Reneske Doorenspleet

PART II

6. Evolution of Parliament–Executive Relations in Zambia — 101
   Jotham C. Momba

7. Longitudinal View on Ghana's Parliamentary Practices 120
Kwame Boafo-Arthur

8. People, Party, Politics, and Parliament: Government and Governance in Namibia 142
Henning Melber

9. Parliament and Dominant Party System in Ethiopia 162
Kassahun Berhanu

10. Parliament as Machinery for Political System Control: The Inner Workings of Bunge, Tanzania 183
Vibeke Wang

11. A Decade of Legislature–Executive Squabble in Malawi, 1994–2004 201
Boniface Dulani and Jan Kees van Donge

12. The South African Parliament's Failed Moment 225
Tim Hughes

13. Conclusions 247
M.A. Mohamed Salih

Bibliography 264

Index 284

List of Figures and Tables

Figures

2.1	Type of Political System and Governance	36
2.2	Type of Electoral System and Governance	37
2.3	Legislature Fractionalization and Governance	38
2.4	Federalism and Governance	39
2.5	Electoral Competitiveness and Governance (Africa)	40
2.6	Democratic Tenure and Governance	41

Tables

2.1	Regression Analyses with Quality of Governance Dependent	33
2.2	Regression Analyses for Africa with Six Governance Components Dependent	35
3.1	Constitutionally Mandated Parliamentary Quotas for Women	50
3.2	Legally Mandated Quotas for Women	51
3.3	Party Mandated Parliamentary Quotas for Women	52
5.1	Mali National Assembly Election Results (July 14, 2002)	82
5.2	Trust in Parliament in Percentage of Population	86
5.3	Influences on Support for the Legislature in Mali	93
7.1	Political Parties Represented in Post-1990s Parliaments, Ghana	131
8.1	Election Results, 1989–1999 for Namibia's Largest Political Parties	146
12.1	South Africa Election Results, 1994, 1999, and 2004	227

List of Abbreviations and Acronyms

ADEMA	Alliance for Democracy in Mali
AFC	Alliance Forces for Change
AforD	Alliance for Democracy
AG	Attorney General
ALF	Africa Leadership Forum
ANC	National African Congress
APNAC	African Parliamentarian Network against Corruption
ARMSCOR	Armaments Corporation of South Africa
BBC	British Broadcasting Corporation
CC	Central Committee
CCAP	Church of Central Africa, Presbyterian
CCM	Chama Cha Mapinduzi
CDC	Constitution Drafting Commission
CEDAW	Convention on the Elimination of Discrimination Against Women
CNID	Congrès National pour l' Initiative Démocratie (National Congress for Democratic Initiative)
CoD	Congress of Democrats
CODESA	Committee of the Convention on Democratic South Africa
CPP	Convention People's Party
CUF	Civic United Front
DA	District Assembly
DCE	District Council Executive
DEC	District Executive Council
DoD	Department of Defense
DTA	Democratic Turnhalle Alliance
ECA	United Nations Commission for Africa
ECN	Electoral Commission of Namibia
ECOWAS	Economic Community of West African States
EHRCO	Ethiopian Human Rights Council

EIU	Economist Intelligence Unit
EPA	Ethiopian Peasants' Association
EPRDF	Ethiopia People's Revolutionary Democratic Front
ETA	Ethiopian Teachers' Association
FDC	Forum for the Defense of the Constitution
FDD	Forum for Democracy and Development
FDRE	Federal Democratic Republic of Ethiopia
FPTP	First-past-the-poste
GCA	Global Coalition for Africa
GCC	Gaborone City Council
GDP	Gross Domestic Product
GNU	Government of National Unity
HIPC	Highly Indebted Poor Countries
HIV/AIDS	Human Immunodeficiency Virus/Acquired Immune Deficiency Syndrome
HOF	House of the Federation
HPR	House of People's Representatives
HRM	Human Resources Management
ICT	Information and Communication Technology
IDEA	Institute for Democratic and Electoral Assistance
IEG	Imperial Ethiopian Government
IFP	Inkatha Freedom Party
IPU	Inter-Parliamentary Union
LASDAP	Local Authority Service Development Plan
LC	Local Council
LCAC	Legal and Constitutional Affairs Committee
MAG	Monitor Action Group
MCP	Malawi Congress Party
MGODE	Movement for Genuine Democratic Change
MMD	Movement for Multiparty Democracy
MP	Member of Parliament
MPR	Mouvement Patriotique pour le Renouveau (Patriotic Movement for Renewal)
NA	National Assembly
NARC	National Rainbow Coalition
NCC	Nairobi City Council
NCOP	National Council of Provinces
NDA	National Democratic Alliance
NEC	National Electoral Commission
NEC	National Executive Committee (Tanzania)
NGOs	Non-Governmental Organizations

NIP	National Industrial Participation
NMB	National Microfinance Bank
NORDEM	Norwegian Institution of Human Rights
NUDO	National Unity Democratic Organization
NWMN	Namibian Women Manifesto Network
OIC	Organization of Islamic Conference
PAC	Public Accounts Committee
PAC	Public Affairs Committee
PDRE	People's Democratic Republic of Ethiopia
PM	Presiding Member
PMAC	Provisional Military Administrative Council
RDR	Rassemblement pour la Démocratie du Ravail (Rally for Labour Democracy)
REWA	Revolutionary Ethiopian Women Association
REYA	Revolutionary Ethiopian Youth Association
RPM	Rassemblement pour le Mali (Rally for Mali)
SADC	Southern African Development Community
SANDF	South African National Defense Force
SCOPA	Standing Committee on Public Accounts
SISCD	State Institutions Supporting Constitutional Democracy
SNNPR	Southern Nations, Nationalities and People's Region
SWAPO	South West African People's Organization
TANU	Tanganyika African National Union
UDF	United Democratic Front
ULA	Uganda Land Alliance
UNCW	United Nations Conference on Women
UNDP	United Nations Development Program
UNIP	United National Independence Party
UNTAG	United Nations Transitional Assistance Group
UPND	United Party for National Development
UWONET	Uganda Women Network
WPE	Worker's Party of Ethiopia
ZAR	South Africa Rand (currency)

Notes on Contributors

Kassahun Berhanu (Ph.D. Free University Amsterdam, The Netherlands) is Assistant Professor and Chair of the Department of Political Science and International Relations at Addis Ababa University. He has published on a range of issues pertaining to elections (*Review of African Political Economy* 1995), refugees and land tenure (*Ethiopian Journal of Development Research*, 1998), and is the author of: *State Building and Democratization in Ethiopia* (Greenwood Press, 1998), *Ethnicity and Social Conflicts in Ethiopia* (Heinrich Boll Foundation, 2000), *The Role of NGOs in Promoting Democratic Values in Ethiopia* (Nordiska Afrika Instituet, forthcoming), *Returnees, Resettlement and Power Relations: The Making of a Political Constituency in Humera, Ethiopia* (Free University of Amsterdam Press, 2000).

Kwame Boafo-Arthur (Ph.D. University of Ghana) is Head of the Department of Political Science at the University of Ghana. He was Fulbright Senior African Research Scholar at the James S. Coleman African Studies Centre, University of California at Los Angeles and Visiting Research Fellow at the Nordic African Institute Uppsala, Sweden. He published widely on Ghanaian politics, democratization, and political economy as well as on African development and international economic relations, conflicts, and democratization in Africa. He has published in prestigious journals such as *African Journal of Political Science* (2000), *West African Review* (2001), and *Journal of African and Asian Studies* (2003).

Reneske Doorenspleet (Ph.D. University of Leiden, The Netherlands) is Postdoctoral Fellow at the Belfer Center for Science and International Affairs at Harvard University, USA. Her current research interests include democracy in divided societies, funded by the Dutch Science Foundation at Leiden University in the Netherlands. She has authored a number of journal articles and book chapters on democratization, freedom, and the press in Senegal, definitions and waves of democracy. She is author of "The Fourth Wave of Democratization" (Ph.D. dissertation: University of Leiden, 2001) and articles in journals including *Acta Politica* and *World Politics*.

Boniface Madaltso Dulani (M.Phil. University of Sussex, UK) is Lecturer in Political Science and Development Studies at the Department of Political and Administrative Studies, Chancellor College, University of Zambia. He has published numerous commissioned papers on political transition in Zambia for the Rockefeller Foundation and the World Bank's Operations Evaluation Department.

Wil Hout (Ph.D. University of Leiden, The Netherlands) is Associate Professor in International Relations and Development at the Institute of Social Studies in The Hague. He is the author of *Capitalism and the Third World* (Aldershot: Edward Elgar, 1993), co-editor (with Jeon Grugel) of *Regionalism Across the North–South Divide* (London: Routledge, 1999), and co-editor of three Dutch-language volumes on issues of international relations and political science. He has published on issues of international political economy in such journals as the *European Journal of International Relations*, the *Third World Quarterly, Development and Change*, and *Acta Politica: International Journal of Political Science*.

Tim Hughes (M.A. cum laude, University of Cape Town, South Africa) is Parliamentary Research Fellow at the South African Institute of International Affairs. Until 2001, he lectured in Political Studies at the University of Cape Town, acted as a policy advisor to EU parliamentarians and as Team Leader on the Southern Africa Development Cooperation Futures Scenario (SADCFS) research program. He recently completed a book on the formulation of South African foreign policy and international best practices. Currently, he is engaged in a long-term project on strengthening parliamentary democracy in southern Africa.

Henning Melber (Ph.D. in Political Science and venia legendi, University of Bremen, Germany) is Director of Research at the Nordic Africa Institute in Uppsala, Sweden. He was Director of the Namibian Economic Policy Research Unit (NEPRU) in Windhoek, Namibia between 1992 and 2000. His latest books (as editor and contributor) include: *It is No More a Cry: Namibian Poetry in Exile and Essays on Literature in Resistance and Nation Building* (Basel: Basler Afrika Bibliographien, 2004); *Re-examining Liberation in Namibia. Political Culture since Independence* (Uppsala: Nordic Africa Institute, 2003); *Limits to Liberation in Southern Africa: The Unfinished Business of Democratic Consolidation* (Cape Town, Human Sciences Research Council, 2003); and *Zimbabwe's Presidential Elections 2002: Evidence, Lessons and Implications* (Uppsala: The Nordic Africa Institute, 2002).

Jotham C. Momba (Ph.D. Toronto, Canada) is Associate Professor of Political Science in the Department of Political and Administrative

Studies at the University of Zambia. He has contributed several journal articles and book chapters on Zambian politics. His most recent publications include "Change and Continuity in Zambia's Southern African Policy: Kaunda to Chiluba" *Africa Insight*, 31/2 (2001) and "Democratic Transition and the Crisis of an African Nationalist Party: UNIP, Zambia" in M. A. Mohamed Salih (ed.) African Political Parties (London: Pluto Press, 2003).

Dele Olowu (Ph.D. Public Administration, University of Ife, Nigeria) is Senior Governance Advisor at the African Development Bank. He was Professor of Public Administration and Local Government Studies at Obafemi Awolowo University, Nigeria, and has also served as advisor to a number of African governments on public sector management reforms, including Nigeria (his home country), Ethiopia, Sierra Leone, and Mozambique. He was resident/consultant advisor to the United Nations Economic Commission for Africa on Governance and capacity building from 1995 to 1998, after which he joined the ISS. His most recent books include *African Perspectives on Governance in Africa* (Asmara: Africa World Press, 2000), *Better Governance and Public Policy: Capacity Building for Democratic Renewal in Africa* (Bloomfield: Kumarian Press, 2002), *Local Governance in Africa: The Challenge of Democratic Decentralization* (Boulder: Lynne Rienner, 2003).

M.A. Mohamed Salih (Ph.D. University of Manchester, UK) is Professor of Politics of Development at both the Institute of Social Studies, The Hague and the Department of Political Science, University of Leiden, The Netherlands. Among his recent books are *African Democracies and African Politics* (London: Pluto press, 2001), *African Pastoralism: Conflict Institutions and Government* (London: Pluto Press, 2001), *African Political Parties: Evolution, Institutionalisation and Governance* (London: Pluto Press, 2003) and *Africa Networking: Information Development, ICTs and Governance* (Utrecht: International Books and Addis Ababa: the United Nations Economic Commission for Africa, 2004).

Aili Mari Tripp (Ph.D. Northwestern University, USA) is Professor of Political Science, Associate Dean of International Studies, Director of the Women's Studies Research Center, and Professor of Political Science and Women's Studies. Her teaching and research interests are in African politics, comparative politics, and gender studies in an international context. She is author of *Women and Politics in Uganda* (Madison: University of Wisconsin Press, 2000) and *Changing the Rules: The Politics of Liberalization and the Urban Informal Economy in Tanzania* (Berkeley and Los Angeles: University of California press, 1997). She is editor of

Sub-Saharan Africa: The Greenwood Encyclopedia of Women's Issues Worldwide (Wesport: Greenwood Press, 2003), and co-editor of *The Women's Movement in Uganda: History, Challenges and Prospects* (Kampala: Fountain, 2002) and *What Went Right in Tanzania? People's Responses to Directed Development* (Dar es Salaam: University of Dar es Salaam Press, 1996). She has also published articles and book chapters on women and politics in Africa, women's responses to economic reform, and transformations of associational life in Africa. She is currently co-authoring a book on the political impact of women's movements in Africa.

Jan Kees van Donge (Ph.D. Wageningen University, The Netherlands) is Senior Lecturer in Public Policy and Management at the Institute of Social Studies, The Hague, The Netherlands. He is the author of *Zambia: A World Bibliographic Series* (Abc-Clio Inc., 2001). Among the journals in which he has published are *Journal of Development Studies* (1999), *Development and Change* (2001), and *Journal of Modern Africa*, and *African Affairs*.

Vibeke Wang (Cand. Polit. Degree, University of Bergen, Norway) is a political scientist focusing on the study of parliaments, watchdog institutions, and democratic accountability in new democracies—in particular, Tanzania, Uganda, and Malawi. She is currently a research assistant at Christian Michelsen Institute, Bergen, Norway.

Preface

Today's intense debate over the role of institutions in peoples' life brings to sharp focus the position of parliaments (also known as legislatures and assemblies) in the relatively new democracies of Africa. As Dr. Roel von Meijenfeldt, Director of the Netherlands Institute of Multiparty Democracy, who endorsed this book that enjoyed the support of his Institute and staff, laments, "For democracy to deepen and to contribute to social cohesion of societies, parliaments and political parties are essential building blocks." I came to this realization when I initiated a research program in 2000 called "Managing Democracies" under the auspices of an "Innovation Fund" arrangement blessed by Professor Hans Opschoor, the then Rector of the Institute of Social Studies (ISS), one of the leading European Development Institutes. The innovative element of the Innovation Fund is to take on board issues that are important for the academic community, yet overlooked or understudied, or issues that could enhance cooperation with other academic institutions and consortia or attract "external" financial support. This particular book falls into the category of important social and political subjects that have not gained the attention they deserve from the academic and publishing communities. This undertaking has also attracted the attention of Mr. Denise Kodhe, Executive Director of the then Institute of Liberal Democracy in Kenya, now renamed the Institute for Democracy in East Africa (IDEA) that have lent it their financial and institutional support.

Not all the papers presented at the Nairobi Conference on African Parliaments in April 2003 found their way into this volume. As contributors to this volume, we benefited greatly from the excellent opening and closing speeches of the workshop offered by the Honorable Professor Anyang Nyong, Kenya Minister for Planning (Social Democratic Party) and the Honorable Mr. Raila Odinga, Kenya Minister for Housing and Public Works (Liberal Democratic Party), respectively. The quality of the debate was enriched by heated discussions lead by the parliamentarians themselves who not only defended their parliamentary record in the new era of multiparty democracy but also challenged our academic and theoretical understandings of African parliaments, which are, by and large, Western—not the least due to our educational backgrounds and, to some extent, socialization to Western democratic values.

This book also received invaluable helping hands from two colleagues known for their passion for supporting women in parliament: Ms. Elizabeth Sidiropoulos, Deputy Director of the South African Institute of International Affairs (SAIIA), who gave permission to Mr. Tim Hughes to publish some of the work he has undertaken for the Institute as a chapter in this volume under the title "The South African Parliament's Failed Moment." The second is Ms. Julie Ballington, the Women in Politics Program Officer at the International Institute for Democracy and Electoral Assistance (IDEA), who gave Professor Aili Mari Tripp permission to publish an intensively revised version of the chapter entitled "Legislative Quotas for Women" in this volume.

I am most grateful to the many colleagues whose opinions I sought in various stages of the production of this book, but they cannot all possibly be mentioned in this preface, and to the contributors to this volume. I know some of them must have been very frustrated by the apparent absence of a single volume or textbook wholly devoted to the study of African legislatures, which would have made the initial journey of writing their chapters much easier. I am also most grateful for their patience and perseverance to be at the receiving end of an unruly and, at times, too vocal an editor. I am also thankful to Ms. Leslie O'Brien who I am yet to meet in person but who has done a remarkable job in making a coherent reading of our diverse English writing styles which expand the African continent in the Netherlands, USA, Norway, and beyond.

Finally, it is my hope that the outcome is worth the effort—the first single volume addressing the thorny issue of the role of parliament in African political life under the new democratic desperations the continent is experiencing.

Mohamed Salih
The Hague, The Netherlands
March, 2005

Part I

1

Introduction: The Changing Governance Role of African Parliaments

M.A. *Mohamed Salih*

Department of Political Science, University of Leiden,
Institute of Social Studies, The Hague, The Netherlands

Interchangeably used, legislatures, parliaments or assemblies are mirrors of the nature of the state (democratic or authoritarian), party systems (one-party, multiparty, or dominant party), and political culture. They are representative institutions ideally established to represent citizens and reflect the range of citizens' preferences as expressed in elections. Legislatures literally legislate and amend laws[1] as well as sanction or amend major policies and policy shifts, and, as such, are caught between fulfilling a significant governance role while acting as part of the machinery of government. On the one hand, legislators hold the executive accountable to citizen representatives. On the other, they hold the power of the burse and assume an important (if not one of the most important) governance role as representatives of the majority political party or parties in parliament. This is particularly so because legislatures are mandated by constitution to maintain oversight in spheres where the executive's private deeds or misdeeds may clash with public interests.

In this sense African legislatures, like other legislatures, are caught between two competing roles as first, part of the machinery that confers legitimacy on governments and makes or breaks governments by exercising the right to a vote of no confidence and second, as pivotal oversight institutions responsible for scrutinizing the activities of government in order to maintain high-quality governance and safeguard the public interest vis-à-vis any attempt by the executive to conflate public and private interests. Generally, the contention between, and the quality of, legislature practice in fulfilling these two roles has eluded politicians and political scientists alike in most democratic governments, old or new.

Informed by the tension between legislature and executives, the objective of this volume is to offer a broad perspective analyzing and explaining African parliamentary developments and their changing governance fortunes emanating from straddling the contested arena between government and governance. This chapter, indeed the rest of the book, traces the development of African parliaments vis-à-vis the principles and practices of democratic systems of government. The chapters grapple with the question as to whether African parliaments are unique and exhibit the specificity of Africa's political culture or, because they oscillate between tradition and modernity, whether African parliaments are more effective in responding to social problems and common public interest issues than governance roles vis-à-vis government determined by their constant quest to adapt to generic parliamentary principles. I will return to these questions in the Conclusion (Chapter 13), which also attempts to tease out the implications of answering these questions for the tension between parliaments' governance role and the executive.

Introduction

Originally, parliaments in their modern form were peculiar to the West and assemblies were common features of Africa's pre-colonial states, historic kingdoms, and centralized chiefdoms, such as Zulu (South Africa),[2] Buganda (Uganda),[3] Ashante (Ghana), Zande (Sudan)[4] and Nupe (Nigeria),[5] mentioning just a few. The rulers of these kingdoms were subjected to the scrutiny of aspirant royals, elders and regularly renegade interest groups that challenged their rule. The assemblies here govern jointly with the princes through the administrative and judicial control of a territory and possession of a monopoly of military force, supported by systematic taxation.[6] There were also centralized as well as dispersed chiefdoms where most African ethnic groups had councils of elders and sophisticated subordinate territorial chiefs, religious officials, among other institutionalized restraints upon autocracy. For example, the Bemba (Zambia), the Lou (Kenya), the Anuak (Sudan), Tiv (Nigeria), Oromo (Ethiopia), etc. qualify as groups with such councils.[7] Coleman[8] observes that, "One found the core of the concept of constitutionalism and the assumption of a measure of popular participation—direct or indirect—in the political process." In addition, "the centralized chiefdoms were not necessarily autocratic; rather, there frequently existed a variety of countervailing forces which acted as checks on the arbitrary exercise of chiefly power."

The colonial experience introduced Africans to the Western concept of assemblies or parliaments and had used, to some extent, residual African political systems to rule the continent and formed political parties in an earlier "political modernization" drive.[9] In the urge to leave behind democratic political institutions, the departing colonial powers decided "to export to Africa their peculiar version of parliamentary government, with several parties and recognized opposition" being created.[10] In some countries, it took the African educated political elite less than a decade from establishing political parties to contesting elections and assuming the role of government in their countries.[11]

In order to establish constituent assemblies responsible for constitution making to prepare the colonies for self-rule, the colonial powers hastily created political parties that contested elections and elected representative assemblies. Due to the accelerated pace with which political development was engineered, ethnic groups were the only widespread institutional framework within which the majority of Africans were organized. The emergent political parties and the educated elite who established them found ethnic associations and groups readily available structures on which modern political parties became vehicles for ensuring representation in the constituent assemblies. Numerous ethnically based parties emerged and in some incidences one ethnic group provided the opposition required by minority ethnic groups. Once these political parties were established, they began to assume the structures and functions of Western style political parties. Upon their founding, they contested elections and assimilated some of the institutional norms and behaviors of their Western counterparts, exhibiting the form rather than the substance.[12] Subsequently, African political parties formed "constituent assemblies" and assumed the role of legislature under colonial rule and guidance. Clearly, the process from creating political parties to forming parliaments or assemblies differed from country to country, as the chapters of this volume will explain.

Large and small political parties represented in African parliaments are to some extent ethnically tented, thus maintaining some continuity as well as affinity between African political and organizational culture and the parliaments that constitute the legislatures as supreme institutions expressing peoples' sovereignty. This is particularly so because, historically, the emergence of African political parties preceded the emergence of parliaments, assemblies, or legislatures.[13] In contrast, in Europe, powerful trends of ideology, opinion, popular clubs, trade unions, the church, philosophical societies, and parliamentary groups emerged before the formation of political parties in the strict sense of the term. Essentially, no real parties in the modern sense preceded the emergence of Western democracies and parliamentary systems.[14]

The precedence of parties over assemblies is important in two senses. First, parliaments, assemblies, or legislatures in Africa emerged as a result of the formation of modern political parties and not as a result of the "natural" evolution Africa's endogenous polity, political systems, chiefly, or monarchical assemblies. Second, at the dawn of independence, Africans' exposure to Western-style political parties and assemblies was too short to ensure the internalization of the political values and practices associated with it, which I will explain in the course of this introduction. However, once established, African early legislatures were miniature indirect rule, up-scaled to operate at the national level as constitutional foundations for the machinery of government. Evidently, when the early parliamentary governments of the post-colonial era degenerated into one-party systems, the loyalty of Members of Parliament to their constituencies superseded their loyalty to the party.[15] The continuity of Members of Parliament as fixtures of ethnic representation after the restoration of multiparty democracy during the early 1990s is glaring evidence of the association between political party, voter behavior, ethnic affiliation, and legislature membership.[16]

Although this is the subject of another volume, it is noteworthy that the recent global resurgence of the debate on governance as part of development aid conditionality has neglected the continuity between African parliaments and assembles, on the one hand, and local governance institutions, on the other. In the bid to conform with the international development conditionality imposed by donor agencies and global economic governance, modernization revisionism has triumphed over tradition.[17] This unfortunate neglect of local governance occurred at a time when legislatures are constantly distracted by violent conflicts (Somalia, Liberia, Sierra Leone, Sudan, Burundi, Great Lakes, etc.) and social problems (HIV/AIDS and other endemic diseases) that require more and not less local participation and locally adapted solutions.

Parliaments between government and governance pose tensions between the two roles and the parliaments' capacity to ensure the fulfillment of their triple heritage in augmenting competitive democratic systems: responsive representation, accountability, delegation, and the rule of law.

The following section deals with African parliamentary development and governance roles from colonial rule to independence.

Parliaments from Colonial Rule to Independence

When Africa began to experiment with the norms of her first advisory councils/legislative assemblies and even contesting the first elections ever in the history of the continent, the political parties were embryonic. There was clearly a diligent African attempt to adopt and practice liberal democracies similar to Europe, particularly under the influence of political development, and the departing colonial powers quest to transplant the seeds of political modernization.[18]

The emergence of Western-style political institutions (government structures, including parliament, constitution and law, bureaucracy, policy, and the army) empowered with the educated African elite took a steady pace toward self-rule. Parliaments became the rallying point embodying the new hope for an Africanized machinery of government operating under the Africanization banner. They represented the growing aspirations for sovereignty conferred on their elected representatives.

Largely, the dominant governance role of parliaments during the colonial period was confined to at least four prominent domains:

1. *Political modernization.* Signaling the shift from traditional to modern assemblies. In this sense, parliaments were conceived as the natural successor, albeit in a modern context of traditional political/judicial institutions shifting loyalty away from traditional assemblies and councils of elders to modern Western institutions operated by Western-style educated elite.
2. *Political socialization.* Following the Second World War and the emergence of a reformed colonial state thereafter, the involvement of educated Africans in the lower levels of administration became more acceptable. The spread of education, the creation of urban associations and trade unions facilitated the emergence of a political community with clear aspirations for independence and self-rule. On its part, the colonial administration was bent on leaving behind political systems similar to those of the West.
3. *Constitutional development.* Political parties similar to those of the West were founded and organized in haste and political elites took their seats in constituent assemblies with the main objective of developing national constitutions to i) empower the state to undertake its responsibility vis-à-vis government; ii) establish unifying governing values and goals; iii) provide government stability; iv) protect freedom; and v) legitimize government.
4. *Legislation.* This role was part of the colonial government policy to establish three distinct branches of government (legislature,

executive, and judiciary) with identifiable functions similar to those of their Western counterparts. The rule of parliament is to legislate in the emerging post-colonial state.
5. *Representation*. Legislatures evolved as a means for representing society, geographical areas, and interests in parliaments and assemblies. This could also be viewed as a shift from the non-representative colonial military-civil administration to an African administration fully dominated by Africans representing Africans.

Because the apparatus of government was still under colonial control in the form of civil–military administration, the role of African Constituent Assemblies, which were sought to prepare Africans for constitutional sovereignty, was limited, but could not be dismissed as unimportant. Socializing Africans to democratic norms is, in my view, the most important endeavor as far as educating Africans with no experience of parliamentary institutions and how they operate in the real world.

Despite misgivings about colonial political engineering, the advisory council and legislative assemblies (not free to decide on all issues that really matter to Africans—the Civil Secretary, as Chair of such Councils, was authorized to suspend the discussion at any time and on any matter that was deemed sensitive) provided the participating Africans with a first glimpse of how modern government institutions operate. It is possible to generalize that the African political elite learned their early political education lessons on governing from colonial officials who, by the very nature of their creed, were second-rate democrats. Some of the worst lessons the African political elite learned from their early exposure to modern political institutions, including political parties and parliaments, persisted and, in so many ways, continue to haunt the continent's independence. One example was the granting of privileges to the leaders of the largest political parties, whose claims to power continued to derive legitimacy from the role their ancestors had as tribal chiefs or from those who played an important role in independence. The performance of these in post-independence party and parliamentary institutions cannot be underestimated, but also the excesses of some are unforgivable. Another negative political ramification particular to the colonial advisory councils and/or legislative assemblies during the closing decade of the colonial period was the selective manner in which important issues were presented for debate. Some issues which were not in Africans' interests were thoroughly discussed and resolutions adopting them were passed quickly, while others (such as land and the Africanization of the civil service) were not fully discussed or were left hanging without a resolution. The powers of such advisory councils or legislative assemblies were entirely advisory and could only be given within certain limits, in accordance with strict rules that were set out, in considerable detail.

In short, despite my critique of the colonial legislative assemblies, advisory councils, and parliaments, they represented the first lessons in modern parliamentary theory and practice. The combined heritage of African traditional governance and, where contradictions existed, the political elite favored modernity over tradition and began to assert the form and not the substance of Western-style assemblies. This could be attested in the manner in which many a political leader had reversed the trend toward strong leaders (presidential systems) with one-party rule and a duck parliament, thus simulating the role of chiefs in traditional African polity. The main difference is that traditional African polity values were superimposed on modern political institutions that have logic of their own.

The governance structures left behind by the colonialists carried with them the insignia of an authoritarian non-democratic state and, with it, governance structures that were state-centered. I argue elsewhere that the leaders of the independence movements were statist, as state-centered leaders. For them, the human security of citizens was subservient to state security. It is for this reason that they accorded the state not only the right to abuse its monopoly over the use of power and coercion, but also to lay claim on the monopoly of the truth whereby the state was always considered right and its opponents wrong. This attitude ushered in the genesis of a wave of constitutional reforms and the slide toward one-party rule in a large number of African states.

African Parliaments in One-Party Systems

The changing role of African parliaments is closely tied to the party systems that evolved since independence. Political parties are products of historical circumstances that contributed to their emergence. In this sense, the substance of political parties mirrors the social, economic, and political relations in society. Due to the speed with which political development occurred, numerous ethnically based parties emerged in opposition to other ethnic parties. Once these political parties were established, they began to assume the structures and functions of Western-styled political parties, poised to engage parliamentary democracy.

After the attainment of independence and the waning of the flare of "decolonization nationalism," the political elite consumed the goal of national unity, the very goal that gave birth to their political ambitions, and fell back to sub-nationalist politics. In some countries (Sudan, Nigeria, Congo, Angola, Mozambique, Uganda, among others), sub-nationalism flared into second wars of what is termed "second liberation" from what some marginalized and minority ethnic political elite conceived as a form of internal colonialism exacted by "the ruling ethnicity." Unfortunately, the majority of African leaders opted for banning political parties, describing them as divisive and a danger to national unity, and instituted one-party systems instead. Some of these political parties, were heirs of power from the colonial rule and others were created by military rulers to bring about development and national integration to what they misconstrued as the threat of division to national integration.[19]

In many a country, civilian politicians who inherited power soon began to ban existing political parties, except their own, and transformed their states into one-party systems in order to achieve goals similar to those pronounced by military leaders, including development and national integration. As recent history and subsequent events have shown, both goals remained elusive. According to Freund, during the struggle for independence, "African political parties provided an all-purpose appeal. The party invariably claimed to represent the African people, but never admitted to speaking for the interests of specific class and/or ethnicity. After independence, a vaguely articulated 'African socialism' was adhered to in an attempt to reconcile the aspirations of the ambitious few with the needs of the majority."[20]

Initially, parliaments became the rallying point, the voice of the people and statehood in newly established national governments still trusted and treated as the unifying institution that galvanized people's hope for development and national integration. It is also true that no matter how we judge the misgivings of these early parliaments, they were able to shoulder the responsibility of statehood and sovereignty (whether ethnic or secular) and the debate of impending national issues with passion and responsibility. However, legislature experiences differ from one country to another, but they largely subscribed to the norms of parliamentary democracy.

In less than a decade after independence, the majority of the African states were transformed by authoritarian leaders into one-party states, military or military socialist regimes. The best example one can give in this respect is Eastern Africa. At the dawn of independence and in common with other ex-British colonies, Kenya's, Tanzania's, and Uganda's independence constitutions embodied liberal democratic principles: the rule of law, separation of powers, independence of the judiciary, impartiality of civil service and armed forces, popular participation through regular, free and fair elections and parliamentary supremacy. The constitutions also provided for a prime ministerial and cabinet system and made a dichotomy between the formal authority of the constitutional Head of State and the real authority of the Head of Government, the Prime Minister the leader of the majority party.²¹ A Series of constitutional amendments had reversed the system either under the one-party system or dominant party systems into dual to unified executive in Tanzania and Kenya, that circumvented the principle of parliamentary supremacy and elevated the chief executive and executive branch to a powerful dominant machinery of government. The legislature was no longer in a position to discipline or vote a government out of office on grounds of incompetence, gross inefficiency, or abuse of power because the vote of no confidence was not provided for in the constitution.

The constitutional amendments of the late 1960s and 1970s weakened parliament and strengthened presidential and executive powers. There is no gainsaying that parliaments suffer under one-party rule, although, to be fair, during the 1990s individual and collective parliamentary revolts by courageous Members of Parliament gave parliamentary debate a sense of seriousness and urgency.

With respect to the parliament role under a one-party system, at least five observations could be made:

1. Parliaments were formed and expected to be loyal to the single and at times constitutional political party or military rulers and ensure that the laws and legislations put forward by government were rubber-stamped. The absence of separation of power made the relationship between the legislature, the executive, and the judiciary so blurred that checks and balances and accountability are non-existent.²²
2. One-party system parliaments were considered all-purpose institutions, which indulged not only in enacting laws and legislations, but also in decision-making, policy implementation, and justification of executive decisions. Therefore, the relationships between legislature and executive, on the one hand, and executive authority and the judiciary, on the other, were muddled so that national political issues could hardly ever be discussed openly.
3. Legislative powers of parliaments were under the scrutiny of the ruling party. Not only were the Members of Parliament not in fact the true representatives of the electorates but were often carefully vetted by the central committee of the ruling party before they were allowed to contest elections. In some one-party system parliaments, more than 25 percent of the members were selected from social forces (army officers, professionals, youths, and women) considered vanguards of the regime (see the cases of Ethiopia and Zambia, in this volume, during one-party rule).
4. One-party system parliaments were not only bound up with the executive in a manner that made a mockery of the doctrine of

the separation of power, they were used to bestow legitimacy on an illegitimate and non-competitive political process. In this sense, the government was not accountable to a parliament freely elected by and responsive to the electorate's preferences and aspirations.
5. Parliaments were the voice of the ruling elite and the oppressive regimes they represented—not the expression of peoples' sovereignty. The role of parliaments was largely the affirmation and confirmation of the status quo, thus leading to political oppression in the absence of judicial independence. In one-party systems, opposition is considered dissent and prosecuted under the watchful eye of the Members of Parliament who pledged their loyalty to the supreme leader and the ruling party.

The governance role of parliament in one-party systems could be described as muted at best and oppressive at worst. In authoritarian state-centered governance such as those of the 1970s, parliament as space for people's participation through their representative legislatures was curtailed and duly made subservient to the whim of an authoritarian state rule by dictats.

In the view of the type of "bad governance" that had prevailed in states governed by a single political party, the changing fortunes of the African parliament during the current era of multiparty democracy could not and should not be underestimated. Governance within this context meant oppression, dictat and rule by decree, without legitimacy or public consent. Parliaments were subdued and their functions were muted to the extent that they were forced to rebel and in some countries contributed significantly to democratic agitations and the transition to democracy. With the transition, African legislatures became part of a new concept of governance referred to in the lexicon of the current neo-liberal paradigm as "good governance," with its national and global reference points.

African Parliaments in Multiparty Democracy

The democratization process which spread during the 1990s contributed to the dominance of multiparty systems and with it a considerable change in the role of parliamentary systems across the African continent. With some apparent exceptions, while one-party systems disappeared, the tendency toward establishing a dominant party system or two-party system under the guise of a multiparty system has not. What we could celebrate, however, is the disappearance of one-party systems and the emergence of competitive politics, where parliaments gained a considerable proportion of the ground they lost during the period from the late 1960s to the early 1990s.

With multiparty democracy, African parliaments began to assume more seriously the six generic roles of political governance:

1. Legislation, where proposals and programs emanate, in the main, from the political executive.
2. Representation by providing the link between government and people.
3. Scrutiny of the executive to ensure that government is accountable, including the power to remove it.
4. Political recruitment of a pool of talent, some of which is expected to find its way to leading political and decision-making positions.
5. Legitimacy through representative legislation, debating public affairs and government performance openly.
6. Conflict management.

The extent to which African parliaments have been able to discharge these generic functions is contingent on several factors, not least the nature of the political environment within which they operate, the strength of political institutions and civil society organizations, and the constitutional arrangements governing the relationship between legislature and executive. However, we must realize that these parliamentary functions must have been reconfigured to respond to the new concepts such as shared governance or the governance continuum linking state-centered and societal-centered governance.

The role of parliament in the governance debate cannot be overstated, particularly in the case of Africa where the current wave of democratic consolidation is in its embryonic stage. In addition to the classic generic roles that I stated earlier (legislation, representation, scrutiny, recruitment, legitimacy, and conflict management), African parliaments are increasingly invited to take a more profound role in anti-corruption campaigns, gender auditing, observance of social justice, and ethnic or violent conflict management.

Generally, political parties historically developed as part of the parliamentary system with the notion that Members of Parliament represent the whole nation. Expressing the will of sovereign citizens and using their own conscience is common to all African legislatures. However, a democratic model with clear disjuncture between party and parliament has never existed with any clarity anywhere in the world, but the degree of intensity of relationship between political groups formed by like-minded political parties is an inseparable part of parliamentary democracy. One of the positive developments in African parliamentary democracy is that party-to-party partnerships are reflected increasingly in coalitions between political parties that share common political orientation.

Another dimension of parliament functions is agenda setting, in particular the ability to amend legislation and respond to major policy shifts proposed by the executive but that harbor goals inconsistent with public interest.[23] Because parliament legislates and sanctions new major policy or policy shifts, it is an arena in which public and private interests may clash and conflict arises between perceived losers and gainers. Like other parliaments, African parliaments are not short of such controversies. From land policy to environmental law and from budget to free or cost-sharing subscription drugs, parliaments try to bring sanity to the debate and contain it within the bounds of institutionalized politics.[24] These debates can only assure citizens of the significant qualitative difference multiparty democracy has contributed to parliamentary oversight and, rather than rubberstamping, genuine debate along party policy agenda has begun to ensue.

Not all African legislatures succumbed to the whim of leaders who treated the constitution with contempt or strived to prolong their term of office at any expense (for example, Chiluba of Zambia, Mugabe of Zimbabwe, Nujoma of Namibia, Paul Biya of Cameroon, Mouseveni of Uganda). African legislatures responded in a variety of ways, ranging from taking severely dividing partisan positions such as supported constitutional amendments in conformity with the personal ambitions of their political party leaders or resisted in favor of defending the constitution (Cameroonian MPs boycott of Paul Biya's inauguration in 2002). However, the constitutional amendments that brought about competitive multiparty politics cannot be underestimated, because constitutional amendments made it possible for people to assume their democratic rights that were denied by one-party states and military or civilian dictatorships.

Legislatures were engaged in implicit and at times explicit critical interventions denouncing government as incapable of responding adequately to social problems such as conflict. In some countries, parliamentarians took up the role of conflict management, or assumed the role of personal representation of aggrieved citizens to the executive branch or local government functionaries. For example, bargaining in ethnically divided societies is an obvious instrument parliamentarians use for conflict management such as the positive involvement of Malian Members of Parliament in conflict management during the civil war. One can even argue that the end of the Malian war in 1999 could have never been possible without the engagement of local Tuareg chiefs, religious and community leaders, civil society organizations supported by political parties and parliamentarians. The whole process started in 1995, when traditional leaders (chiefs) used

potential consequences of national policies on their
rom the few cases where I tried to gauge Members of
nstituencies in rural Africa I had the impression that gone
ien Members of Parliament visit their constituencies only to
)tes. The "absentee" Members of Parliament was common
ng Africa's early parliamentary period, but, as competition
increas... ie Member–Constituency relationship must have improved and more intense contacts must have developed.

The legislature roles described above co-existed with other generic functions, including oversight, legislation, and administrative review. If we consider the judiciary services committees as an example, according to Krafchik and Wehner,[26] in Zambia and Mozambique the Constitutions do not provide for the composition of the judiciary services committee, leaving this to an Act of Parliament and attaching less importance to the institution. In a substantial number of African countries (Malawi, Tanzania, Botswana, Lesotho, Uganda, and Zimbabwe) and in the case of Lesotho, persons appointed by the president or prime minister dominated the commissions. However, in all cases, the Chief Justice and his Deputy are disqualified from being appointed to the judicial services committee. In the same vein, Wehner purports that in many African countries the auditor general (for instance, in Kenya) is appointed by the president.[27] In most cases, parliament is required to endorse the appointment, as is the case of Zambia.[28] A number of African constitutions specify the exclusive grounds upon which the Auditor General may be removed. These are usually limited to incapacity or misconduct, as for example in the Constitutions of Kenya, Malawi, and Namibia.

However, I am aware that the actual delivery of governance functions by legislatures hinges more on practice than theory. The technical expertise parliamentary committees bring to parliament cannot be shrugged off as mere formalities (see Wang's chapter in this book). The variety of expertise and specialized knowledge needed to act upon issues of vital significance to citizens makes parliamentary governance functions diverse and complex. Ideally, parliamentary committees are not only assisting Members of Parliament to adopt, amend, or reject laws and policies, but also to know for sure what is to be adopted, amended, or rejected, and why, and whether what is legislated is in the public interest.

African Parliamentary Systems

Uni-cameralism is the dominant parliamentary system in Africa. Currently, 39 African parliaments are uni-cameral and 16 are bi-cameral.[29] Whether uni-cameral or bi-cameral, parliamentary systems have a major role to play in regulating the relationship between and maintaining the separation of legislative and executive power. However, it is difficult to discern whether African uni-cameral or bi-cameral parliamentary systems are more capable of providing political stability and accountability and better oversight over the executive. The chapters dealing with African bi-cameral parliamentary systems illustrate that, under absolute majoritarianism, they are as much prone to executive manipulation as uni-cameral (Kassahun, Melber, and Hughes in this volume).

The advantages of bi-cameral parliaments are not new. For instance, IPU stated that,

> The arguments for a bicameral system are of two kinds: a) Concern with a more stable balance between the executive and the legislature, the unbridled power of a single chamber being restrained by the creation of a second chamber recruited on a different basis; b) The desire to make the parliamentary body operates, if not more efficiently, at any rate more smoothly, by having a so-called "revision" chamber to maintain a careful check the sometimes hasty decisions of a First Chamber.[30]

Two important considerations that have eluded parliamentary democrats are, first, the way the members of the second chamber should be elected or selected and second, the relative extent of their power as compared with those of the lower chamber. The counter view, according to IPU,[31] is that the uni-cameral system is more appropriate to democracy; bi-cameral systems are essentially designed to restrain and moderate the ebullience of popular sovereignty, which would operate in too ruthless a manner if there were only a single chamber. Ideally, the single chamber is elected by direct universal suffrage, and that is in fact the most common practice in all African bi-cameral parliaments.

The current views on bi-cameralism are polarized. Some consider it the centerpiece of liberal constitutionalism, offering the possibility of representing powerful economic and social interests in the governing institutions. It also operates within the principles of polycentrism, fragmenting legislative power in order to prevent its monopoly (a few powerful interests) while safeguarding against executive domination.[32] Others are skeptical, offering more critical viewpoints on its merits and de-merits (for example, Riker 1992 and Tsebelis and Money 1997). In bi-cameral assemblies, the second chamber thoroughly scrutinizes legislation in order to ensure the collection of possible mistakes and offers an opportunity for more public debate. Among the drawbacks is the possibility of considerable delay, the check on democratic rule, particularly when members are not elected or are indirectly elected, and the reinforcement of social forces (chiefs and a powerful political elite) vis-à-vis democratically elected institutions such as the first chamber.

It is not difficult to observe the uneasy relationship between bi-cameral assemblies and federal states in the cases of Ethiopia and Nigeria and other severely divided states such as Namibia, Mauritania, and South Africa. However, in African states where bi-cameralism prevails, the general belief is that it will manage social and political conflicts emanating from regional disparity, ethnic cleavages, and/or severe center-periphery contradictions. What is important here is whether bi-cameralism contributes to political stability or to lesser executive manipulation of the legislatures. It seems that the former rather than the latter is the objective of African bi-cameral parliamentary systems. This, however, should not imply that such problems do not exist in states that have adopted uni-cameral legislature arrangements.

Admittedly, the absence of serious attempts to introduce new constitutional arrangements (such as bi-cameral parliaments) other than those inherited from the colonialists explains African polity's fear of any developments that might be perceived to inflame national sentiments and even portray those who advocate them as separatists or tribalists. Although the bi-cameral arrangements may delay legislation by soliciting a broader range of opinions, as has often been argued, the possibility for the executive to manipulate bicameral legislature is less likely and even remote.

The prominent role of chiefs in Botswana, Swaziland, Lesotho, and Mauritania are examples of how both uni-cameral and bi-cameral parliamentary systems provide more space for integrating and giving voice to a wider range of political representatives who emerge from chiefs and other similar local entities that reflect the "state" as the state of the nations or nationalities. For example, in uni-cameral Botswana, the House of Chiefs is an advisory 15-member body consisting of the chiefs, of the eight principal tribes, four elected sub-chiefs, and three members selected by the other 12. In Lesotho, the Senate has 33 members (22 principal chiefs and 11 other members appointed by the ruling party). In Swaziland, the Parliament (or Libandla) is an advisory body consisting of the Senate with 30 seats (10 appointed by the House of Assembly and 20 appointed by the monarch). Members serve five-year terms. In Mauritania, the Senate (or Majlis al-Shuyukh) has 56 seats (17 up for election every two years) and members elected by municipal leaders serve six-year terms.

The relatively new democratic parliaments of Namibia and South Africa, with their "proportional representation" electoral systems are also bi-cameral[33] (see Wiese 2003 for Namibia and O'Brien 1997 for South Africa). In Namibia, the National Council consists of 26 seats, two members chosen from each regional council to serve six-year terms. In South Africa, the National Council of Provinces with 90 seats (10 members elected by each of the nine provincial legislatures for five-year terms) has special powers to protect regional interests, including the safeguarding of cultural and linguistic traditions among ethnic minorities. Three Federal African states (Ethiopia, Nigeria, and the Comoros) also differ. In Ethiopia, the House of People's Representatives or lower chamber has 548 seats; and its members are directly elected by popular vote from single-member districts.

It is difficult to generalize whether bi-cameralism offers a better foundation for political stability, delegation, and accountability than uni-cameralism. However, constitutional structures that protect legislatures from the executive dominance are generally better served by bi-cameralism than uni-cameralism.[34] If adequately practiced, bi-cameralism, could provide a better chance of representation at the regional level, protect linguistic and cultural differences, as well as reflect the full extent of a country's ethnic and regional diversity and disparity.

From the governance perspective, bi-cameralism implies greater subsidiarity between central and regional bodies of government and therefore contributes to wider citizen participation at the lower organs of government. Bi-cameralism is also better suited for severely divided societies by checking more effectively the power of the executive and exposing the failings of Government. It allows more thorough scrutiny of legislation by double-checking with a broader spectrum of citizens', representatives. In the case of chiefly representation, bi-cameralism is also more inclusive and hence more appropriate in representing divergent ethnic, religious, linguistic, and cultural entities than otherwise. As mentioned in the introduction to this section, the cases of Ethiopia, Namibia, and South Africa (Kassahun, Melber, and Hughes, respectively) will shed light on these countries' recent legislature–executive alignment and struggles in bi-cameral legislatures.

However, van Cranenburg[35] is of the opinion that African parliaments (whether bi-cameral or uni-cameral) are under severe executive dominance. Upon closer examination of a number of African countries, she illustrates that some semi-presidential systems lean heavily toward pure presidential systems, yielding a considerable degree of executive dominance. Van Cranenburg therefore observes that African presidentialism (or prime ministerialism for that matter) is not characterized by the separation of power between the executive and legislative branches of government. They are separated by linkage or fusion between the two branches: functionally through holding the confidence of the majority in the legislature, and personally through the absence of the rule of incompatibility of the office of a minister with membership of the legislature.

The chapters of this volume reveal some general trends of African parliamentary development, the relationship between parliaments and government and its implications for the current debate on parliament's role in the governance debate. These developments cannot be isolated from the broader economic and political structures that inform the evolution of African parliaments and their conjuncture with the current democratic development.

An Enhanced African Parliamentary Governance Role

Governance in this introduction, indeed in all chapters, is defined as institutional arrangements "consist[ing] of basic rules and practices, as well as individual purposes and intentions and involves frameworks within which citizens and officials act and politics occurs, and which shapes the identities and institutions of civil society." [36] It also borrows from Ostrom[37] the notion that democratic governance is about how institutional frameworks are organized to achieve democratic ideals and how institutions are constituted and changed within the processes they define. Defining processes, making rules, managing conflicts, and ensuring compliance are only a few of the whole range of functions and activities in which democratic governance institutions are involved. As I will further explain in the conclusion, democratic governance is a product of the historical as well as the socio-economic and political circumstances in which they are conceived and performed.

When the Constitutional arrangements that make up the democratic governance of society are broadly defined, it is obvious that parliaments or legislatures are at the heart of governance and of the national integrity system that citizens entrust with the burdensome task of ensuring that democratic states, aided by the Constitution, fulfill their functions in the interests of citizens. Managing Constitutional crises emanating from the political whim of leaders who attempt to extend unconstitutionally their presidential mandate or who acquire powers to ensure their supremacy over all other braches of government are major governance issues that have occupied African parliaments and will continue so to do.[38] The functions of parliament narrated earlier in this introduction are important governance instruments at the disposal of the legislature in order to protect the citizen's liberties by ensuring that the Constitutional provisions are not empty jargon. As part of the machinery of government, parliaments are important governing partners because, according to Johnson and Nakamura:

> Parliaments represent, shape laws, and exercise a degree of oversight or control over the executive. Performing these functions contributes to good

government by increasing its capacity to monitor and respond to public sentiments/dissatisfactions, by playing a part in passing legislation capable of withstanding critical scrutiny, and serving as a vehicle for improving the degree of probity, efficiency and responsiveness in the administration of laws.[39]

In particular, the reference to the democratic state distinguishes the post-1990s African legislatures from those of one-party states and authoritarian regimes. Beyond their normative functions, parliaments are democratic governance institutions representing the citizens, who expect them to develop political identities, govern solidarities, manage conflict, and constitute an arena where the representatives of citizens build, diffuse, and mobilize capabilities that match democratic hopes.[40] It is in parliaments that political accounting for deeds or misdeeds is expected to be consistent with transparent democratic governance and where deliberations are open to citizens and of debates are resolutions made public. Citizens cannot be asked or that have not been compelled to comply with laws that they do not know or made public. There are at least three implications of this, clearly demonstrated throughout this book: first, competitive politics, at least at the level of the political parties, ensure that parliament is not the ultimate expression of the ruling party and that opposition political parties represented in parliament can exploit the failings of the party in government to their advantage. In the words of Johnson and Nakamura,

> Constituents have greater access; they are often more likely to feel that they have a claim on a representative than on other government officials. And legislative proceedings are often organized to maximize public attention to particular controversies and to offer participation opportunities ranging from contacting individual representatives to organized hearings.[41]

Citizens' support of parliament (see Doorenspleet) and civil actions against the government to express solidarity with parliament (Dulani and Van Donge) illustrate that under democratic conditions civil society is an aid to legislatures. Second, pluralistic politics, especially the prevalence of competing political parties, means that parliaments have become representative of a wide range of opinions, "ideological" trends and interest groups and as such are symbols of the citizen's sovereignty, and by extension an exercise of overseeing on their behalf. Third, access to information is made easier through the development of parliamentary websites containing the daily journal, legislative summaries, and texts of legislation. ICT made it possible for citizens, particularly the educated and politically inclined elite, to air their views to parliamentarians and parliamentary committees. On their part, parliamentarians have taken advantage of the political space pluralistic politics has created to inform citizens or outsmart their political opponents.

The chapters in this book reveal that African or any other parliament could hardly exercise the full range of its functions and concomitant governance role without the support or synergies they develop with several other governance institutions (e.g. Auditor General, Ombudsman, and Attorney General) and non-state actors such as NGOs and civil society organizations concerned with advocacy and integrity. Other non-state actors include international finance institutions, regional banks, bilateral and multilateral development agencies. Internal and external pressures are brought to bear on both parliament and the executive through the direct and indirect force of at least being seen to be acting in the public interest.

The Structure of the Book

This book consists of 13 chapters divided into two parts dealing with the changing governance role and the relationship between African parliaments, assemblies, or legislatures and the executive as well as their governance role. Part I consists of five chapters (Salih, Hout, Tripp, Olowu, and Doorenspleet). It introduces a larger synthesis intended to explain the broader socio-economic and political context within which African parliaments operate. The contributors move from explaining the specificity as well as the universal characteristics of African parliaments (Salih) to examining data sets comparing the performance of African parliaments with other parliaments in developing countries (Hout). Others explain the increasing role of African women parliamentarians and attitudes toward the quota system of representation (Tripp); local assemblies' assertiveness in their struggle to instill the ethos of governance from below (Olowu); and public opinion formation and the extent to which Africans support their parliaments, using data sets, with Mali as a case in point (Doorenspleet).

Part II deals with parliamentary development from a political–historical perspective either from colonial rule to independence, with special reference to current developments in the struggle between legislature and executive (Momba, Boafo-Arthur, and Melber) or from imperial to multiparty democracy (Beshanu), examining the cases of Zambia, Ghana, Namibia, and Ethiopia, respectively. The historical depth of these chapters is deliberately intended to avoid the mishaps reminiscent of some current trends in scholarly work, which assumes that African democratic institutions such as constitutions, parliaments, political parties, and the like are products of the recent democratization processes. These chapters also explicate the changing fortunes of the relationship between the legislature and executive in different political party systems (one-party, dominant-party and multiparty) and ideologies (broadly defined as military, socialist, or democratic/pluralistic, operating under multiparty democracy).

The second set of chapters in Part II offers case studies that respond directly to the question as to whether African parliaments have actually been effective in holding the executive accountable (Wang, Dulani and van Donge, and Hughes, elucidating the cases of Tanzania, Malawi, and South African, respectively), including instances of legislature success or failure to exercising its cherished accountability functions.

Rephrased in today's dominant discourse on democracy, African parliaments would probably fall short of fulfilling the whole range of governance responsibilities expected of them, particularly the quest to bring about the ethos and practice of good governance in the form of developing political accounts. I will return to these points in the conclusions presented separately in Chapter 13. This final chapter also aims to offer the reader a synoptic analysis of the salient features that give the book a sense of coherence and attempts to tease out the recent developments in the relationship between African legislatures and executive and the factors that constrain their governance role.

As this is the only collection of essays solely devoted to the study of contemporary developments of African parliaments, we hope that this volume will plug an important gap in the study of African legislatures and therefore encourage students of political development in Africa and elsewhere in the developing world. Our greatest satisfaction will be realized when students of African politics take up and elaborate on some of the issues which we have only briefly introduced, knowing that African parliaments would probably fall short of fulfilling the whole range of the governance responsibility expected of them. However, this should not draw our attention away from the fact that they constitute the main governance pillar entrusted with bringing about the ethos and practice of good governance.

Notes

1. Olson 1994: 1.
2. Elliot 1991.
3. Lloyd 1964.
4. Evans-Pritchard 1971.
5. Ibrahim 1992.
6. Coleman 1960: 254.
7. For elaborate description of these groups and others, see Fortes and Evans-Pritchard 1940.
8. Coleman 1960: 255.

9. Lord Hailey Report 1979.
10. Mazrui and Tidy 1984: 85.
11. Salih 2001.
12. Salih 2003.
13. Ibid.
14. Duverger 1958.
15. See, for example, Clapham 1982; Van Donge 1995a; Salih 2003.
16. Salih 2001.
17. Ibid.
18. Salih 2003.
19. Ibid.
20. Freund 1984: 246–247.
21. Mwakyembe 1995: 51.
22. Kjekshus 1974a; Hindess 1983.
23. Bynton and Kim 1975: 17.
24. Examples of this include the heated parliamentary debates such as Malawi land policy (Jan. 2002), South Africa land policy (Nov. 2003), Mozambique energy and transport sectors privatization (2004), among others.
25. Nykuri 1997: 13. For more on the role of parliament in conflict management, see European Parliamentarians for Africa, 2001.
26. Knofchik and Wehner 1998: 238.
27. Wehner 2002: 226.
28. See Burnell 2003 for a fuller account of legislative–executive relations and the parliamentary reform agenda in Zambia.
29. Uni-cameral African parliaments are Algeria, Angola, Benin, Botswana, Cape Verde, Chad, Comoros, Côte d'Ivoire, Djibouti, Equatorial Guinea, Eritrea, Guinea, Gambia, Ghana, Guinea Bissau, Kenya, Liberia, Libya, Malawi, Mali, Mauritius, Mozambique, Niger, São Tomé and Príncipe, Senegal, Seychelles, Sierra Leone, Sudan, Tunisia, Uganda, Tanzania, Zambia, and Zimbabwe. The bi-cameral parliaments are found in Burundi, Congo, DR Congo, Egypt, Ethiopia, Gabon, Lesotho, Madagascar, Mauritania, Morocco, Namibia, Nigeria, Rwanda, South Africa, and Swaziland.
30. Inter-parliamentary union 1961: 8.
31. Ibid.
32. Heywood 2002: 320.
33. See Wiese 2003 for Namibia and O'Brien 1997 for South Africa.
34. See Patterson and Mughan 1999 on bi-cameralism in the contemporary world.
35. Van Cranenburgh 2003.
36. March and Olsen 1995: 6.
37. Ostrom 1990.
38. For more on this refer to Okoth-Ogendo 2000.
39. Johnson and Nakamura 1999: 1.
40. March and Olsen 1995.
41. Johnson and Nakamura 1999: 2.

2

Parliaments, Politics, and Governance: African Democracies in Comparative Perspective

Wil Hout[1]

Institute of Social Studies, The Hague, The Netherlands

This chapter focuses on the relationship between features of national political systems, many of which relate to the functioning of national parliaments, and the quality of governance. Throughout, I make use of data from a number of recent datasets on political institutions and governance.

At the general level, the expectation that wealthier countries tend to have better governance is corroborated. African democracies have, on average, a much lower quality of governance than democracies in Asia, Latin America, and the Caribbean. There is, however, a clear disparity in the quality of governance among African countries, with the poorest scoring least well. Moreover, the impact of international dependence (reliance on primary products) appears to have a negative effect on governance quality in African democracies.

A second set of analyses demonstrates that only some institutional features related to parliaments have a noticeable impact on the performance of democracies. In particular, the role of parliament vis-à-vis the executive, federalism, degree of electoral competitiveness, and length of democratic experiences tend to influence the performance of African democracies in a positive direction.

Introduction

Over the past decade or so, because of the rise of institutionalism in political science and economics, researchers have paid considerable attention to the role of (political) institutions in the development process. Most empirical research in the institutionalist tradition focuses on general characteristics of national political systems, such as the level of democracy and the extent of political stability, rather than on specific national political features. Moreover, economic growth is usually the primary indicator of the performance of political systems.

This chapter takes a different approach to the empirical research on institutions and development. The current analysis focuses on the relationship between political characteristics and the quality of governance. Governance quality—that is reflected in, among other things, the degree of openness and accountability of decision-makers, the effectiveness of government, and the absence of corruption—is arguably an important indicator of political performance, on a par with economic growth. This chapter is limited in its geographical orientation in that it zeroes in on African countries, although it tries to compare the experience of African minimal and liberal democracies with that of similar political systems in other parts of the developing world (in particular, Asia, Latin America, and the Caribbean).

The focus of the analysis is on the democratic experience in developing countries; in particular, on some important features of minimal and liberal democracies. Parliament occupies a central place in the comparisons because it clearly is the key institution in minimal and liberal democracies around the world. This chapter does not study day-to-day affairs in developing country parliaments, but rather concentrates on certain "structural" features of parliaments, such as legislative–executive relations, the type of electoral system, and the degree of parliamentary fragmentation.

Apart from the fact that it is legitimate to study governance quality per se, it is relevant to include this variable in the equation because there appears to be quite significant controversy about the contribution of governance to (the lack of) development in many developing countries, most notably those in Africa.[2] The current focus on a particular group of developing countries in Africa is appropriate because these countries have certain characteristics in common that set them apart, as a group, from other countries. As Mick Moore phrased it,[3] political underdevelopment—which he suggests as a summary term for the existence of ineffective, arbitrary, and unaccountable regimes that has resulted from their historical insertion into the global capitalist system—distinguishes the political systems of many developing countries from those of the industrialized world.

In this chapter, I analyze the relationship between political institutions and governance in African countries. The chapter starts with a discussion of several approaches relevant for the understanding of this relationship. The next section contains a discussion of the research design and data that are used in the chapter. The subsequent two sections offer the results of the analyses on the interrelations among institutions and governance. The concluding section contains a discussion of the chapter's main findings and the implications of these for ongoing discussions about the role of political institutions and the quality of governance.

Understanding Institutions and Governance

Since the publication of Seymour Martin Lipset's seminal article on the social requisites of democracy,[4] political scientists have accepted the relationship between a country's level of (economic) development and its political system almost as a given. Although Lipset's original findings have been corroborated in several recent analyses,[5] and have almost come to assume the exceptional status of a "political science law," most analyses have been limited to assessing the impact of countries' level of development at a given moment on the level of democracy.

The recent attention for issues of governance and the attempts to measure the quality of governance[6] produced a greater interest in the effects of certain institutional arrangements on the performance of political systems. Many studies, in particular those informed by the new institutional economics, emphasized the impact of institutions on economic growth.[7] Political scientists started to analyze what implications certain institutional arrangements have for the quality of governance.[8]

Most analyses of the relationship between institutional features and the performance of political systems—whether those focusing on economic performance or those relating to the quality of governance—failed to assess the influence of world-systemic forces that condition both domestic institutions and the output of political systems. The research of Kick et al.,[9] which springs from the world-system tradition, has drawn attention to the conditioning effect of the international political economy—in particular, dependency—on countries' level of achievement. Based on a quantitative–empirical research design, Kick et al.[10] showed that "[d]emocratization and political stability in the core and capitalist semicore have paid off handsomely . . . The spread of polyarchy nevertheless has had no impact whatsoever on economic growth in either the semiperiphery or periphery".

This analysis was broadened by Mick Moore,[11] who provided an explanation of "bad governance" in developing countries in terms of political underdevelopment. In Moore's view, political underdevelopment relates to the fact that the state in many developing countries is (a) relatively ineffective, meaning that it is unable to rule and pursue collective interests in an authoritative fashion, and (b) relatively arbitrary, despotic, and unaccountable.[12] Moore locates the causes of political underdevelopment in the structure of the international system:

> these [causes] lie to a large degree in the ways in which interactions with the rich (or "metropolitan") countries have shaped, and continue to shape, the states of the poor world. "Bad governance" is neither inherent in the culture or traditions of the people of poor countries nor a product of poverty. It is rather the result of the ways in which state authority in the South has been constructed—and is being maintained—through economic and political interactions with the rest of the world.[13]

Looking at more specific features of political systems, comparativists such as Arend Lijphart paid more attention to the roles played by parliaments.[14] Among other things, these comparativists analyzed how majoritarian and consensus-oriented political institutions are related to the performance of political systems. Van Cranenburgh pointed out that the degree of power concentration and dispersion is an important political feature in the explanation of political performance.[15] Inclusion of institutional variables related to the type of political system may enhance knowledge of the distribution of political power in countries and may help to redress the "electoral fallacy" (the almost exclusive focus on the process of elections; see Karl, quoted by van Cranenburgh)[16] that so often dominates the study of politics. Features related to the distribution of power include the nature of the political system in terms of legislative–executive relations (presidential versus parliamentary systems), the nature of the electoral system (first-past-the-post or more proportional systems), the degree of fragmentation or concentration of important political institutions, such as parliament, and the existence of territoriality-based power dispersion, as in federal political systems.

Ferree and Singh focused on one specific institutional feature—namely, electoral competitiveness—and its relationship with the performance of political systems in Africa.[17] They argue, "executives elected in competitive multiparty elections are more likely to choose good policies than those who are not elected in competitive elections".[18] Such "good" policies are growth-enhancing policies, and it is expected by these authors that more competitive political systems will, on average, perform better.

A final dimension concerning political institutions relates to their durability. Although one might hypothesize, pace Olson,[19] that the longer democracies exist, the more vested interests (so-called "distributional coalitions") reduce their performance level, Przeworski et al. have shown that "there is no reason to think that growth in the countries where regimes were stable was different from that in countries where regimes changed."[20]

Research Design and Data

Hypotheses

This chapter takes the elements discussed in the previous section as the building blocks of the analysis of the relationships among political characteristics and governance. Five hypotheses are tested in this chapter.

The first hypothesis is derived from the research tradition inspired by Lipset's analysis of development and democracy,[21] and links the general expectation of a positive relationship between the two variables to Moore's interpretation of good and bad governance.[22] This hypothesis states that countries that have achieved a higher level of economic development will tend to have, on average, a higher quality of governance.

Linked to this is a second hypothesis which ties the quality of governance in the developing countries to their structural position in the world-system. As Moore and Kick et al. have made clear,[23] dependency can be an important factor in the explanation of poor governance. The second hypothesis is, therefore, that countries that occupy a more dependent position in the world-system will tend to have, on average, a lower quality of governance.

The third hypothesis concerns the distribution of power discussed in relation to Lijphart's distinction between different types of political institutions and van Cranenburgh's application of these ideas to Africa. The general expectation is that the dispersion of political power will enhance the performance of political systems. The third hypothesis is that countries that are characterized by a greater dispersion of political power will tend to experience, on average, a higher quality of governance.

The fourth hypothesis derives from Ferree and Singh's analysis of electoral competitiveness and its relationship to performance, through the selection of better policies. This hypothesis is that countries that are characterized by more electoral competitiveness will tend to have, on average, a higher quality of governance.

The final hypothesis relates to the durability of democratic rule. Following Przeworski et al. it can be expected that there is little to no difference between the performance of old and new democracies.[24] The sixth hypothesis is, therefore, that countries with long-existing and those with newly democratic political systems will not show substantial differences in terms of the quality of governance.

Data

The hypotheses are tested with the use of quantitative data derived from several datasets. The data were collected for a sample of low and middle-income countries[25] in Africa, Asia, Latin America, and the Caribbean that were ranked as minimal or liberal democracies by Freedom House.[26] The countries included in the sample are listed in the Appendix, along with the scores on some key variables.

The Freedom House dataset makes a distinction among three types of democracies:

- minimal democracies that had been free or partly free for less than five years in 2002 (score 0);
- minimal democracies that had been free or partly free for at least five years in 2002 (score 1);
- liberal democracies that had been in existence for at least five years in 2002 (score 2).

The democracy type variable can be seen as an indicator of the consolidation of democratic systems where a higher score reflects a higher degree of consolidation.

Data on the quality of governance in 2002 are taken from the Governance Matters III dataset, compiled by Kaufmann et al.[27] Applying a so-called "unobserved components model,"[28] Kaufmann et al. distinguished six dimensions of governance, with scores ranging between $+2.5$ and -2.5:

- voice and accountability: the extent to which citizens of a country are able to participate in the selection of governments;
- political stability and absence of violence: the likelihood that the government in power will be destabilized or overthrown by possibly unconstitutional and/or violent means, including domestic violence and terrorism;
- government effectiveness: the quality of public service provision, the quality of the bureaucracy, the competence of civil servants, the independence of the civil service from political pressures, and the credibility of the government's commitment to policies;
- regulatory quality: the incidence of market-unfriendly policies such as price controls or inadequate bank supervision and the burdens

imposed by excessive regulation in areas such as foreign trade and business development;
- rule of law: the extent to which agents have confidence in and abide by the rules of society;
- control of corruption: the limitation of the extent to which public power is exercised for private gain.

A summary variable ("quality of governance") has been created on the basis of the scores of countries on the six dimensions.[29] This summary variable (ranging between $+1.0$ and -1.0) is used in place of the six dimensions in some analyses.

Data on specific aspects of the political systems of the African, Asian, Latin American, and Caribbean sample countries are taken from the Database of Political Institutions, which was assembled by researchers from the World Bank and published in 2001.[30] These data are applied in the analyses of specific political features and their impact on the quality of governance and economic growth. Variables included in the tests performed below are:

- type of political system, which has a score of 0 for presidential systems, 1 for systems with an assembly-elected president, and 2 for parliamentary systems;
- type of electoral system, which has a score of 1 for majority systems in which the first-past-the-post principle is applied, and 0 for other systems (variants of proportional representation);
- fractionalization of the legislature, which is calculated as the probability that two deputies picked at random from the legislature are of different parties (recoded into quartiles);
- federalism, which is operationalized as the absence (0) or existence (1) of autonomously operating regions or states;
- the legislative index of electoral competitiveness, which is recoded into a trichotomy that expresses the competitiveness of elections: 1 means that there is either no or an unelected legislature or that elections are held with only one candidate, 2 means that only one party, with multiple candidates, is allowed to take part in elections or that only one party has been able to win seats, and 3 means that multiple parties competed and have been able to win seats;[31] and
- tenure of the democratic system, which is calculated as the number of years that a country has been democratic (recoded into four groups: 0–5 years, 6–10 years, 11–15 years, 16 years or longer).

Data on economic achievement are taken from the World Development Indicators.[32] Gross national income per capita in 2000, based on purchasing power parity, is taken as indicator of the relative wealth level of countries.

The position of developing countries in the world-system, and the ensuing degree of dependency, is measured with data on the exports of primary products. Data on the exports of agricultural raw materials, fuels, ores, and metals as a percentage of total exports, for the most recent year available,[33] are used as the operationalization of the structural position of developing countries.

Research Design

Two different types of analysis are used to test the hypotheses that were formulated above. In the first place, several multiple regression analyses are performed to assess the relative explanatory power of sets of independent variables (expressed in the proportion of variance explained, or R^2) and the contribution to that explanation of several individual variables (expressed in standardized regression coefficients or beta weights). In the second place, bar charts are drawn to analyze the relationships between several political characteristics of African, Asian, Latin American, and Caribbean democracies and the quality of governance, and to assess the differences in these relations across the three groups of developing countries.

Regression Analyses of Institutions and Governance

The first set of multiple regression analyses relates to the first and second hypotheses concerning the relationships between the level of economic development and the structural position of developing countries in the world-system, on the one hand, and the quality of governance, on the other. Table 2.1 presents the findings of a set of multiple regressions where the quality of governance is regressed on the type of democracy, the level of development (operationalized as gross national income per capita) and the structural position of developing countries (measured as primary export dependence).

The results of the analyses reported in table 2.1 show quite an interesting pattern and produce remarkable differences among the three groups of democracies. The general pattern for all three groups of developing countries, as captured in equation 1, is that more consolidated democracies have, overall, a much higher quality of governance. Similarly, the quality of governance—which receives a negative average score for African and a positive average score for Latin American and Caribbean democracies,

Table 2.1 Regression Analyses with Quality of Governance Dependent

	All countries (1)	Africa (2)	Asia (3)	Latin America and Caribbean (4)
Type of democracy	.44***	.41**	.54**	.51***
Gross national income per capita	.46***	.39**	.33	.65***
Primary export dependence	−.19**	−.36**	−.18	−.14
Adjusted R^2	.65	.71	.48	.64
F	35.2***	16.0***	5.3**	13.6***
n	56	19	16	22

Note: * = significant at .10 level; ** = significant at .05 level; *** = significant at .01 level.

with the Asian countries taking a middle position (see appendix)—tends to increase significantly with increases in the level of wealth of countries; this finding corroborates the "Lipset law." Finally, the level of dependence appears to have a significantly negative effect on the quality of governance. The first equation is able to explain about two-thirds of the variance in the quality of governance among all developing country democracies.

Equations 2, 3, and 4 show that the explanatory power of the three independent variables differs when the three groups of developing countries are analyzed separately. The general pattern, expressed by equation 1, also applies to Africa. Equation 2 shows that the negative effect on governance quality of the dependence on primary exports is almost twice as strong for Africa as it is for all minimal and liberal democracies in the developing world (−.36 as opposed to −.19). Thus, the influence of countries' structural position in the world-system on the quality of governance appears to be much more evident in Africa than it is in all democracies in the developing world. On top of this, equations 3 and 4 make clear that the dependence of countries on the exports of primary products does not have the same explanatory power for Asian, Latin American, and Caribbean democracies as it had for African ones. The beta weights related to this variable in equations 3 and 4 show a negative sign—a finding that supports the conclusion of the overall analysis—but the coefficients appear to be non-significant, thus casting doubt on the robustness of the findings. The effect of democratic consolidation, as expressed by democracy type, on the quality of governance appears to be much stronger in Asia, Latin America, and the Caribbean than in Africa. Per capita gross national income, the indicator of relative wealth, shows a very strong positive relationship with the quality of governance in the western hemisphere, but has a non-significant (though positive) effect in Asia.

On the basis of the above, it may be concluded that hypothesis 1, related to the effect of the level of economic development on the quality of governance, has been corroborated for more or less democratic developing countries, with the exception of those in Asia. It is quite interesting that the general "Lipset law" gets support in an analysis of African, rather than Asian, democracies, but the finding is less surprising when it is realized that the group of Asian minimal and liberal democracies experienced, during the 1990s, on average substantially lower economic growth than the African countries in the sample (see the appendix).

Upon closer inspection of the data on the quality of governance (appendix), it becomes apparent that African democracies stand out negatively. The data reveal that African democracies, on average, have a negative overall score on the composite measure created on the basis of the Kaufmann et al. dataset on governance (-0.35 in a range between -1.0 and $+1.0$). The Asian democracies score 0.02, while the Latin American and Caribbean democracies reach a score of 0.38.

This finding about the average quality of governance is remarkable in the light of the corroboration of the "Lipset law," which postulates a positive relationship between the average wealth of countries and the quality of their governance. As the average per capita gross national income of African democracies ($2,303 in terms of purchasing power parity) is much higher than that of Asian democracies ($1,543), it is apparent that the average quality of governance cannot be attributed only to the average level of wealth of the democracies. In this case, it is necessary to look beyond mere averages. Although the average per capita gross national income in African democracies appears to be higher than in Asian democracies, the finding may be skewed significantly by the inclusion of five African democracies with incomes over $5,000 (Botswana, Gabon, Mauritius, Namibia, and South Africa) versus only one Asian country (South Korea).

The second hypothesis, on the effect of developing countries' structural position in the world-system, tends to get support that is less straightforward. Although the analyses report a generally quality-depressing effect of primary export dependence, the effect appears to derive mainly from the relatively strong influence that this dependence seems to have in African countries.

The general findings related to the quality of governance in Africa, which were presented in table 2.1 are disaggregated in table 2.2, where the six components of the quality of governance are regressed separately on the three independent variables (type of democracy, level of wealth, and structural position in the world-system). The results that are displayed in

Table 2.2 Regression Analyses for Africa with Six Governance Components Dependent

	Voice and Accountability (5)	Political Stability (6)	Goverment effectiveness (7)	Regulatory quality (8)	Rule of law (9)	Control of corruption (10)
Type of democracy	.61***	.29	.23	.66***	.27*	.24
Gross national income per capita	.32*	.32	.38*	−.03	.43**	.37
Primary export dependence	−.03	−.38***	−.44**	−.02	−.49***	−.38*
Adjusted R^2	.62	.41	.49	.31	.70	.44
F	12.2***	5.4***	7.2***	3.8**	15.1***	5.7***
n	22	20	20	20	20	19

Note: * = significant at .10 level; ** = significant at .05 level; *** = significant at .01 level.

table 2.2 show that the explanatory power of the three independent variables tends to be moderate (as in equations 6, 7, and 10) to high (equations 5 and 9). Only in the case of the regulatory quality dimension (equation 8), which is an expression of a country's relative market-friendliness, the proportion of variance explained is below one-third.

The beta weights that are presented in table 2 reflect, overall, the general pattern that was found with respect to Africa in equation 2 (table 2.1). The consolidation of democratic rule and the level of economic wealth tend to have a positive influence on the six dimensions of governance quality, while the structural position of countries in the world-system (their reliance on primary exports) tends to have a negative influence. The impact of democratic consolidation appears to be particularly positive in the case of voice, accountability, and regulatory quality, whereas the influence in most other cases is found to be weak to moderately strong.

The influence of economic wealth on the governance indicators tends to be in the range of .32 to .43 (indicating a moderately strong impact) in all but one case, regulatory quality. This implies that relatively wealthier African democracies tend, overall, to score better on most dimensions of governance quality than poorer ones.

The impact of the structural position in the world-system on the dimensions of governance quality is found to be moderately to strongly negative in four out of six dimensions. The exceptions to the rule are voice, accountability and regulatory quality. Therefore, it may be concluded that African democracies that are more dependent on the export of agricultural products and raw materials tend to have a lower quality of governance than less dependent democracies.

Political System Characteristics and Governance

As a sequel to the tests performed in the previous section, this section contains an analysis of the impact of several specific political system characteristics on the quality of governance in African, Asian, Latin American, and Caribbean minimal and liberal democracies.

The third hypothesis, related to the distribution of power, is tested by establishing the effects of four different variables on the quality of governance. These four variables are the type of political system (presidential versus parliamentary) and electoral system (majoritarian versus non-majoritarian), fractionalization of the legislature and federalism. The results of the tests are pictured in figures 2.1 to 2.4.

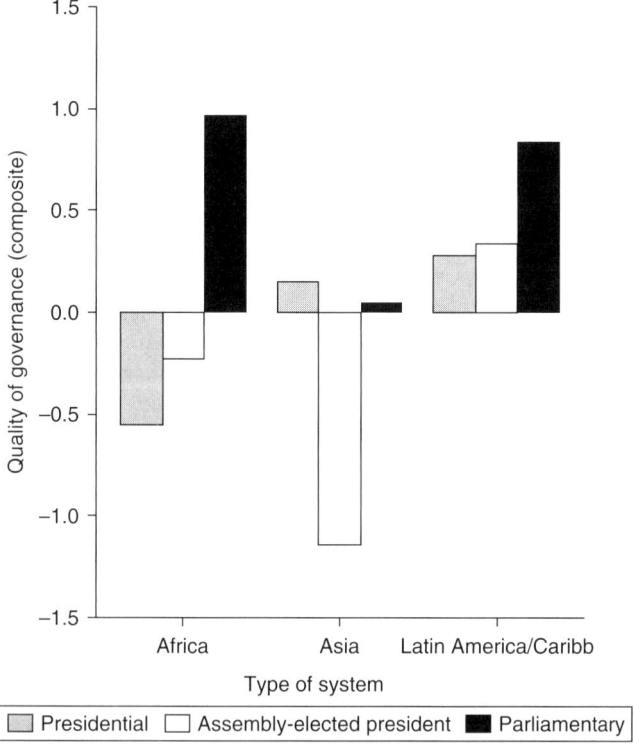

Figure 2.1   Type of Political System and Governance.

Figure 2.1 makes clear that there is not a clear-cut relationship between the type of political system in developing countries and their performance in terms of the quality of governance. With respect to governance, the African, Latin American, and Caribbean cases show that power sharing among executives and legislatures tend to improve the quality of governance. With respect to Asian democracies, systems with assembly-elected presidents appear to fare much worse in terms of the quality of governance than countries with either a presidential or a parliamentary system.

Figure 2.2 displays some interesting differences. Whereas the type of electoral system (majoritarian or non-majoritarian) appears to have no influence on the performance of African democracies with respect to governance quality, the electoral system seems to matter in Asia, Latin America, and the Caribbean. Asian democracies with a majority system tend to perform much worse than non-majoritarian systems in terms of governance quality. Non-majoritarian democracies in Latin America and

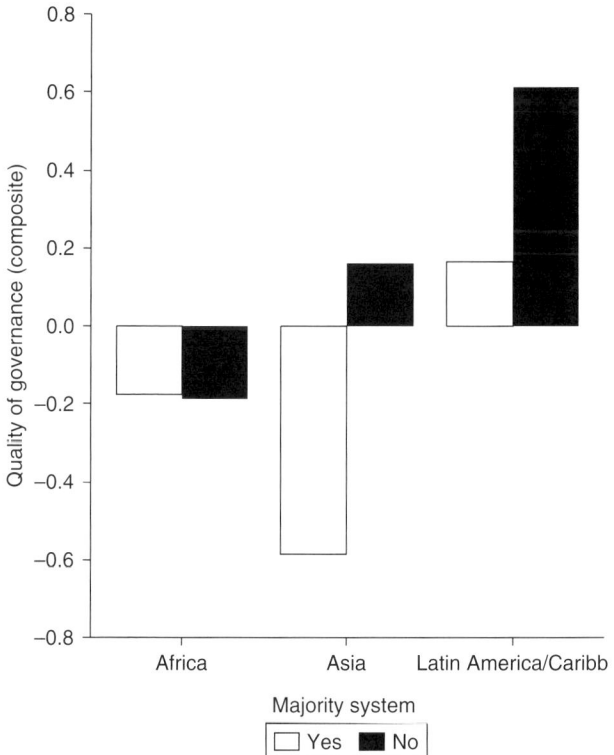

Figure 2.2 Type of Electoral System and Governance.

the Caribbean appear to have a much higher quality of governance than the majoritarian systems in the region.

Figure 2.3, on legislature fractionalization, again demonstrates that is it hard to generalize about the effect of power dispersion on the performance of political systems in the developing world.

Whereas Latin American and Caribbean countries with the least fractionalized legislatures tend to perform best in terms of governance, and countries with the highest degree of fractionalization have the lowest quality of governance, this relationship does not hold among either African or Asian democracies. In Africa, countries in the second and third quartiles tend to have a much higher quality of governance than countries in both extreme quartiles. There is almost no pattern to report on Asia.

Figure 2.4 pictures the relationship between federalism and the performance of political systems. In African and Asian democracies, the institution

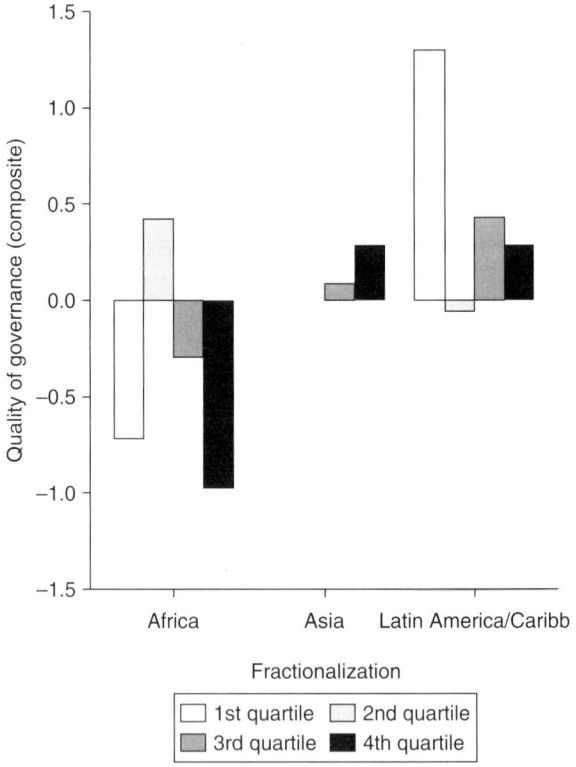

Figure 2.3 Legislature Fractionalization and Governance.

of federalism appears to have mattered for the quality of governance. Latin American and Caribbean democracies seem to benefit much less from federalism, because the quality of governance appears to be much higher in non-federal systems, although countries with federal systems of government still report positively as to governance quality.

The overall conclusion about the first set of four hypotheses must be that there are some signs that power dispersion has a positive effect on the performance of political systems in Africa (notably, in the case of parliamentary versus presidential systems and federalism), but that this effect does not extend to all possible indicators (in particular, the electoral system and fractionalization of the legislative). Most certainly, the impact of power dispersion is not identical across all developing countries, as the analysis suggests the existence of a wide variety of experiences.

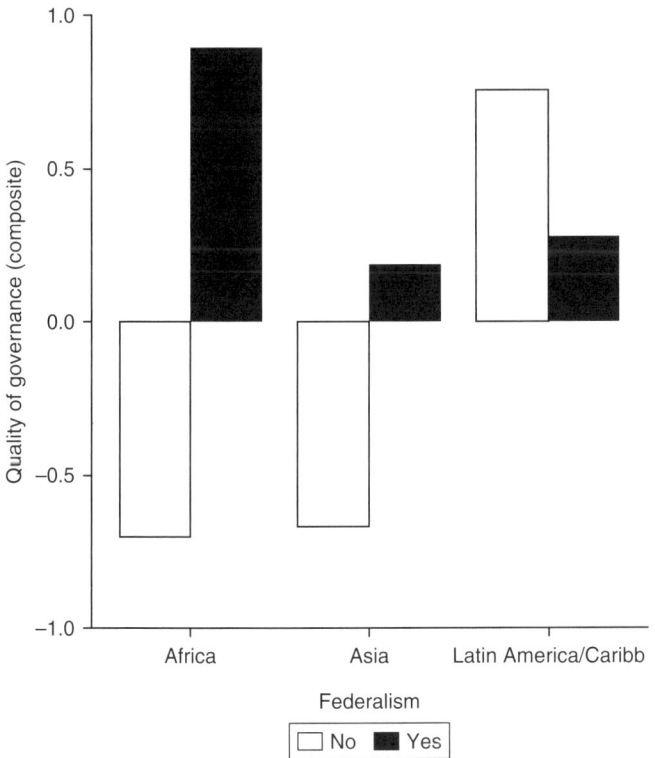

Figure 2.4 Federalism and Governance.

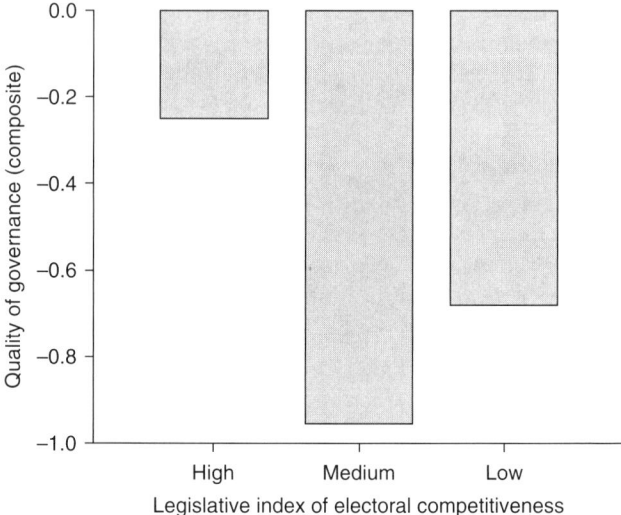

Figure 2.5 Electoral Competitiveness and Governance (Africa).

Figure 2.5 shows the relationship between the degree of electoral competitiveness and governance quality among African democracies. The other two groups of countries have not been included in figure 2.5 since there proved to be little to no variance as to the index of electoral competitiveness (possibly caused by the selection of countries for which data are available). The graph shows that the countries in the middle category (countries with limited competition for seats in the legislature) perform much worse in terms of governance than the non-competitive and the highly competitive countries. Thus, the fifth hypothesis is not fully corroborated by the data.

Figure 2.6 documents the relationship between democratic experience and performance. The graph shows quite clearly that developing countries with longer democratic experience perform, on the whole, (much) better in terms of the quality of governance. This relationship appears to be almost linear, the only exception being the long-existing Latin American and Caribbean democracies. These findings go against the expectation laid down in the sixth hypothesis and seem to cast doubt on both Mancur Olson's analysis of the effect of distributional coalitions and Przeworski et al.'s findings about the effect of democratic experience and systemic performance.[34]

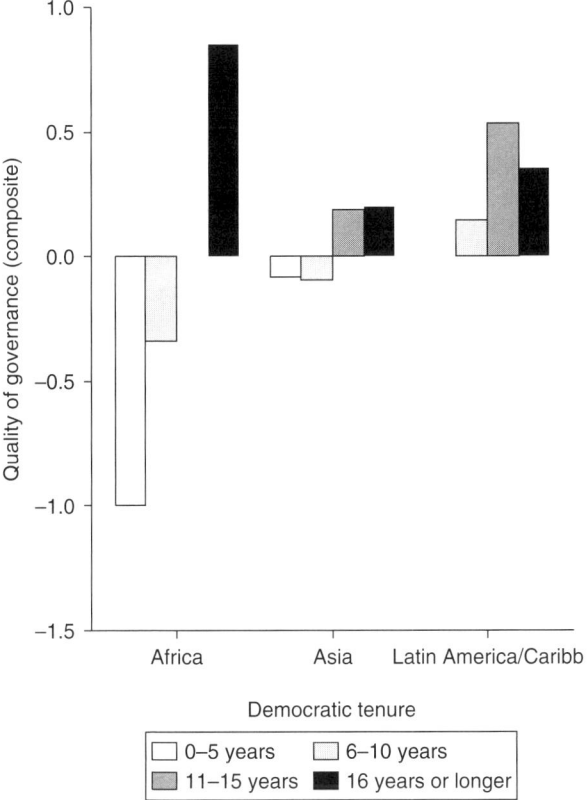

Figure 2.6 Democratic Tenure and Governance.

Conclusion and Discussion

The analyses in this chapter focused on some strongly held beliefs about the effects of political system characteristics on regime performance, where the latter variable was operationalized with data on the quality of governance. The focus of the analyses was on African minimal and liberal democracies, and comparisons were made to similar democracies in other parts of the world in order to see to what extent, if at all, African democracies stand out. The chapter's findings reveal that many of the expectations brought forward in the literature on institutions and development have not been corroborated in analyses using data drawn from several comparative datasets.

The analyses of the "Lipset law" produced corroboration, at the general level, of the expectation that there is a positive relationship between countries' average level of wealth and the quality of their governance. Looking beyond the immediate results, it becomes clear, however, that democracies in Africa and Asia display important variation within the general pattern. While the average national income per capita in African democracies is much higher than in Asian democracies, the overall quality of governance in Africa appears to be much worse than in Asia. The positive relationship between development level and governance quality in Africa seems to reflect the fact that the poorest democracies of the continent (for example, Congo, Guinea-Bissau, Niger, Nigeria, and Sierra Leone) perform relatively poorly in terms of governance, while the richer countries (such as Botswana, Mauritius, and South Africa) show up as very good performers and compare favorably even to well-governed countries in Asia and Latin America. This finding lends support to programs that aim to integrate support to improve governance into more general assistance strategies. The gap in governance quality that exists between the poorest and the wealthiest African countries may actually be reduced by continued attention to improvement of the economic situation of the least developed countries, coupled with progress on the governance front.

The analyses have shown that the structural (world-systemic) position of democracies in the developing world has an overall negative impact on the quality of their governance. The effect of international dependence appeared to be negative across the board, although it was found to be much stronger (and statistically significant) for African democracies. This finding supports the interpretation of bad governance in terms of political underdevelopment, and reinforces the position that improvement of the quality of governance in developing countries cannot be achieved by focusing only on the political system. Developing countries, in particular the more or less democratic ones, need better access to world markets and more foreign investment in order to diversify their economic structure and, on the basis of this, achieve a sustainable democratic political system.

An important element in the chapter concerned the impact of the distribution of power on the quality of governance in non-western democracies. Some indicators of power dispersion (in particular, the role of parliament vis-à-vis the executive and federalism) appeared to have a positive impact on the performance of political systems in Africa. At the same time, power dispersion as measured by other important indicators (such as the nature of the electoral system and fractionalization of parliament) did not seem to have a similar impact in African democracies, nor did it appear to apply identically to democracies in other parts of the developing world. The highly varying patterns that can be witnessed across the developing world require more in-depth research before credible explanations can be developed.

The analyses have indicated that the degree of electoral competitiveness of political systems has a noticeable impact on governance only in African democracies. The findings demonstrated, however, that African countries with a medium degree of competitiveness performed much worse in terms of governance than highly competitive and non-competitive systems. This puzzling result, which does not fully support Ferree and Singh's expectation that more competitive systems tend to adopt 'better' policies,[35] merits further exploration.

A result of the analyses in the chapter is related to the impact of the democratic experience in developing countries. In almost all cases, longer democratic tenure appears to go together with better performance of political systems in terms of their governance. This finding contradicts both Olson's and Przeworski et al.'s expectations.[36] The result—which may be a consequence of the exclusion of industrialized democracies—is encouraging, because it would mean that democratization really pays off for developing countries. At the same time, the finding prompts further investigation of the factors that set democracies in the developing world apart from those in other parts of the world.

The overall conclusion of this chapter is that political system characteristics do really matter as determinants of the performance of democracies in terms of the quality of their governance. Importantly, it was found that there were some important structural prerequisites (related to, among others, the level of development and dependence) for the performance of democratic systems in the developing world. Using Mandelbaum's words, democracy may rightfully be considered one of "the ideas that conquered the world,"[37] but this does not mean that democratic political regimes can be built by targeting the political system in isolation of the social and economic context. Strategies aimed at democratizing political regimes in the developing world should be accompanied by policies that address the structural problems of countries (such as their lack of development or external dependence) to make the democratic order sustainable. While democracy, as an idea, may have conquered the world, the minds of policy makers still need to be conquered by the idea that reform of the economic and international order is required if democratic regimes in the developing world are here to stay.

Appendix: Countries Included in the Analyses

	Type of democracy	Quality of governance	Average yearly economic growth	Per capita gross national income (PPP)
AFRICA				
Benin	2		4.8	980
Botswana	2	1.87	4.7	7,170
Burkina Faso	1	−0.45	5.0	970
Cape Verde	2		5.8	4,760
Central African Republic	1		1.7	1,160
Comoros	1		0.2	1,590
Congo (Brazzaville)	0	−1.76	0.4	570
Côte d'Ivoire	0	−1.07	2.7	1,500
Djibouti	0		−0.9	
Ethiopia	1	−0.86	4.0	660
Gabon	1	−0.43	2.4	5,360
Gambia	0	0.40	3.5	1,620
Ghana	1	0.24	4.3	1,910
Guinea-Bissau	1	−1.58	2.1	710
Lesotho	1		3.9	2,590
Liberia	1	−1.43		
Madagascar	1	−0.33	1.8	820
Malawi	1	0.04	3.8	600
Mali	2	−0.34	3.9	780
Mauritania	0	−0.99	4.1	1,630
Mauritius	2	1.89	5.3	9,940
Mozambique	1	0.13	5.7	800
Namibia	2	1.43	4.4	6,410
Niger	0	−1.01	2.0	740
Nigeria	0	−1.34	2.6	800
São Tomé e Príncipe	2		1.9	
Senegal	1	−0.07	3.4	1,480
Seychelles	1		2.6	
Sierra Leone	0	−1.63	−3.8	480
South Africa	2	0.89	1.7	9,160
Tanzania	1	−0.17	2.9	520
Togo	0	−1.35	1.6	1,410
Uganda	1	−0.96	6.6	1,210
Zambia	1	−0.32	0.7	750
Average score for Africa		−.35	2.9	2,303
ASIA				
Armenia	1	−0.85	−2.4	520
Azerbaijan	1	−1.02	−4.4	600
Bangladesh	1	−0.52	4.8	370
East Timor	1			
Fiji	1	0.56	1.2	1,820

Continued

Appendix Continued

	Type of democracy	Quality of governance	Average yearly economic growth	Per capita gross national income (PPP)
Georgia	1	−0.82	−11.0	630
India	1	0.36	5.5	450
Indonesia	0	−1.14	4.4	570
Kiribati	2		2.4	950
Korea, South	2	1.30	6.2	8,910
Malaysia	1	0.76	7.2	3,380
Marshall Islands	2		−1.1	1,970
Micronesia	2		2.1	2,110
Mongolia	2	1.01	0.1	390
Nauru	2			
Nepal	1	−0.55	5.0	240
Palau	2		2.2	
Papua New Guinea	1	−0.63	4.8	700
Philippines	2	0.19	2.9	1,040
Samoa	2		2.6	1,450
Solomon Islands	1		1.5	620
Sri Lanka	1	−0.33	5.2	850
Taiwan	2	1.72		
Thailand	1	0.72	4.5	2,000
Tonga	1		3.2	1,660
Turkey	1	−0.29	3.6	3,100
Tuvalu	2			
Vanuatu	2		2.6	1,150
Average score for Asia		0.03	2.2	1,543
LATIN AMERICA AND CARIBBEAN				
Antigua and Barbuda	1		3.4	10,000
Argentina	1	0.75	4.7	12,050
Belize	2	1.30	4.6	5,240
Bolivia	2	−0.05	3.8	2,360
Brazil	0	0.48	2.7	7,300
Chile	2	2.32	6.7	9,100
Colombia	1	−0.68	2.8	6,060
Costa Rica	2	2.04	5.2	7,980
Dominica	2		1.7	
Dominican Republic	1	0.64	5.9	5,710
Ecuador	1	−0.80	1.8	2,910
El Salvador	2	0.48	4.6	4,410
Grenada	2		3.6	6,960
Guatemala	1	−0.69	4.1	3,770
Guyana	2	0.34	5.0	3,670
Honduras	1	−0.41	3.2	2,400
Jamaica	2	0.56	1.0	3,440

Continued

Appendix Continued

	Type of democracy	Quality of governance	Average yearly economic growth	Per capita gross national income (PPP)
Mexico	1	0.43	3.6	8,790
Nicaragua	1	−0.40	3.3	2,080
Panama	2	0.81	4.5	5,680
Paraguay	1	−1.24	2.0	4,450
Peru	1	0.12	4.1	4,660
St. Kitts and Nevis	2		3.9	10,960
St. Lucia	2		2.7	5,400
St. Vincent and the Grenadines	2		3.3	5,210
Suriname	1	0.15	2.4	3,480
Trinidad and Tobago	1	1.35	3.0	8,220
Uruguay	2	1.89	3.1	8,880
Venezuela	1	−0.69	2.1	5,740
Average score for Latin America and the Caribbean		0.38	3.5	5,961

Notes

1. I would like to thank Renske Doorenspleet and the participants in the Conference on African Parliaments (Nairobi Apr. 19–22, 2004) for their comments on earlier versions of this chapter.
2. Olowu 2002: 4–5.
3. Moore 2001: 386.
4. Lipset 1959.
5. See Burkhart and Lewis-Beck 1994: 906–907; Doorenspleet 2001: 115–120.
6. Kaufmann et al. 2003.
7. North 1987; 1995.
8. Lijphart 1999.
9. Kick et al. 2000.
10. Ibid. 147.
11. Mick Moore 2001.
12. Ibid., 390.
13. Ibid., 386.
14. Arend Lijphart 1999.
15. Van Craneburgh 2003: 188–189.
16. Ibid., 188.
17. Ferree and Singh 2002.
18. Ibid., 92.

19. Olson 1982: 65.
20. Przeworski et al. 2000: 156.
21. Lipset 1959.
22. Moore 2001.
23. Moore 2001; Kick et al. 2000.
24. Przeworski et al. 2000.
25. As defined in World Bank 2002.
26. Freedom House 2003.
27. Kaufmann et al. 2003.
28. Ibid., 2–4.
29. Applied principal components analysis, a common way of data reduction, revealed that the six dimensions of governance could be summarized by one principal component that contains 71.6 percent of the total variance of the data. The factor loadings of the six dimensions on the summary variable quality of governance are: .86 (voice and accountability) .85 (political stability) .91 (government effectiveness) .80 (regulatory quality) .87 (rule of law) and .79 (control of corruption).
30. Beck et al. 2001.
31. Ibid., 165–166; cf. Ferree and Singh 2002: 96.
32. World Bank 2002.
33. Ibid.
34. Olson 1982; Przeworski et al. 2000.
35. Ferree and Singh 2002.
36. Olson's 1982; Przeworski et al. 2000.
37. Mandelbaum 2002.

3

Legislative Quotas for Women: Implications for Governance in Africa

Aili Mari Tripp[1]

International Studies, Women's Studies Research Centre,
Northwestern University, USA

Introduction

Today, women in some African countries have the highest rates of representation in legislatures in the world. Rwanda, for example, became the country with the highest female legislative representation in 2003, as the women of that country claimed 48.8 percent of parliamentary seats—surpassing even the Nordic countries. Other countries like Namibia, Uganda, Seychelles, South Africa, Mozambique, and Swaziland (only the upper house has 30 percent women) are at or exceed the 25 percent mark in female legislative representation. These represent significant increases in the presence of women in these bodies, especially between 1990 and 2005 when the numbers increased from an average of 8 percent to 14.5 percent. In part, this can be attributed to the increased use of legislative quotas for women. In many countries, women's rights activists are currently debating the introduction of quotas, some with the intent of increasing women's representation to 50 percent.

The expansion of women in legislatures has a number of implications for improving governance in African polities. It expands the pool of talent that is incorporated into governing institutions. Women bring their own perspectives to the table and can influence legislation in ways that reflect the diverse interests of a wider range of societal actors. Women's increased representation enhances equality, fairness, and justice in representation as a group in society that has been marginalized from governance regardless of whether women as a group have shared interests. Even though there have been active women's movements in many African countries, it cannot be assumed that women as a group are always going to share common concerns any more than one can say this of men. Nevertheless, women's interests, including conflicting interests among women, are represented; thereby leveling a playing field that has up until now been seriously skewed with respect to gender representation. Quotas can thus expand the legitimacy of a regime by addressing the concerns of this half of the electorate.

The utility of quotas in terms of enhancing the ability of women parliamentarians to be effective in legislative bodies and to enhance governance is more complex and problematic. Generally, it appears to depend greatly on 1) the extent to which the regime in question is democratic; 2) on the genuine commitment of the regime to advancing women more generally; and 3) on the extent to which a women's movement is active in working with women parliamentarians around issues of key concern, both around gender-related bills as well as more general legislation. This is evident in a comparison between the Ugandan and South African cases explored in this chapter. Thus, the extent to which quotas can make a difference in improving women's ability to participate effectively in the key institutions of governance is constrained or facilitated by the broader political framework within which they find themselves.

Reasons for the Expansion of Electoral Quotas

What accounts for the expansion of the use of electoral quotas for women in Africa? In part, these quotas result from pressure applied by women's movements in African countries, as well as by international women's movements. They are a product of changing international norms regarding female representation, as evident in various United Nations (UN) conventions and resolutions and in relation to the legislative targets set by key African regional organizations like the African Union, the Southern African Development Community (SADC) and the Economic Community of West African States (ECOWAS). With the rise of multipartyism and the decline of mass women's organizations tied to the single party, there was a need to find new symbolic ways to appeal to women voters as well as to create new bases for patronage networks. In some predominantly Muslim countries, the women's quota became part of an effort to contain the growing influence of Islamists.

Quotas fall into two main categories in Africa. One category, involving about half the countries with quotas, includes constitutional or legal provisions for reserved seats or executive appointments that are intended to determine the number of seats to be held by women in an election. Women may run for reserved seats in their districts and can be elected either by an electoral college of men and women (Uganda), or by women in each district/province (Rwanda). Another variant of the reserved seats system is the women-only list in which only women can vie for these seats on a nationwide basis regardless of party affiliation or district. In Tanzania, a reserved seat quota for women is allocated to political parties based on the proportional number of parliamentary seats won in an election.

The other half of countries with quotas belongs to the second category, which involves measures adopted voluntarily by political parties aimed at influencing the number of women candidates (for example, placing women higher on the party list, alternating women and men).

Cross-national studies of women's representation have to date largely ignored the impact of such legislative quotas.[2] One explanation for this

Table 3.1 Constitutionally Mandated Parliamentary Quotas for Women

Country	Women in legislature %	Constitutional provision of quota for women[a]	Quota introduced	Year quota
Djibouti[b]	10.8	10 percent of all party seats allocated for women	10%	2002
Eritrea	22.0	Reserved seats for women; uni-cameral	30%	1995
Kenya	07.1	Executive appointment; uni-cameral	3%	1997
Morocco	10.8	Women-only nationalist[c]	10%	2002
Rwanda	48.8	• Reserved seats for women in upper and lower house	30%	2003
		• Electoral college of women's Councils	~20%	
Tanzania	22.3	Special seats; uni-cameral	20%[d]	2000
Uganda	24.7	Reserved seat; uni-cameral	18.4%	1989

Source: Based on Inter-Parliamentary Union data, www.ipu.org/wmn-e/classif.htm. Figures refer to lower house or single house in case of uni-cameral legislature.
[a] Based on Parline database on the Inter-Parliamentary Union website www.ipu.org and on data from the Global Database of Quotas for Women, joint project of International IDEA and Stockholm University, www.quotaproject.org. Bi-cameral unless indicated otherwise.
[b] The special seat quota for women is allocated to political parties based on the proportional number of parliamentary seats won in an election.
[c] Only women can vie for these reserved seats regardless of party affiliation, not based on constituency as in reserved seats.
[d] The special seat quota for women is allocated to political parties based on the proportional number of parliamentary seats won in an election. Each party determines its own mechanism for filling the seats, with some nominating the women and others allowing women party members to elect their candidates.

Table 3.2 Legally Mandated Quotas for Women

Country	Women in legislature %	Legal provision of quota for women[a]	Quota	Year quota introduced
Niger	11.5	Elected	10%	
		Nominated; uni-cameral	25%	2000
Somalia Transitional National Government	10.0	Women-only lists[b]	10%	2001
Sudan	09.7	Reserved seats	9.7%	2000
Swaziland	10.8	Upper house: Executive appointment[c]	28%	2003

Source: Based on Inter-Parliamentary Union data, www.ipu.org/wmn-e/classif.htm. Figures refer to lower house or single house in case of uni-cameral legislature, with the exception of data for Swaziland, which indicates upper house figures.

[a] Based on Parline database on the Inter-Parliamentary Union website www.ipu.org and on data from the Global Database of Quotas for Women.

[b] Only women can vie for these reserved seats, regardless of party affiliation and not based on constituency as in reserved seats.

[c] Applies only to upper house.

omission may have to do with the fact that the phenomenon is new in much of Africa and Latin America. With the increased adoption of quotas in Latin America since the 1990s and in Africa since 1995, the findings of these earlier studies need to be modified to take account not only of quotas, but also of women's movements that have advocated for these changes in domestic and international norms.

Characteristics of Countries Adopting Quotas

By 2005, approximately 23 African countries (half of all African countries) had adopted some form of legislative quotas for women; some, like Angola, had plans to adopt quotas, while others, like Gambia, Kenya, and Nigeria, were engaged in ongoing debates on quotas. With a few exceptions, the majority of the countries with quotas had adopted them after 1995, which was the year that the UN Conference on Women was held in Beijing. The countries and parties that introduced quotas often cited the Convention on the Elimination of Discrimination against Women (CEDAW) and the 1995 UN Conference on Women in Beijing and the Beijing Platform for Action, which laid out guidelines for increasing the political representation of women. These were clear indications of the impact of the international women's movement on the adoption of quotas in Africa. Only three African countries with quotas in 2003 had adopted

Table 3.3 Party Mandated Parliamentary Quotas for Women

Country	Women in legislature %	Party mandate of quota for women[a]	Quota	Number of seats held by party	Year quota introduced
Botswana	07.0	• Botswana Congress Party	30%	21%	1999
		• Botswana National Front	30%	2%	1999
Burkina Faso[b]	11.7	• Alliance pour la Démocratie et la Fédération	25%	13%	2002
		• Congrès pour la Démocratie et le Progrès	25%	50%	2002
Cameroon	08.9	• Cameroon People's Free Movement	25–30%	83%	1996
		• Social Democratic Front	25%	12%	
Côte d'Ivoire	08.5	• Front Populaire Ivoirien	30%	43%	
Equatorial Guinea	18.0	• Convergencia para la Democracia Social		5.8%	
Ethiopia	07.7	• Ethiopia People's Revolutionary Free Front	30%	85%	2004
Mali	10.2	• Alliance for Democracy	30%	40%	
Mozambique	30.0	• Frente de Libertação de Moçambique (Frelimo)	30%	49%	1994
Niger	11.5	• National Movement for a Society in Development	5 seats	42%	
Senegal[c]	19.2	• Senegalese Free Party	33%	74%	2001
		• Parti Socialiste	25%	8%	
South Africa	32.8	• African National Congress	33%	70%	1994
Tunisia	22.8	• Democratic Constitutional Rally	20%	80%	

Source: Based on Inter-Parliamentary Union data, www.ipu.org/wmn-e/classif.htm. Figures refer to lower house or single house in case of uni-cameral leigislature.
[a] Based on Parline database on the Inter-Parliamentary Union website www.ipu.org and on data from the Global Database of Quotas for Women, joint project of International IDEA and Stockholm University, www.quotaproject.org. Bi-cameral unless indicated otherwise.
[b] Election not yet held under new quota arrangement.
[c] In 1982, Parti Socialiste reserved 25 percent of all posts in the party for women. In 2001, 14 political parties in Senegal urged political parties to reserve at least 30 percent of the places on their candidate lists for women.

them prior to 1995. This excludes the adoption of a quota for ten women by the Convention People's Party in Ghana in 1960 and the introduction of eight percent quotas in Egypt between 1979 and 1986.

In those African countries with quotas, on average, 17 percent of legislative seats were held by women, compared with nine percent of seats in countries without quotas. Those countries with reserved seats of more than 20 percent or where the ruling party or top two parties had targets or quotas of more than 20 percent were able to raise female representation in the legislature to 23 percent.

A number of countries with quotas recently emerged from civil wars (Eritrea, Mozambique, Rwanda, Somalia, and Uganda) or wars of liberation (Namibia and South Africa) after which they drew up new constitutions and re-established their parliaments from scratch. Similarly, countries with quotas in Africa are more likely to be newly independent states: hence, they are also countries where women most recently received the right to vote and to run for office. Africa is different from other parts of the world in this respect, where the end of conflict and the lateness of independence have not mattered as much. In Africa, the end of major turmoil and conflict meant that there was greater openness in relation to creating new rules that included female leadership. Moreover, women were not contending with entrenched male incumbents as they sought political representation. Female quotas have generally been difficult to introduce when they meant ousting a male incumbent from his seat, especially in places where large numbers of incumbents are usually re-elected. Therefore, it has been easier to introduce quotas in situations where women could compete for vacant seats—newly recreated parliaments (after a civil conflict) provided such a venue.

Some of the countries that adopted quotas have left-leaning parties in power: Eritrea, Mozambique, Namibia, and South Africa. Seychelles also had a left-leaning party in power in 1991 when it had female representation of 46 percent, suggesting that some kind of informal preferential treatment was applied within the party in regard to the selection of candidates. Overall, however, there is no particular relationship between left-leaning parties and the adoption of quotas in Africa.

Many of the countries with quotas have the most active women's movements in Africa (Botswana, Mali, Mozambique, Namibia, South Africa, Tanzania, and Uganda), while approximately one-third of the countries have relatively weak women's movements (Burkina Faso, Cameroon, Côte d'Ivoire, and Djibouti), co-opted women's movements (Eritrea) or suppressed women's movements (Sudan). If the number of women's organizations attending the Beijing conference in 1995 is taken as a rough indicator of the strength of the women's movement, countries with quotas tended to have more of these organizations at the conference.

In many parts of the world, the electoral system is said to influence women's ability to gain legislative representation. Of the eight (Rwanda, Mozambique, South Africa, Namibia, Uganda, Tanzania, Seychelles, Eritrea) countries with female representation of more than 20 percent in Africa, all but two have quotas, four have party list systems and five have proportional representation systems. In Africa, about 33 percent have party list proportional representation; 31 percent have first-past-the-post (FPTP) plurality systems; 18 percent have two round-majority systems and ten percent have FPTP semi-proportional systems.

The countries that have adopted quotas divide evenly into three categories in regard to regime type: democratic, semi-authoritarian, and authoritarian. This suggests that regime type in Africa does not determine whether countries are more or less likely to adopt quotas, although democratic countries with quotas average some four percentage points more in terms of female representation in parliament than semi-authoritarian and authoritarian regimes with quotas. About 25 of Africa's sub-Saharan states would fall into the semi-authoritarian regime category based on Freedom House data, and, of these, nine have some form of legislative quota for women (Burkina Faso, Côte d'Ivoire, Ethiopia, Kenya, Uganda, Tanzania, Senegal, Mozambique, Niger). In the nine African countries that would be considered democratic according to Freedom House, three have quotas (Botswana, South Africa, and Mali) and Namibia has local level quotas. Finally, of the ten authoritarian regimes in sub-Saharan Africa, four have quotas (Rwanda, Equatorial Guinea, Eritrea, Cameroon). In other words, slightly less than half of the countries representing each regime type have some kind of quota. If one compares countries with and without quotas, differences regarding democratic status and civil and political liberties are minimal. However, the more democratic-leaning countries in Africa (Botswana, Mali, Mozambique, Namibia, Senegal, and South Africa) have tended to prefer quotas or targets set by parties themselves rather than adopting reserved seats or quotas mandated by legislatures or constitutions.

Countries adopting quotas include the wealthiest in Africa, Botswana, Namibia, and South Africa, as well as the poorest, including Cameroon, Eritrea, Mali, Mozambique, and Tanzania. Generally, though, the countries with quotas tend to be less wealthy with gross per capita domestic product (GDP) of approximately $2,646, compared with $3,361 for those without quotas, according to figures from the UNDP *Human Development Report 2003*. Countries that have the highest rates of female representation in parliament (more than 20 percent), however, do have, on average, higher per capita GDP ($4,433) than those with lower rates of female representation ($3,315).

About half of the countries adopting quotas have a population of 50 percent or more that considers itself Muslim, although in several of the predominantly Muslim nations like Djibouti, Somalia, and Sudan, the quotas are relatively small (ten percent). Nevertheless, overall, countries with quotas are less likely to have a high percentage of Muslims or

Catholics and are more likely to have higher Protestant populations when compared with countries without quotas. Female representation rates in predominantly Muslim states still tend to be lower than those of other countries in Africa.

Factors Giving Rise to Quotas

Domestic Women's Movements

Women's movements have been closely associated with the adoption of quota systems in most African countries. The best-documented cases of pressure applied by women's movements in regard to quotas are found in southern Africa. In South Africa, the African National Congress (ANC) Women's League spearheaded the initiative to increase female representation in parliament, achieving a 30 percent quota.[3] In Namibia, before the 1999 National Assembly elections, a coalition of women's organizations and other non-governmental organizations (NGOs), the Namibian Women's Manifesto Network (NWMN), convinced several parties to adopt resolutions providing for party lists in which 50 percent of the candidates were women, resulting in 26.4 percent female representation in parliament in 1999, a jump from 12.5 percent in 1994.[4] (More women would have been elected had the parties stuck to their resolutions. For example, only 20 of the ruling party's 72 candidates were women.) In September 2000, the NWMN launched the 50/50 Campaign to fight for 50 percent female representation in the legislature. The Parliamentary Women's Caucus and the Namibia Elected Women Forum (including elected women from the local, regional and national levels) have also been involved in this campaign.

International Women's Movements

Another factor giving rise to the increased adoption of quotas has been pressure from international bodies. Not only did pressure come from international conferences like the 1995 UN Conference on Women in Beijing, but it was also applied throughout the region. Women activists pressed regional bodies within Africa to pressure member states to increase female representation. The African Union's 2003 Protocol on the Rights of Women in Africa calls for equal gender representation, as do the 1997 SADC Declaration on Gender and Development and the 2001 Protocol on Democracy and Good Governance of ECOWAS. There have also been efforts to bring about one-third female representation in these regional bodies themselves. The East African Legislative Assembly (EALA) has a provision for one-third female representation and the ECOWAS Female Parliamentary Association (ECOFEPA) is working to increase the number of parliamentarians in that organization.

Diffusion Factor

Another related explanation for the adoption of quotas is the diffusion factor, both from country to country and within countries.[5] It is especially evident within countries in Africa. If one party adopts quotas, other parties may feel compelled to do the same lest they lose the votes of women. During the 2001 parliamentary elections in Senegal, a group of women's organizations instigated a Citizen Campaign to address the under-representation of women in parliament. They sought to reverse a situation in which only 19 of 140 legislators (13.5 percent) had been women.[6] In an unprecedented development, the majority of the 25 political parties in Senegal fielded more than 20 percent female candidates in national lists in the run-up to the 2001 parliamentary elections, with the list of the Parti Démocratique Sénégalais (PDS) amounting to more than 33 percent.[7] As a result, women ended up with 19.2 percent of the seats in Senegal, an increase of about six percent.

Symbolic Appeal

Quotas sometimes served as symbolic gestures to appeal to women voters. In a multiparty context, some countries sought new methods of winning the political allegiance of women voters after the demise of the single parties and their attendant mass women's organizations. With the proliferation of independent women's organizations, the use of quotas became a way to indicate support for women and women interested in political representation.

Impact of Quotas

The success of quotas in enhancing women's role in parliaments and governance depends on the political will of the government to support women's rights and the strength of the women's movement in pushing for changes in the status of women. However, more importantly, it depends on the broader conditions established by regime type and the extent to which the regime is committed to democratic governance.

The contrast between the experiences of women in South Africa and Uganda illustrates some of the ways in which the impact of quotas is constrained by regime type with South Africa being a democracy, while Uganda has remained under semi-authoritarian rule. Both countries have active women's movements that became especially galvanized at the same time in the 1990s with respect to women's role in parliament. Women parliamentarians themselves in both South Africa and Uganda have improved their skills as legislators over time and become more effective.

As Hannah Britton, who has studied the women parliamentarians, points out in the case of South Africa: "In the span of four years, from 1991 to the 1994 elections, the women of South Africa moved from the silent backbone of the nation to a force of considerable political power and public influence."[8] She shows how women parliamentarians, through the Joint Committee on Improving the Quality of Life and Status of Women, had a positive impact on many key pieces of legislation, including laws impacting women, e.g., the 1996 Choice on the Termination of Pregnancy Act allowing women the right to abortion; the 1996 Films and Publications Act that protects against the degradation of women and children; and the 1998 Domestic Violence Act, which increases the legal and institutional protection for victims of domestic abuse. Britton shows how women parliamentarians made important contributions to the Maintenance Act, the Employment Equity Act, the Skills Development Act, and the Labour Relations Act. In particular, they ensured that the Labour Relations Act recognized maternity rights and women's rights against sexual harassment in the workplace and lobbied for the Employment Equity Act requiring employers to hire fairly across race, gender, and disability. Moreover, women activists together with the parliamentarians were able to put in place a Commission on Gender Equality through the 1996 Commission for Gender Equality Act to ensure that such laws were fully implemented. In addition, they fought to be part of the budget process so that the budget might better reflect women's interests.

In contrast, in Uganda, although women were vocal and active in parliamentary debates, they had more difficulty pushing through legislation that would have provided key supports to women. For example, although leading women parliamentarians and activists were able to insert key gender related provisions into the 1998 Land Act, they failed to get the inclusion of key co-ownership clauses into the passage of the 2000 amendments to the Land Act. The Uganda Women's Network (UWONET) and the Uganda Land Alliance (ULA) coordinated lobbying efforts and were very active around this issue. The insistence on the co-ownership clause stems from the fact that current legislation, given customary practices, provides limited possibilities for women to own land. Thus under customary law, which prevails in Uganda, a woman may have jointly acquired land with her husband and may have spent her entire adult life cultivating the land, but she cannot claim ownership of the property. If he dies, the land generally goes to the sons, but may also be left to daughters. Nevertheless, he may still leave the wife with no land and therefore no source of subsistence.

Up until this conflict, the women's movement had been enthusiastic about President Museveni and his pro-women policies, including reserved seats for women in the legislature and in local councils, political appointments of women to key government posts, affirmative action policies for women in university admissions, etc. In February 2000, when the Minister of State for Lands brought the amendments to the Land Act before Cabinet, it was the president, by his own omission, who decided to pull out the co-ownership clause and used some parliamentary procedure technicalities through which to justify their omission even after the parliament had voted to approve the amendments.[9] The action was an enormous disappointment for women's rights activists and parliamentarians supporting the amendments. They believed that the lack of governmental support for the amendments were a clear indication of a lack of governmental support for key demands regarding women's rights. However, had the process been transparent and had the parliamentary vote in support of the amendments been recognized, such irregularities would not have occurred.

Another way in which undemocratic governance impacts on women have to do with the way state patronage networks operate. In some countries, the introduction of quotas was linked to the attempt to create new state patronage networks. Uganda is a country that has adopted female legislative quotas in response to pressure from a vibrant women's movement to increase the number of female political leaders. By 2003, women held 25 percent (77) of the seats in parliament. The use of reserved seats—one seat that only women compete for in each of Uganda's 56 districts—has contributed to a change in the political culture. Today, by and large, the population accepts women as public figures.

Many women parliamentarians, however, owe their positions to President Yoweri Museveni and the existing system of patronage. While the relatively large number of women in parliament is an indication of the success of lobbying by women for greater representation, many of the elected women officials have been restrained from supporting women's issues. As one activist explained to me in 2002: "Our voice has been hijacked at the highest organs, at parliament. Our voice there has been killed." Some argue that the affirmative action seats in parliament have created a group of legislators more beholden to the regime in their loyalties than to the cause of women's emancipation.[10]

One factor that accounts for the consolidation of parliamentary loyalties is the fact that the District Women Representatives in parliament are elected by an electoral college of roughly 200 people who can potentially be manipulated via bribery and vote buying. Other interest groups (youth, disabled, and workers) with special reserved seats in parliament directly elect their own representatives through their own organizations. Women District Representatives, however, are not representatives *of* women, but, rather, they are women representatives of the district, which has translated into a different mode of election for the women representatives. Efforts to open up the election process to universal suffrage were voted down because of pressure applied by the president, who argued that it would be too difficult for women to canvas votes across an entire district.[11] Many of the women parliamentarians who have been elected to the reserved seats have been used to vote for anti-democratic legislation (such as the 2002 Political Parties and Organizations Bill) and against legislation that would promote women's rights (such as the co-ownership amendment to the 1998 Land Act).

Thus, the introduction of quotas in Uganda served many purposes. It signaled to ordinary women the government's commitment to women's leadership and opened up new avenues for women to become political leaders. At the same time, it created a block of loyalist women who could be used when needed to suppress various demands of the women's movement or of democrats when they ran counter to government wishes.

Thus, the broader context within which quotas are introduced can make a dramatic difference in the capacity of women activists and parliamentarians to have an impact on legislation as is evident in the above contrast between efforts to pass women friendly legislation in South Africa and Uganda.

Conclusion

The introduction of legislative quotas in about half of Africa's countries has served multiple purposes for different actors. Women's movements, domestic and international, have sought legislative quotas to increase the representation of women. Parties have sometimes introduced quotas under pressure from other parties to keep up with their competitors. Governments, in turn, have often sought quotas for symbolic reasons to appeal to women voters and to signal an interest in women's rights and voices. They may be responding to changing international norms regarding female representation, but they may also be seeking to create a modern image for themselves in order to challenge more conservative societal forces, including Islamist movements in predominantly Muslim countries (Morocco and Tunisia, for example). In other instances, government leaders may be seeking to create new lines of patronage and to ensure loyal support as old networks become problematic or threatening (Rwanda and Uganda). The introduction of gender-based quotas has the potential to improve government legitimacy if it is tied to other measures to enhance the status of women and women's leadership. Quotas can be used as a mechanism to enhance equality and societal justice if used within a democratic framework. As in the South African case, it is evident that quotas can improve women's status if introduced with the active participation of a women's movement and in a manner that keeps women's interests at the core and that, the terms are acceptable to women. However, overriding political considerations of patronage as in the Ugandan case within an undemocratic context, can lead to quotas being manipulated for political purposes other than the advancement of women and the promotion of democratic governance. In an undemocratic environment, the utility of quotas is considerably diminished. Future research should explore varying reasons why countries adopt legislative quotas for women and how they make use of them in varying contexts.

Notes

1. The chapter is largely adapted from Aili Mari Tripp, "The Changing Face of Africa's Legislatures: Women and Quotas" in Ballington, J (ed.), *The Implementation of Quotas: African Experiences*", International IDEA: Stockholm, 2004.
2. Paxton 1997; Kenworthy and Malami 1999; Reynolds 1999; Norris and Inglehart 2001.
3. Geisler 2000.
4. Bauer 2003.
5. Matland and Studlar 1996.
6. Diop 2001.
7. Beck 2003.
8. Hannah Britton 2002.
9. Tripp 2004b.
10. Tamale 1999.
11. Gawaya-Tegulle 2001.

4

Local Assemblies and Local Democracy in sub-Saharan Africa

Dele Olowu

African Development Bank, Tunis, Tunisia

Introduction

This chapter is about local assemblies and local democracies. Its main objective is to plug the scanty attention given to comparative local democracy in much of the discourses on Africa's democratic renewal. The need for articulating this issue stems from the fact that despite the significant role they play in effective governance and economic development in many regions, local governments have not been major players in African governance or development before the second democratic upsurge in the continent. Africa's local governments for instance are the weakest among the world's regions judged by personnel size or expenditure profile.[1] The rationale for stronger local governments is premised on the following considerations. First, there is the argument that democracy cannot be consolidated at the central level if it is not devolved to the locality. Second, some contend that the revitalization of local government is critical because local democracies serve as the training ground for recruiting national level democratic leaders and for citizenship training in democratic practices and norms. Within this view, some analysts point out that many of the huge economic mistakes made in Africa's development governance up to the late 1980s are attributable to excessive centralization of power.[2] Countries as disparate as Ethiopia, Uganda, Mali, Rwanda, and Republic of South Africa, to mention a few, are turning away from centralized approaches to decentralized ones. Third, because most global public policy initiatives such as the millennium development goals (MDGs) are actually delivered by local governments (basic health, education, water, and sanitation), it is vital to develop the capacity of local governments so that they can complement the efforts of national government. It is at the local level that the process of democratizing development, combating poverty and mobilizing resources within and outside the state can become a guarantee for accessing basic services.[3]

I intend to provide a critical review the performance of selected Africa's growing number of local assemblies. The number is growing because many countries in the region have embarked on a new round of decentralization closely tied to their national democratic renewal program. In some important respects, these reforms are different from previous experiments at decentralization in that authority (or responsibility for delivering specific services) and resources (human and financial), are actually devolved to local communities—in sharp contrast to similar efforts in the past. More than two-thirds of countries in the region embarked on some new rounds of democratic decentralization in which responsibilities, resources (human and financial), and accountability arrangements are transferred from national to local levels.[4]

Another attribute of the new decentralization is that local government councilors in these countries are actually elected by the people not appointed by the state as in the past. Hence, these newly created local assemblies are expected to function like the national assemblies and the question is how have they been performing their roles of legal and policy development, oversight and representation? I have been fortunate to have access to information from diverse data sources including two most recent studies. These are, first, a seven-nation study of local governance and democratic decentralization [5] and, second, an assessment of the quality of local democracy in eastern and southern Africa cities undertaken by the International Democratic Electoral Assistance (IDEA) in 2004.[6]

I will start by discussing the models of local democratic governance before presenting and assessing the cases on which I focus and in the third section I provide a distillation of the main lessons before concluding.

Models of Local Democratic Government

At the heart of the different models of local government is an attempt to forge an effective relationship between the local assembly or legislature and the executive in a way that ensures maximum effectiveness and energy in policy articulation and decision-making (largely through the executive), while at the same time ensuring accountability of the governors to the governed. I content this is essentially through the local legislature.

In contrast to national level arrangements, local assemblies, in many countries, combine executive and legislative responsibilities—although there are also wide variations by country, history, and political ideology.

For instance, the British and French arrangements have been particularly dominant in Africa, largely due to the colonial experience. Even though Britain and France have made substantial changes to their systems of local government, former colonies have held to the legacies of the colonial past rather than the realities of the present.

In the Westminster or British model, council members are elected in electoral wards to represent their local population. This council then elects the mayor and his deputy. In fact, the mayoral office in this *weak mayor model* is largely ceremonial. The work of the council is carried out mainly by council committees that work closely with professional administrators under the general direction (traditionally not effectively coordinated) of the Town Councilor. Since the late 1960s, the British have sought to bring stronger coordination to the work of councils at the political and administrative levels, but most African countries continue to use the original concept of the Town Councilor and the weak mayor. There are two implications of this for the legislative role of the council. First, the council provides the policy direction through committee work. It also has responsibility for determining who will serve as mayor (and deputy) and, at least in theory, has wide powers of control over the budget and the administration of the council. The mayor is not only heavily dependent on the council members for his/her office but s/he can be replaced anytime the latter can muster a majority to do so. The mayor is further weakened by the fact that the incumbent has no executive control of the council, being a ceremonial rather than an executive head of the council. As already noted above, many commonwealth African countries have adopted this British system—although, as shown below, a few countries have made changes to this model. Legislative functions, such as passing by-laws (laws that require approval by the national government before they become effective) and policy as well as the budget formulation and review are actually performed by professional departmental heads through committees and these committees bring them to the full council for ratification.[7]

A major modification to the weak mayor system is what operates in a number of large American cities. Referred to as *the strong mayor model*, the mayor is elected directly like the councilors by the full electorate thus giving him/her a strong hand in running the council's affairs. In addition, he/she appoints heads of the various departments of the council with people selected from within and outside the council who serve with him/her as a form of cabinet. To complete the picture of the full separation of powers as at national and state levels, the mayor can use veto powers to block council legislation or policy initiatives. The council's responsibility of law-making, oversight, and representation is thus separated from executive work. Many countries have made variations to this arrangement. For instance, some South African large cities—Cape Town, Durban, and Johannesburg—are run under this model with the mayor able to hire his/her own city manager who then hires senior members of the council's professional leadership. The strong mayor system works well in the United States in big cities where party politics dominate and class divisions are strong.[8] The Zimbabwe government also adopted this model for the governance of its cities in 1998.

Most African French-speaking countries use the French model, which is different from the pure British and American models. French commune mayors have independent powers to appoint officials and make by-laws, they also exercise powers on behalf of the state but the council elects such mayors indirectly in a typical weak mayor system. French mayors have substantial political clout at the national and local levels, in the African variant; however, the prefect, an appointee of the central government who enjoys equal and more prominent legislative and executive power than the mayor, exercises most of the powers of the mayors.

Other lesser-used models are the *city manager* and *commission plan*. Many countries also try to find an accommodation for traditional system of governing within the modern system of local government.[9] The latter is not discussed in this chapter as it is only tangentially related to the work of local councils.

The main elements of the city manager system are that it follows the corporate plan of the private sector. The city manager is hired by the council to run the council. H/she has wide powers to hire and fire and to spend resources once approved by the council. In the United States, research has shown that the city manager works best in small cities rather than in large cities. In small cities consensus on what constitutes good governance is not so easy to secure. The Windhoek municipality is run under this arrangement and since Windhoek is a well-governed city, it is a system that is worth studying. One of the Nigerian regional governments also adopted the city manager plan in the late 1960s; however, the city managers could not be hired and fired by the council, they were civil servants—and it was not surprising that the system was abandoned after a few years. It is important to note that the city manager does not replace either the mayor or the council in terms of their latent roles in the executive and legislative branches of the local government system.

In the commission plan, electorates elect a board of management for the city. This board of management oversees the work of each department and reports directly to the public. In essence, the board members combine executive and legislative work of the local council. The use of portfolio councilors (Nigeria under the initial reform of local government in 1976) is a variant of this arrangement. The problem of the commission plan is that of coordination.

The most dominant forms in Africa are the weak mayor and the *prefectoral models*. The latter is actually a form of deconcentration or administrative decentralization rather than of devolutionary decentralization even though there is usually a committee to advise the prefect. This was the dominant model in Anglophone and Francophone Africa until the 1990s, when many countries embraced democracy at the national level and new efforts were made to institutionalize democracy at the local level as well. The important point is that prefectoral models do not give legislative authority (or any substantive authority for that matter) to the council. The prefect combines the executive and legislative roles. The committee or local assembly serves as adviser to the prefect who is regarded as the representative of the national government in the province or locality. The Ghanaian case, discussed later in this chapter, approximates this model.

The litmus test for an effective local assembly is whether it is able to promote two types of accountability of the local council—the accountability of the local bureaucracy to elected officials and the accountability of elected officials to the bureaucracy.[10]

Since this study is on local assemblies, we focus on the composition, size, and effectiveness of local assemblies in terms of their key roles—policy-making, oversight, and representation of citizens. In particular, we shall try to pose the question of the effectiveness of these arrangements in terms of influencing policy-making by the councils and also of the exercise of oversight over the executive, whether this is viewed in terms of the mayor (in a strong mayor system), the prefect, or the heads of departments (in a weak mayor system).

City Case Studies

Municipal governments are the most advanced local governments in Africa. They confront problems arising from rapid population growth, economic management and global and national influences that make them significant political and economic actors. We focused on these municipalities first before reviewing national cases below.

Lusaka City Council, Zambia

Lusaka has a total population of 1,084,703. It is the capital city of Zambia, a country whose governance has undergone significant change since the departure of the country's long-term president, Kenneth Kaunda, who was deposed at the country's first multiparty election in 1992. Since then, the country has had two ivilian presidents: President Chiluba, currently under investigation for corruption charges and President Mwanawasa, the present incumbent. Economically, Zambia has become one of Africa's poorest countries (poverty increased from 70 percent to 73 percent between 1991 and 1998) and has qualified for the Highly Indebted Poor Countries (HIPC) facility. Only a small minority of the Lusaka population is employed (9 percent) in the formal sector, the rest operate in the sprawling informal sector. A majority (70 percent) of the population is also estimated as poor. Life-expectancy has fallen from 55 to 50 years between 1990 and 2000.

The city of Lusaka has 30 wards from which local government councilors are chosen using the first past the post (FPTP) system. The national political party system dominates local electioneering and in the elections in 1992, 1998, and 2001 the ruling Movement for Multiparty Democracy (MMD) was formally in opposition and controlled the local council. However, in the last year, Lusaka city council has fallen to two opposition parties: the United Party for National Development (UPND) and the Forum for Democracy and Development (FDD). The process of selecting candidates for local elections is the same as for national elections—the local committee initiates a recommendation, which is ratified by the national committee. It is significant that issues that dominated the election campaigns were provisions regarding potable water, market stalls, upgrading squatter compounds, construction and maintenance of roads, and anticorruption in plot allocation.

These are all local issues, but the Zambian local governments are not effectively resourced to provide them. The government's decentralization program encapsulated the 1991 Local Government Act, that promises authority and resources to local governments. On the other hand, new national bodies have been created to handle basic healthcare and large municipal housing was privatized. Lusaka is completely dependent on its own sources to finance its annual budget of 46.5 billion kwachas.[11]

Unlike other countries in the region, Zambia has no quota for women although the issue is still being discussed openly. Nationally, only 6.3 percent of councilors were women in the last three elections, even though women constitute 52 percent of the electorate. It is also felt that not enough educated persons are councilors, but this might be due to the perception that these organs have little resources under their control.

Voter participation at local election is about 10 percent compared with 75 per cent at national level elections.

Besides the 30 elected councilors, Lusaka city council has seven Members of Parliament. The council is run by council committees and co-opted persons. There are four main committees—finance, personnel, works, housing, and social services. The town clerk is the chief executive officer and has eight directors and a workforce of 2,200 employees working under him. Management makes recommendations to the council committees that are then recommended (or rejected or deferred) to the full council, which meets monthly.

Lusaka city council, like other councils in the country, is run under the weak mayor model. Councilors rather than the electorate elect the mayor and his position is largely ceremonial and carries no executive powers. Nevertheless, the position is significant especially in terms of relations with the central government and the growing number of development partners among the NGOs and international organizations working at the local government level. The council lacks resources to tackle many of the problems it confronts. It does not receive grants from the government and is forced to rely on levies and rates from citizens. The latter complain that these levies have rarely been translated into services. It is estimated that about 80 percent of total expenditures is spent on servicing the administration.

It is significant that the council committees can be quite effective and have suspended seven of their own members for improper conduct in the sale of land plots. The minutes of the council meetings, budgets, and information on land plots available for sale are also available to the public at a nominal fee. The council has a website (www.lcc.gov.zm) and invites the public to its budget discussions. The tendering procedure makes it mandatory for the local tenders committee to include representatives of two outside bodies—the Christian Council of Churches and the Lusaka Chamber of Commerce. The council has the power to hire and fire its staff.

Gaborone City Council, Botswana

Gaborone population has grown rapidly from 3,800 when it became the national capital in 1963 to 186,007 (2001). Thirty-six percent of urban residents in the country live in Gaborone—although large tracts of territory and people are now living outside the formal boundaries of the city. As a government capital city, Botswana is credited as one of the better-governed countries in the continent. It is important to appreciate the fact that even though the city is largely dependent on the central government to finance most of its expenditure requirements, up to 72 percent of the total budget (in 1999/2000 it was Pula 99 million[12]), the opposition has been in power for many years.

Gaborone has 13 wards and uses the British system of FPTP constituency-based local council electoral system. The local government structure is also found in the British weak mayor system as described above. In recognition of the growing number of the city's population, the number of councilors was almost doubled in 1994 with restructuring of the city into 25 wards.

The most serious problem confronting GCC is that most of the responsibilities undertaken by local governments in other southern African regions are actually managed by central government agencies—housing, land, planning, water and these activities also undermine potential revenue bases of the council. Even then, the poor sections of the city of Gaborone are poorly served with services such as sanitation, recreational facilities, and security and this is traced to the fact that these sections of the city are poorly represented in the council.

The city council is governed through committees of councilors. The opposition party, the Botswana National Front since 1984, has dominated the council at elections. As in other parts of the region, party members can cross the carpet after their election. Moreover, since parties are structured around national rather than local issues, local democracy tends to be marginalized in the elections as in the council operations.

There is much apathy in local council elections partly because of the perceived weaknesses of local government, there is a national unified local government commission responsible for all senor staffing into all local governments, as well as their weak constitutional status. They are only statutory with huge powers given to the Minister of Local Government for the management or dissolution of local governments. Both the recurrent and capital budgets of GCC is the subject of close scrutiny by the Ministry of Local Government and Housing and Finance.

On the other hand, councilors in GCC are quite alert to their responsibilities. They are in effective engagement with civic bodies. GCC in 1995 received permission to make grants to small civic bodies and most councilors understand their primary responsibilities as meeting their constituents and seeking feedback, informing the council of the needs for their constituents, defending the council's decisions before constituents, meeting with area committees, and encouraging self-help activities. However, the councilors are part-timers and most council meetings begin in the evenings when many civic officials have retired for the day. It is also not easy for them to keep abreast of issues presented to them by full-time professionals, and generally competent officials whom they cannot hire or fire.

The mayor sits as an ex-officio member of all the council committees, each of which has its own chairperson. To date, out of the 11 mayors that came to power in GCC, only two have been female. Moreover, the position of Mayor is a largely ceremonial one, with little authority.

Nairobi City Council, Kenya

This is one council that has known better days in the early years of the country's independence before the central government clamped down, took over most of its functions and resources, and, for a time, even its management, having appointed a commission to manage it. The reassertion of democracy nationally has brought new life back to the NCC.

Nairobi is a millionaire city of some 2.1 million people as of the last census (1999). Almost one million is less than 20 years old making it a largely youthful population that requires many services including education, health, and recreation. Almost all of Kenya's ethnic groups are represented in Nairobi, as the city is the main source of urban formal employment, involving 30 percent of the total active population, but also the largest majority of those in the informal sector. It is not surprising that NCC has a largely youthful population and a racially structured society in which white communities control most of the economic resources followed by Asians, with Africans constituting the largest bulk of the city's poor population.

Electoral turnout in NCC is more impressive compared to other cities—it was 44 percent in 2002 compared to 57 percent at national elections. There are 74 councilors. 55 elected from single wards and 19 nominated, previously by the Minister for Local Government but since 1977 by each political party reflecting their electoral strength. As in other English-speaking countries, the first-past-the post electoral system of councilor constituency is used. The councilors work in committees and elect the mayor, resulting in a weak mayor system. This reflects not only in poor mayor–citizen–council relationships but also in the inability of the councils to hold senior officials who run the departments accountable. This is because a unified commission under the control of the Ministry of Local Government rather than the local governments manages senior local government personnel. In addition, senior managers accuse councilors of wanting to micromanage and ensuring that council services benefit them and their cronies. Council elections are undertaken every five years.

The new (2003) decentralization policy of the national government requires local governments to make consultations with civic bodies in drawing up their strategic development plans (Local Authority Service

Development Plans—LASDAPs). It also requires that in implementation there must be decentralization beyond the local governments into wards. The central government contributes 10 percent of national revenues to support this initiative.

It is significant to note that each of these three cities has a functioning system of local democracy—elected councilors are recruited through elections to perform functions on behalf of the community. On the other hand, in all three cities we find that municipalities are severely constrained from addressing some of the most important problems confronting these cities—their powers are severely constrained by the national government legislation and their own capacity. In particular, the legislative systems used in all three cities are based on the inherited British system of constituency-based councilors who elect one among them to be mayor. The council functions through committees but these committee members are part-timers and no match for the full-time professionals. In only one city is the council the employer and manager of full-time personnel.

The next three cases take national samples of the functioning of local assemblies.

National Case Studies

Ghana

Ghana's district assemblies (DAs) were designated as "the highest political and administrative, planning, development, budgeting and rating authorities".[13] The assemblies have been assigned 86 functions as a part of Ghana's decentralization and democratization program in 1988. In 1992, it was fully embodied in the new constitution. DAs are the sole taxing authorities in their localities and have powers to make by-laws (subject to the approval of the Ministry of Local Government and Rural Development), and are corporate bodies.

However, the devolutionary authority of the council is subject to strict limitations. First, DA activities are monitored by the Regional Coordinating Council headed by a regional minister, an appointee of the national government. The central government reserves the power to investigate the performance of the DAs and may dissolve the assembly. According to Ayee, the reality of devolution of authority to the DAs remotely influences national policy. Their ability to persuade the government to modify its policies has been severely constrained.

Even though competitive party elections exist at the national level, DA members are elected through non-party-based elections. The argument of the government is that local government deals with bread-and-butter issues that should not be subject to partisanship, although some observers see this as a ploy to keep contending parties from occupying top positions in local government.

While the DAs elect their own officers, including the presiding member (PM), government appointees, called District Council Executives (DCE), head the district executive councils (DEC). The argument for this arrangement is that it will help to reduce corruption at the local government level. Anecdotal and other evidence point to the fact that this arrangement has not prevented corruption, Indeed 25 of these DCEs were dismissed on the basis of corruption charges in 1997. On the other hand, the government normally requests that the DAs endorse anyone proposed as DCE before formal appointment. The PM is not even a member of the all-powerful DEC—ostensibly to promote the separation of powers. Unfortunately, the council members cannot remove an erring DCE. In addition, the president of the republic appoints 30 percent of the membership of the DAs in order to represent special interests and chiefs, but, again, this is used to further the political support of the party in power at the center.

Ghana's DA members are expected to maintain close contacts with their constituency, but this has been endangered by two institutional factors. First, constituency relations are often financially demanding, yet DA members are only paid a sitting allowance of 10 US cents per sitting. Second, they are often overshadowed by Members of Parliament who have much more institutional largesse to maintain their constituency relations. For poorly performing DA members there is a provision for recall by 25 percent of the registered electorate. This has not been applied to date due to its cumbersomeness. A petition must be lodged with the District election committee, which must in turn organize a referendum on this petition with at least 40 percent of the electorate voting and 60 percent supporting the recall request. The only ground for suspending council members is for non-attendance at three consecutive meetings and this is a growing reality as the members see their roles undermined by the DCE.

DA members are also required to work closely with civil society organizations in the development of their communities, but there has been no love lost between these two sets of institutional actors. The DA members believe that CSOs are heavily dependent on donors thus becoming competitors for resources that councils would have used for development programs. On the other hand, the CSOs believe that they have a better track record than the DAs and, therefore, bypass them leading further to loss of legitimacy. This is of growing importance, as many international NGOs are becoming major players in development work.

In summary, the Ghanaian council is a mixture of old and new decentralization. The DAs are empowered legally to undertake development in its area of jurisdiction. However, it is undermined by several central government institutions, which directly control their personnel, working on centralized responsibilities. DAs have no control of their own senior personnel by the fact that there are two parallel councils—the DA under the leadership of PM and the DEC under the leadership of the DCE, with the latter an appointee of the central government, with impressive powers.

Nigeria

Nigeria's democratic decentralization program is one of the oldest in the Africa region. Nationwide democratic decentralization was initiated in 1976 and successive governments—both civilian and military—have sustained and supported the initiative. The Nigerian reforms transferred major responsibilities, including financial and human resources to the local communities. Each community chooses its own local political leadership. Nigerian local governments are second only to Uganda in terms of the level of total public expenditures for which they are responsible— 12 percent against Uganda's 21 percent. Even then, Nigerian local governments dispose of more resources as a percentage of GDP than Uganda's (5 percent and 4 percent respectively).[14]

Nigeria is also the only country in the sub-region with a strong mayor system. Each council has a mayor elected by the whole electorate and those who comes to office, including six supervisory councilors, each of whom is responsible for heading a department. By a reform of 1988, all councils have six departments—four sectoral and two generic dealing with administration (HRM) and finance.

The country settled for the strong mayor system because it was felt that this ensured that political representatives would be able to provide direction to the permanent administration. It also represented a replication of the American presidential system at the local government level with full separation between the executive and the legislature. The problem is that the chair of councils has been more dominant in the local government system and is not always subject to control by the local councilors. Neither can one argue that the councilors are subject to the citizens, given the regular and widespread reports on corruption at the local government level, as at other levels of government.

On the other hand, where effective leadership at departmental and managerial levels matches local government leadership, the results have been positive for the local government system. The community responded by providing much more resources than was mandated (through donations and special fund-raising projects). Community members also utilized effectively their networks to ensure that the federal and state governments were supportive.

In spite of the elaborate provision of the Nigerian constitution to promote effective accountability, full-time council membership and provisions for recall of councilors and decentralization to wards below the local government council areas, chairs of local government have been able to dominate council deliberations. Part of the problem arises from the fact that the councilors tend to lobby the executive directly for their constituency and for personal contracts rather than act as a body in the scrutiny of budgets and policy presented to it by the executive. Two other important problems are, first, the heavy reliance of the local government system on federal revenue transfers (up to 96 percent) with little effort at revenue generation and, second, the absence of any effective support from either the federal or state government to assist local governments in tackling problems of personnel, structure or inter-local cooperation.

Uganda

Decentralization came to the top of the Museveni government early. The government had reasoned that excessive centralization was a part of the problem of governance in Uganda. In fact, the ruling National Resistance Movement had organized the territories it took from the government during its guerilla struggle on the basis of village-based resistance councils. Since 1986, the structure had been systematically implemented and refined. In addition, since the government has an aversion to party political competition, local governments become major centers of political activity. Moreover, the government has transferred extensive responsibilities and financial and human resources to local governments.

There are five levels of local governments in Uganda, although in reality only three levels actually operate as multi-purpose local government councils. These are the local council (LC1), sub-county (LC3), and district (LC5). Major responsibilities including basic education and health, water and sanitation, economic development, justice, and security have all been transferred by constitution to local governments. The government also assigned new financial resources to local governments. Each district council also manages its own personnel. However, the most basic councils have been regarded as most successful in two areas (judicial and security functions) at the LC1 level. It is also their responsibility to assure peace and security (36 percent) and problem-solving (22 percent) or a combined score of 57 per cent. LC1 are courts of original jurisdiction for all petty and non-capital crime. This often does not involve the formal legal system, which is based on a wholly different set of principles and conducted in a language that is not accessible to the majority of the population. On other functions administered by higher-level local governments there are serious problems. For instance, planning and budgeting for the four major services are not effectively integrated, often lack any needs assessment or strategic thinking and cost was always rudimentary at best. Council personnel tended to produce budgets that could not be justified by the financial resources and, yet, the local councilors failed to use this opportunity to discipline decision-making by administrative personnel.

Even then, Uganda, like Nigeria, utilizes the strong mayor system with a cabinet. These cabinet members work with council committees and it is not surprising that the major problem of the local councils is the weakness of the committees. In a sample of six districts, only one of the councils had committees that met regularly and made autonomous decisions based on information obtained from the executive. Other met more irregularly, at times once a quarter instead of monthly. Five major weaknesses of the committees were identified. These included educational levels of councilors, frequency of meetings, understanding of roles by councilors, paucity of resources actually available to councils (more than 60 percent of grant support from national government comes in the form of unconditional grants) and, finally, internal fragmentation and factionalism in competition for constituency projects and personnel promotion to cabinet status. Uganda has a quota for women councilors—30 percent of the council must comprise women.

Uganda city councils present a mixed record. It is strongest where it is weakest. It is stronger in terms of citizen effectiveness at LC1. Yet, this level of local government has much more limited resources than higher levels of local government (LC3, LC5, or the district), which has more resources at their disposal but weaker in terms of citizen effectiveness. The reason for this is the poor structure of accountability at these higher levels.

Finally, the Ugandan local government system improved dramatically compared with what existed before reforms in terms of their decision-making ability (though limited by central directions and council ineffectiveness), available resources at their disposal, and the engagement between local governments and civil society. On the other hand, the system of multiple-tiered councils shows variable performance. Those closest to the village communities (LC1) are far more successful than the ones farther away. The challenge of integration between higher- and lower-level organs of local government and between the executive and legislative remains a tough one for Uganda local democracy.

Chad

Finally, we review the case of one country that did not have a national program of decentralization. In the absence of formal structures of local government, Chad rediscovered its embedded or indigenous structures of local governance. It has used these to provide itself with decentralized systems of health, water supply, and other public services. The education service is the most celebrated and most documented. Whereas the national government has been able to offer 45,000 places in the last 25 years, other communities have financed an increase of more than 835,000. They achieved this by the operation of community schools, which currently constitute more than one-quarter of all of the country's primary schools. How was this achieved?

In each village, male household heads select or elect a small group of men to oversee basic education on behalf of the community. There could be different structures for different functions. Responsibilities are assigned to this small group of overseers—president, secretary, and treasurer. This body organizes fund-raising activities, disburses the funds for school building or whatever specific actions are required, and account for the use of the resources. The resources are in two parts—user fees or tuition as distinct from basic community charges for every member of the community whether or not it has children in school. This is graded by the perceived income of the family. An important element of this arrangement is that it ensures high performance levels by students and teachers as the community are directly involved in the delivery of this service. Pass rates are much higher in these community schools than in government-run schools. It is also significant that these community schools actually use guidelines prepared by the government to ensure that they recruited the most competent teachers.

As earlier pointed out, these same principles are used to organize other services and the government is beginning to experiment with using these community structures as the basic institutions of governance. The advantages of the system are astounding and challenge the current practices that heavily depend on imported structures in other countries. Overheads are small, accountability is high, and resources are mobilized to finance resources in an equitable manner.

The Chad case may contain the seed of genuinely functioning local government systems in the region that combine indigenous structures of the past with the challenges of modern times. Over time, intermediate structures have developed to serve as intermediaries between this large number of community governments and the state as well as international NGOs.

Lessons of Experience

There are several important lessons from the cases examined here. We focus only on five of these.

First, local governments are still in infancy in Africa compared to other regions of the world—in terms of authority, resource autonomy, and capacity. Nevertheless, since the early 1990s, many African countries have sought to enhance the authority, legitimacy, resources, and capacity of the local government system. An important area of weakness remains in the local government council. It is surprising that this is an issue that has not occupied a much more important place in local government and decentralization policy discussions given its importance in ensuring effective and accountable local government.

Second, not all countries have allowed local governments to engage in partisan politics, Ghana and Uganda have not, but where local party-based elections are permitted in the large cities, the opposition is in control of these councils. This is currently the case in all the cities studied in this chapter—Nairobi, Gaborone, and Lusaka but this is also the case in Harare and other cities not included here.[15]

Third, there exists very little comparative analysis of available information on this subject. It is surprising, for instance, that political activists and analysts in eastern and southern African countries are demanding a switch to the strong mayor system without bothering to find out what has been the experience of other countries—Nigeria, Uganda and RSA, Zimbabwe (cities only)—that adopted this system.

Fourth, local government councils have not succeeded in working with civil society organizations. The two institutions have tended to undermine one another instead of providing mutual support. Another difficult area is the relationship between councilors and council executives—where strong council executives exist, the latter becomes the stronger party with councilors struggling to win favors from them for their respective constituencies rather than act as a corporate body to ensure effective oversight and/or push for important by-laws. Effectively, the permanent local government bureaucracy is in charge as it has expertise, longer tenure and familiarity with data relating to each function compared to the political representatives in these councils. This explains why it might be important to invest more in building meritocratic local bureaucracies that are responsive to the needs of the local community rather than seconded bureaucrats whose loyalties are firmly with the central government as is the case in some of the studied cities (e.g. Nairobi) and country cases (Ghana).

Finally, local government councils are still relatively weak and need support. Their weakness is attributable to the overall nature of the local government system but also to the peculiar conditions in each country including the choice of local government structure and the quality of councilors found in local government. They need support because globalization and democratization make decentralization necessary and at times, more effective, as they help to align excessively centralized political with highly decentralized economic systems. Many countries in the region were pressed into decentralization by a combination of external and domestic forces, but they are beginning to see the need for reforms of this nature. More local champions of decentralized governance are emerging.

Local councils also need support because of the huge challenges that lie ahead; especially as the pace of urbanization and other social changes in the region pick up. Africa currently has the highest rate of urbanization among the world's regions. This is bound to have important implications for local and municipal governance. More importantly, there is a need for fresh ideas on what type of local governments are needed and what political and administrative structures best promote the values of democratic decentralization. The Chad case seems to suggest that a combination of endogenous and exogenous structures will need to be struck. Most importantly, local councils will need to raise resources internally to finance infrastructure development and sustenance. The huge inequalities in practically every community mean that this is possible, but also difficult given the tendency of those who wield economic power to resist such moves. The experience of many countries in the region, however, suggests that community solidarity is strong and local government representatives might tap into this huge bank of social capital.

Conclusion

This chapter has argued that local governments and local assemblies are acquiring growing importance on the continent but in tackling the challenges they face there is a need for more systematic research and reflection before policy actions are proposed. One area of local government and municipal research that has been sorely neglected is the structure of management of local governments. In particular, the relationships between the legislative and executive branches as well as the movement in favor of direct democracy at the local level, as signified by participatory budgets, currently supported for adoption in some select cities, should be placed within this wider framework of research, thought, and reflection before policy action. Such actions should also constantly be evaluated for their effectiveness. The chapter has suggested some interesting lines of research in this area.

Notes

1. Schiavo-Campo 1998; UNDP 1993.
2. Wunsch and Olowu 1990; Mamdani 1996.
3. WHO 2003; World Bank 2004.
4. Olowu and Wunsch 2004.
5. Ibid.
6. IDEA 2004.
7. Steffensen and Trollegaard 2000; Olowu 2004.
8. Smith 1985.
9. Mamdani 1996.
10. Blair 2000.
11. US $1 is equivalent to 4,760 kwachas (2005).
12. US $1 equivalent to Pula 45 (2005).
13. Ayee 2004: 129.
14. Olowu and Wunsch 2004: 54.
15. Rakodi 1998.

5

Citizen's Support for Legislature and Democratic Consolidation: A Comparative Study with Special Focus on Mali

Reneske Doorenspleet

Department of Political Science, University of Leiden, Leiden, The Netherlands

Introduction

What is the role of legislatures in recently democratized countries? In theory, legislatures are believed to have important latent or symbolic functions for the consolidation of democratic regimes. Consolidation can be obvious, such as (1) the stabilization and effective functioning of the basic principles and institutions of the new system, e.g. legislatures and (2) the process of adaptation of behavior and attitudes that promote such stabilization and effective functioning of the new democratic institutions.[1] In a consolidated democracy, the legislature is stabilized and functions in a democratic way, and democratic rules are accepted "as the only game in town."[2] Most political scientists regard mass support for democracy in general or democratic institutions in particular as a key variable in the consolidation process.[3]

In practice, however, the contributions of legislatures in new democracies are more controversial. Many scholars have debated whether new African democracies suffer from a "democratic deficit." Few legislatures actually legislate, many have limited power and most are clearly overruled by the executive power. The weakness of parliaments in Africa allows only for limited accountability and responsiveness producing a democratic deficit. In addition, political scientists use this deficit in order to explain the lack of support for democratic institutions in African democracies. Until now, empirical research on these issues has been very meager. It is not clear to what extent citizens of a new democracy support their institutions, such as their legislature, and how to explain this support.

This chapter concentrates on the role of the legislature in the consolidation process of a recently democratized country in Africa, namely Mali. Mali is an interesting case that could provide useful insights into the consolidation of democracy on the continent in general, since this country is representative or typical for other African countries that have recently undergone some form of transition toward democracy. Just like some other African countries, like Benin and South Africa, Mali has experienced extraordinary changes leading to a transformation of the political system from a dictatorship to a new democracy in the beginning of the 1990s. However, while the *transition* to democracy in Mali may be successful, the *consolidation* of democracy may be more fragile and in a very preliminary stage.

Firstly, this chapter gives a short overview of the political developments and the power of the parliament in Mali. This overview will demonstrate that the transition to democracy and the creation of democratic institutions occurred rapidly. Secondly, it describes how the composition of the electoral system determines the composition of parliament, and whether it is overpowered by the executive. Thirdly, the chapter intends to illustrate that the mass support for the legislature in Mali is remarkably widespread, despite its weak power. Finally, the analyses demonstrate that the support for the legislature varies with perceptions of economic performance, the level of interpersonal trust, and the level of support for democracy in general. When our understanding of citizen's support and the actual functioning of parliaments in new African democracies is greater, it will expand our knowledge of the quality of the consolidation of these new democracies.

Political Developments in Mali: A Short Overview

Transition Process to Democracy

In the early 1990s, Mali quickly made a regime change toward democracy, but for a long time it was considered a consolidated dictatorship. After achieving independence from France in 1960, military or one-party dictators ruled Mali for more than 30 years. Modibo Keita was appointed first president of a young republic that was leaning toward Marxist policies that were not in line with army leaders, and Keita was eventually overthrown in November 1968. The dictatorial regime of Moussa Traoré was defunct in 1991, when soldiers loyal to him killed more than 100 demonstrators demanding a multiparty state; he was overthrown by his own military.

Lieutenant Colonel Amadou Toumani Touré came to power and signed a peace treaty intended to prepare for the country's first free multiparty elections. Traoré and his wife Mariam were sentenced to death in January 1999 for embezzlement. Traoré had also received the death sentence in 1993 for ordering troops to fire on demonstrators in 1991. However, sentences for both Traoré and his wife were commuted to life imprisonment.

After the 1991 coup, Mali's people first chose their government relatively freely and fairly in presidential and legislative elections in 1992. Konaré and his Alliance for Democracy in Mali (ADEMA) party won the elections. In 1997, little more than a quarter of the registered voters participated. Former President Alpha Oumar Konaré was overwhelmingly re-elected against a weak candidate who alone broke an opposition boycott of the presidential contest. ADEMA was again the overwhelming dominant party in the legislature.

Konaré's ADEMA party suffered a split in 2001, adding more competition ahead of the 2002 presidential election, and 24 candidates participated. After the first round of voting, the Constitutional Court canceled more than 500,000 ballots cast. Several presidential candidates had petitioned the court to annul the results entirely, alleging fraud and vote rigging. The court reported voting by non-registered voters and missing election reports as some of the irregularities of the first round. International observers said the polls were well managed and conducted in the spirit of transparency. However, they also noted several logistical and administrative irregularities. Amadou Toumani Touré, who ran as an independent candidate, and Soumaila Cissé, of ADEMA, went to a second round of voting. Touré won with 64 percent, compared with 36 percent for Cissé. Touré has a strong international profile because he headed Mali during the transition period to multiparty politics in the early 1990s, and thereafter he has been active in regional peace and humanitarian efforts as a UN envoy.[4]

Low voter turnout marked the legislative elections held in July 2002. The coalition Espoir 2002 dominated the voting for the National Assembly elections in July 2002, gaining 66 seats. The dominant position of ADEMA in parliament was broken: a coalition led by ADEMA won only 51 seats. Smaller parties won the remainder (see table 5.1).

Table 5.1 Mali National Assembly Election Results (July 14, 2002)

Assemblée Nationale	Number of seats (160 = total)	
Espoir 2002 — Rassemblement pour le Mali (Rally for Mali) Congrès Nationale pour l' Initiative Démocratie (National Congress for Democratic Initiative) — Mouvement Patriotique pour le Renouveau (Patriotic Movement for Renewal) — Rassemblement pour la Démocratie du Travail (Rally for Labor Democracy)	66	RPM 46 CNID 13 others 7
Alliance pour la République et la Démocratie ARD — Coalition lead by Alliance pour la Démocratie en Mali and Parti Pan-Africain pour la Liberté, la Solidarité et la Justice (Alliance for Democracy in Mali and Pan-African Party for Liberty, Solidarity, and Justice)	51	ADEMA 45 Other 6
Alternance et Changement (Alteration and Change)	10	
Solidarité Africaine pour la Démocratie et l'Indépendance (African Solidarity for Democracy and Independence)	6	
Non-partisans	6	
Annulled elections	8	
Malians from abroad	13	

Source: *Agence France* Press, July 14, 2002.

The Electoral System and the Composition of the Legislature

Not only the actual transition process—with the holding of elections and the creation of the political parties—but also the establishment of the new democratic institutions went rapidly. The design of the electoral system, for example, is an important one with different consequences. This choice is not neutral: it determines the way in which votes are translated into seats and thereby the extent to which some groups of the society are represented in parliament, while others are excluded.

The electoral system in Mali changed dramatically. After the 1991 coup, a 129-seat National Assembly was established with 116 seats elected by the domestic electorate and 13 by Malians residing overseas. The 116 domestic seats are allocated based on population (one seat per 60,000 people) among 55 constituencies (circonscriptions) corresponding to the country's 49 administrative divisions (cercles) and the 6 communes in Bamako, the capital. Because of population disparities, the district magnitudes range from one to six seats per constituency.

While independent candidates are permitted, political parties are required to submit closed-party lists with the same number of candidates as available seats. Voters can vote for only one independent or party list of candidates. A two-round majority-runoff system is used whereby, in the absence of an independent candidate or party list winning an absolute majority in the first round, only the top two finishers in the first round compete in the second round, with the winner decided by an absolute majority. In the case of the multi-member districts, the two highest party lists from the first round compete in the second, with the winning list gaining every seat in the district. A similar two-round majority formula is used in the presidential election. It was thought that a two-round majority-runoff system for legislative elections would encourage coalitions in the second round between smaller and larger parties.

The consequences of this electoral system were too important to overlook.[5] Combined with the entry of large numbers of small parties with limited electoral support (a phenomenon that is typical of new democracies established after an extended period of authoritarian rule) Mali's new system produced the expected political impact on vote–seat disproportionality and multipartyism. Thus, the two-round majority formula produced a high level of disproportionality (between seats and votes), a moderate degree of electoral multipartyism (3.3 effective electoral parties), and a moderately low legislative multipartyism (2.2 effective legislative parties). Another problematic consequence of the electoral system was that the very use of party lists weakens the constituency linkages of elected representatives. Moreover, due in part to the electoral formula, the incumbent ruling party ADEMA won disproportionately large percentage (66 percent) of seats.

These consequences provoked opposition demands for electoral reform. This led to political negotiations between the opposition parties and ADEMA, which produced agreements on three issues prior to the April 1997 legislative elections. They used PR formula for allocating National Assembly seats, subsequently declared unconstitutional by the judiciary. Twenty-seven percent increase in the size of the National Assembly from 116 to 147, with a reduction in single-member and a corresponding increase in multi-member constituencies, gave the opposition parties a degree of electoral advantage, and the creation of a broadly representative Electoral Commission.

The results of the 2002 legislative elections indeed broke the dominance of ADEMA in parliament (see table 5.1). ADEMA lost it majority in the National Assembly. Opposed to ADEMA's former dominance, the majority party Espoir 2002 is only a loose alliance of parties.

In short, the electoral system in Mali changed significantly and quickly during the democratization process in the 1990s. Moreover, the type of electoral system has considerable impact on the number of parties in parliament, and thereby on the character of the legislative power.

The Power of the Legislature in Mali

The Malian Constitution accords separate powers to the three branches of government: executive, legislative, and judicial. In practice, however, the executive branch exercises more effective authority.[6]

The Malian judiciary could hardly be called independent of the executive. On the other hand, the judiciary has shown considerable autonomy in rendering anti-administration decisions, which the government has in turn respected, and reforms are under way. Mali's human rights record is generally good, although there are reports of police brutality. Prisons are characterized by overcrowding, inadequate medical care, and limited food. The government permits visits by human rights monitors and independent human rights groups operate openly and freely.

Although libel is a criminal offense and press laws include punitive presumption-of-guilt standards, Mali's media are among Africa's most open. At least 40 independent newspapers operate freely, and more than 100 independent radio stations, including community stations broadcasting in regional languages, broadcast throughout the country. The government controls one television station and many radio stations, but all present diverse views, including those critical of the government.

Not only the judiciary but also the legislature is subject to executive influence. The president has authority to appoint the government and the prime minister, although the constitution holds them accountable to the legislature as well. The legislature meets twice a year for approximately five months in total. The National Assembly possesses only a limited capacity to check executive authority, since institutionally its powers remain weak relative to the strong executive presidency. The president, as an independent, formed a battle government in October 2002 in consultation with all parties to work with a nearly evenly divided legislature.

The Degree of Trust in the Legislature in Mali

The previous sections showed that the transition process toward democratization has taken place quite rapidly in Mali. Within a few years, democratic institutions such as reasonably free and fair elections, an electoral system, new political parties, a functioning parliament (although with weak powers) and an open media, were established. As we already learned from experiences in other new democracies, we know that these democratic institutions can be a democratic façade without the support of the Malian citizens, which is necessary to sustain the new system. Support and democratic beliefs might have not yet had sufficient time to mature in the

Malian context. It is therefore important to examine the extent of public support for legislatures in new democracies, such as Mali.

High levels of support for democracy in general and democratic institutions in specific are important ingredients for consolidation of the new regime. Diamond (1999) suggests that the concept of democratic consolidation can be measured along two dimensions—beliefs and behavior—and on at least three levels. At the higher level are the country's elites, the top decision-makers and political activists. For Diamond, a democracy may be considered consolidated if the elites accept the legitimacy of democracy, and if they respect each other's right to compete peacefully for power, and obey the democratic laws and mutually accepted norms of political conduct. At the intermediate level, a regime is democratically consolidated if all politically significant parties, interest groups, and social movements endorse the legitimacy of democracy and of the country's specific constitutional rules and institutions. At the lower level, the level of the mass public, consolidation is indicated by acceptance of the overwhelming majority of citizens that democracy is the best form of government in principle and that it is the most suitable form of government for their country.

The rest of this chapter concentrates on the belief dimension, the mass level and support for a particular democratic institution (namely the legislature) in order to say something about the consolidation of democracy in Mali. In other words, the extent and causes of public support for the legislature are investigated. The average level of trust of institutions in Mali can be analyzed by using the data of the Afrobarometer. By the end of Round I (July 2001), Afrobarometer surveys had been conducted in the following countries: Botswana, Ghana, Lesotho, Namibia, Nigeria, Malawi, Mali, South Africa, Tanzania, Uganda, Zambia, and Zimbabwe.[7] The sample was designed as a representative cross-section of all citizens of voting age in a given country. Among many other questions, respondents were asked how much they trusted their parliament.[8]

Let us first make a comparison between the levels of mass trust in several parliaments on the African continents. Table 5.2 presents more detailed descriptive statistics of the support for the parliaments in 11 African countries. In this cross-national comparison, the evaluations of Africans show remarkable differences. In Zimbabwe, for example, the parliament is rated on average much worse than in the other investigated African countries. This reflects the severe political crisis in Zimbabwe. Over the past several years, the government has taken numerous actions restricting civil liberties and political rights, including legislating severe curbs on press freedom. The political arena has been significantly reduced caused by governmental repression of political opponents. Legislation passed by parliament in the pre-2002 election period includes the Public

Table 5.2   Trust in Parliament in Percentage of Population

Botswana	54.4%
Ghana	74.1%
Lesotho	44.6%
Malawi	35.0%
Mali	63.6%
Namibia	61.3%
Nigeria	59.3%
South Africa	35.3%
Tanzania	90.7%
Zambia	25.2%
Zimbabwe	19.5%
Average of African countries	51.2%

Source: Afrobarometer 1999–2001. Categories 3 and 4 are collapsed as "trust."

Order and Security Act, which forbids criticism of the president, limits public assembly, and allows police to impose arbitrary curfews. People in Zimbabwe have clearly limited trust in their parliament.

In Mali, in contrast, the level of mass support for the parliament is more than 63 percent, which is quite high, and clearly above the African average, which is 51.2 percent. The data show that mass support for the legislature in Mali is remarkably widespread, especially when compared to other African countries. This is a positive indication for the consolidation of democracy in this country, but it is not clear why this is the case, and under which conditions Malian people support the new system. Therefore, the sources of legitimacy of the legislature in Mali need to be investigated now.

Explaining Trust in the Legislature in Mali

Socio-Economic Development

A central tenet of modernization theories is that socio-economic development exerts a positive influence on the support for democratic institutions and, consequently, for the democratic consolidation.[9] Lipset argued that when the people of a state are more developed, the people are more inclined to believe in democratic values and will support a democratic system with its institutions. Only in a wealthy society can a situation exist in which "the mass of the population could intelligently participate in politics and could develop the self-restraint necessary to avoid succumbing to the appeals of irresponsible demagogues. A society divided between a large impoverished mass and a small favored elite would result either in oligarchy . . . or in tyranny."[10] Social transformation will result in more democracy because "a large middle class plays a mitigating role in moderating conflict since it is able to reward moderate and democratic parties and penalize extremist groups."[11] According to modernization researchers, "Certain levels of 'basic' socio-economic development appear to be necessary to elevate countries to a level at which they can begin to support complex, nation-wide patterns of political interaction, one of which may be democracy."[12]

Several indicators can be used to measure people's actual socio-economic situation. One measure is the level of education, ranging from no formal education (score 1) to postgraduate university level (score 9). Another question measures the poverty of people by asking, "Over the past year, how often, if ever, have you gone without cash income." The answers range from never (score 0) to always (score 3).

Not only people's *actual* socio-economic situation, but also their economic evaluations or perceptions are important influences on their support for democratic institutions. In addition, in established democracies, most citizens have little understanding of what legislatures do. Nevertheless, because legislatures are highly visible institutions, citizens will probably judge them based on public policy. Evaluations of the economy can be of several types. A continuing controversy concerns the extent to which citizens make egocentric evaluations of the economy according to their personal or family economic experiences or make sociotropic evaluations, judgments based on general economic experiences.[13] Reflecting these distinctions, the Afrobarometer includes a battery of questions measuring satisfaction both with general macroeconomic conditions and with economic conditions in the respondent's households.

Egocentric economic evaluations are measured by three questions that ask individuals in Mali to evaluate their satisfaction with their own living conditions, their economic satisfaction compared with one year ago and their expected satisfaction with their life's prospects in one year. Sociotropic evaluations are measured by questions that ask individuals to evaluate the general situation and the current economic circumstances in Mali. It appears that Malians are ambivalent about the general and the economic situation in Mali, but they are very optimistic that their own living conditions will improve within a year.

Interpersonal Trust

One strand of research has emphasized how cross-national differences in trust toward the regime and its institutions are related to support for, and satisfaction with, the political system and its democratic institutions. Theories of post-materialism and, more recently, post-modernization suggest that a deep-rooted process of value change is gradually transforming citizens' relationships toward government.[14] In this view, attitudes such as personal trust and positive feelings about life are personal characteristics that create a positive individual outlook on the community and the political system. This contributes to optimism about one's ability to participate in, and have an impact on, the political system.[15] These values develop through social interaction in the home, schools, and community, and are associated with the democratic citizen, an individual who is critical of the government but is satisfied with how the system works.[16]

Banfield emphasized in 1958 that interpersonal trust plays a crucial role in democracy. He found that southern Italian society had much lower levels of trust than northern Italy, which hindered the large-scale cooperation between strangers that is essential to both economic development and successful democratic institutions. Almond and Verba[17] also argued that interpersonal trust is important. They found that the publics of Italy and West Germany were characterized by lower levels of interpersonal trust, readiness to participate, and other attitudes conducive to democracy than the British and American respondents were. The relative weakness of civic culture in Germany and Italy contributed to the failure of democracy in those societies in the period before the Second World War. Testing these ideas in a broader cross-national study, Inglehart[18] found that interpersonal trust was indeed strongly related to economic development and democracy. He pointed out that this factor is a variable and not a constant: although interpersonal trust tends to change slowly, it can and does change. Starting from an amazingly low level in the Almond and Verba study in the 1950s, only eight percent of the Italians believed that "most people can be trusted," but this figure rose to 27 percent in 1981 and to 30 percent in 1986. Even in 1990, Italy ranked much lower than the United States and Britain, but it showed a gradual upward trend.[19]

The level of interpersonal trust in Mali is measured by an Afrobarometer question asking, "Generally speaking, would you say that most people can be trusted or that you must be very careful in dealing with people?" It appears that interpersonal trust is not very high in Mali with more than 87 percent of the respondents having no trust in other people.

Organizational Networks

Alexis de Tocqueville stressed the importance of networks of voluntary associations, arguing that democracy had emerged and flourished in America because its people participated in numerous and extensive networks of voluntary associations. Such participation promoted cooperation and trust, which were essential to the successful functioning of democratic institutions. Lipset[20] followed Tocqueville's argument that economic development increases the likelihood of a democratic regime via a vigorous associational life, that is, a strong civil society.

> [Civic organizations] are a source of countervailing power, inhibiting the state or any single major source of private power from dominating all political resources; they are a source of new opinions; they can be the means of communicating ideas, particularly opposition ideas, to a large section of the citizenry; they serve to train men in the skills of politics; and they can help increase the level of interest and participation in politics.[21]

Putnam[22] also emphasized the impact of voluntary organizations, arguing, "social capital" plays a crucial role in both political and economic cooperation. According to Putnam, social capital "refers to features of social organization such as trust, norms and networks that can improve the efficiency of society by facilitating coordinated action." Social capital consists of a culture of trust and tolerance, in which extensive networks of voluntary associations emerge. These networks provide contacts and information flow, that are, in their turn, supportive of a culture of trust and cooperation. Participation in associations develops skills of cooperation, a sense of shared responsibility for collective activities and a means of engaging in broader political systems. Thus, "a dense network of secondary associations both embodies and contributes to effective social collaboration"[23] Citizens in countries with higher levels of social capital are expected to be able to keep their governments more responsive and more honest, and improve democratic institutional performance.

Inglehart's findings[24] support the hypothesis that membership in voluntary associations is linked strongly with stable democracy. He uses the data of the World Values surveys to analyze the rates of organizational memberships across 35 mainly high-income countries. The lowest level of membership was recorded in Argentina, while the Netherlands had the highest rate. Inglehart discovered that societies with high rates of membership are far more likely to be stable democracies than those with low rates of membership.

The Afrobarometer survey provides useful information to measure the rate of membership in voluntary associations in Mali. The respondents in Mali were shown a list of different types of voluntary associations and asked, "For each one, could you tell me whether you are an official leader, an active member, an inactive member or not a member of that type of organization?" The list covers the following types of organizations: religious (church or mosque), sport or recreational, educational, trade unions or farmers' organizations, professional or business, community development, pro-democracy or human rights organizations, and environmental associations.[25] It appears that more than a quarter (26 percent) of the Malian respondents are not a member of any of these organizations. On the other hand, 27 percent of the respondents are members of one of these organizations, 18 percent are members of two organizations, and the rest (29 percent) are members of *at least* three organizations.

Interest in Politics

According to Lipset[26] and others, civic organizations serve to train citizens in the skills of politics, and they can help increase the level of interest in politics, which is conducive for democracy. Hence, a positive relationship between interest in politics and the support for democratic political institutions, such as the national parliament, is expected.

The measure of political interest is based on the question, "How interested are you in politics and government?" According to the Afrobarometer surveys, more than 65 percent of the Malian people are not interested in politics, while almost 24 percent is somewhat interested, and less than 11 percent is very interested in politics.

Political Knowledge

Based on the theory of cognitive mobilization, a *positive* relationship between political knowledge and support for democratic institutions is expected. Persons with more political knowledge may find the existence of a parliament in Mali less threatening (see Inglehart's studies). Alternatively, however, a *negative* relationship between knowledge and support for democratic institutions can also be expected. Malians who are politically well informed may be more likely to know that their parliament, even though relatively freely and fairly elected, is not in control of policymaking in Mali and subordinate to the dominant executive power. Those individuals who lack the political knowledge may fail to see the democratic deficit of their parliament. Moreover, Malians who are politically knowledgeable may show greater concern over questions of the level of accountability and responsiveness of the democratic institutions of their country.

In short, political knowledge may bring greater awareness of the democratic deficit or the costs and benefits of having democratic political institutions, such as a national assembly. On the other hand, political knowledge may also foster greater support of the new democratic institutions. Although the level of knowledge is low in general, those Malians who have more knowledge may be more or less satisfied with the way democratic institutions, such as the parliament, works, depending on the theory.

This chapter focuses on the factual political knowledge of Malians. Two questions measure the knowledge of national figures, that is, the minister of finance and the president of the national assembly. Three questions include knowledge of sub-national political leaders; these questions include identifying the mayor of the council in the area of the respondent, the name of the deputy for the Commune, and the name of the Governor of the respondent's region. These five items form a reasonably reliable index (alpha = 0.60). Therefore, one index of political knowledge is constructed which includes the five questions and runs from 0 (no knowledge) to 5 (a lot of knowledge). It appears that almost one-third of the Malians have no political knowledge at all, in the sense that they do not know the answers to any of the five questions (they reply that they don't know the answer, or they give an incorrect answer). One-third of the respondents know the answer to one question, and one-third knows more than one answer.

Support for Democracy

The support for democracy in general may also be an important explanatory factor for the support of parliament. Although the relationship between support for the legislature and support for a democratic regime is reciprocal, Mishler and Rose [27] discovered that support for legislatures is more a consequence than a cause of support for the democratic regime. Why should this be the case? According to Mishler and Rose, support for regimes is holistic. The public perceives the regime, not as an assemblage of institutional parts, some good, others bad, but as an undifferentiated whole. While evaluations of specific institutions, such as the parliament, may have only modest effects on evaluations of the regime, perceptions on the regime have profound effects on how citizens evaluate specific institutions. "For new democracies, at least, the real value of legislatures may be less anything they do than in what they are. By providing opportunities for citizen participation in elections, legislatures are important symbols of democracy."[28] Consequently, it can be expected that Malians who support democracy in general, are more likely to support specific democratic institutions such as the parliament.

This variable of "support for democracy" can be measured by question 34 in the survey of Mali by the Afrobarometer: "Which of these three statements is closest to your own opinion?" The answers are recoded to "Democracy is preferable to any other form of government" (score = 3), "A non-democratic government can be preferable" (score = 1), and "does not matter" (score = 2).

In addition, question 33 of the survey is used, which measures the "supply of democracy": "In your opinion, how much of a democracy is Mali today?" The answers can be as follows: 0 = Not a democracy, 1 = Major problems, but still a democracy, 2 = Minor problems, but still a democracy, 3 = Full democracy.

Analyses

The following 13 hypotheses can be formulated, based on the discussion above:

A. The impact of people's *actual* socio-economic situation
   1. The level of education has a positive impact on support for the legislature in Mali
   2. A higher level of poverty is associated with less support for the legislature in Mali
B. The impact of egocentric evaluations of the economy
   3. The level of satisfaction with your own living conditions has a positive impact on support for the legislature in Mali
   4. The expected satisfaction with your own living conditions has a positive impact on support for the legislature in Mali
   5. The level of satisfaction with your living conditions compared to your living conditions of one year ago has a positive impact on support for the legislature in Mali
C. The impact of sociotropic evaluations of the economy
   6. A higher level of satisfaction with the general situation in Mali is associated with more support for the legislature in Mali
   7. A higher level of satisfaction with the current economic circumstances in Mali is associated with more support for the legislature in Mali
D. The impact of interpersonal trust
   8. A higher level of interpersonal trust is associated with more support for the legislature in Mali
E. The impact of organizational membership
   9. The rate of membership in voluntary associations in Mali has a positive impact on support for the legislature in Mali
F. The impact of interest in politics
   10. A higher level of interest in politics is associated with more support for the legislature in Mali
G. Political Knowledge
   11. A higher level of knowledge of politics is associated with more support for the legislature in Mali

H. Support Democracy
  12. Support for democracy in general has a positive impact on support for the legislature in Mali
  13. Malians who believe that Mali is a full democracy are more inclined to support the legislature than Malians who believe that Mali is not a democracy.

In order to test the hypotheses above, regression analyses were used, and the results are presented in table 5.3. By calculating the beta scores, the relative strength of the influences can be measured. Beta scores give a standardized indication of the strength of the relationships and indicate whether the influence is positive or negative. Moreover, the strength of

Table 5.3 Influences on Support for the Legislature in Mali

	Nonstandardized coefficients		Standardized coefficients	
	B	Std. Error	Beta	Level of Significance
(Constant)	1.07	0.23		0.00
1. education	0.02	0.02	0.03	0.41
2. poverty: without cash income	−0.09	0.03	−0.08	0.003
3. satisfaction own living conditions	0.03	0.04	0.02	0.44
4. expected satisfaction with own living conditions	0.13	0.03	0.14	0.00
5. satisfaction with living conditions compared to one year ago	0.03	0.03	0.03	0.28
6. satisfaction with Malian economy	0.01	0.04	0.01	0.78
7. satisfaction general situation Mali	0.01	0.04	0.01	0.76
8. trust people	0.32	0.09	0.10	0.00
9. organizational membership	0.004	0.02	0.01	0.79
10. interest in politics	0.13	0.04	0.09	0.002
11. knowledge of politics	−0.10	0.03	−0.12	0.00
12. support democracy	0.09	0.04	0.07	0.02
13. supply democracy	0.27	0.03	0.23	0.00
14. age	−7.5E−06	0.002	0.00	0.99
15. gender	0.05	0.06	0.02	0.47

N = 1251

indirect and direct effects can be measured. The final column of table 5.3 shows whether the impact of the independent variable is significant or not. In the following sections, only the significant influences on the support for the legislature in Mali will be described.

Just as was expected based on the modernization approach, a higher level of poverty is associated with less support for the legislature in Mali. Hence, rich people support the legislature more than poor people do. Not only people's *actual* socio-economic situation, but also their economic *evaluations* or *perceptions* are important influences on their support for democratic institutions. The expected satisfaction with people's own living conditions has a positive impact on people's support for the legislature in Mali.

The analysis supports Putnam's social capital thesis. A higher level of interpersonal trust is indeed associated with more support for the legislature. Civic organizations serve to train citizens in the skills of politics and they can help increase the level of interest in politics, which is in its turn, conducive for democracy. Hence, a positive relationship between interest in politics and the support for democratic political institutions, such as the national parliament, is expected. The empirical analyses find support for this theoretical expectation: a higher level of interest in politics is associated with more support for the legislature in Mali (although the strength of the impact is very weak; see the beta coefficient of 0.09).

The theory of cognitive mobilization, which predicts a *positive* relationship between political knowledge and support for democratic institutions, is not supported. On the contrary, a significant *negative* relationship between knowledge and support for democratic institutions was found in the case of Mali. Malians who are politically well informed may be more likely to know that their parliament is not in control of policy-making in Mali and subordinate to the dominant executive power. Those individuals who lack the political knowledge may fail to see the democratic deficit of their parliament. Moreover, Malians who are politically knowledgeable may show greater concern over questions of the level of accountability and responsiveness of the democratic institutions of their country. In short, political knowledge may bring greater awareness of the democratic deficit or the costs and benefits of having democratic political institutions, such as a national assembly.

Although support for democracy in general has a positive impact on support for the legislature, but the 13th variable (supply of democracy) has the strongest impact on support for the parliament in Mali. Malians who believe that Mali is a full democracy are more inclined to support the legislature than Malians who believe that Mali is not a democracy.

Conclusion

What have we learned? It appears that the transition process toward democratization has taken place quite rapidly in Mali. Within a few years, democratic institutions such as reasonably free and fair elections, new political parties, a functioning parliament (although with weak powers), and an open media, were established. As we already learned from experiences in other new democracies, we know that these democratic institutions can be a democratic façade without the support of the Malian citizens, which is necessary to sustain the new system. Support and democratic beliefs may not (yet) have had sufficient time to be nurtured in the Malian context. It is therefore important to examine the extent of public support for legislatures in new democracies, such as Mali.

The analyses in this chapter show that mass support for the legislature in Mali is remarkably widespread. Moreover, the conditions under which Malian people support the new system vary greatly. This chapter showed that legislative support varies with the level of poverty and people's perceptions of economic performance. The poor are less likely than the wealthy to support democratic institutions such as the legislature. Not only people's actual socio-economic situation, but also their economic evaluations or perceptions are important influences on their support for democratic institutions. It appears that civic organizations serve to train citizens in the skills of politics, and they can help increase the level of interest in politics, which is in its turn conducive for democracy. The level of interpersonal trust, people's interest in and knowledge of politics, and the level of support for democracy in general are all important in order to understand the level of support for democratic institutions specifically. So, the mass support is considerable in Mali and the sources of legitimacy for the legislature are diverse and numerous.

In conclusion, largely, Mali seems to be a consolidated democracy. The transition from an authoritarian regime to a democratic system was an abrupt one, and it should be emphasized that the creation of the democratic institutions went very quickly. The new institutions are not yet well rooted in the democratic soil. It is, for example, desirable for the consolidation of the democratic regime to extend the power of the legislature in Mali. On the other hand, the amount of mass support for democratic institutions such as the parliament is substantial and remarkable. The fact that the sources for support of the legislature are diverse indicates that the institution of the legislature has a firm basis in the new democratic system of Mali.

This is good news for other new democracies that are comparable with Mali. Based on the analyses of the case of Mali, it is very likely that comparable countries such as Ghana and Senegal, of which the regimes recently went through remarkable changes toward more democratic characteristics, can count on a high level of support for their new democratic institutions. Moreover, the sources of this support are expected to vary, thereby providing a diverse and vast basis for the consolidation process in the new democracies.

Scholars of African politics should keep a critical eye on the *actual power* of the legislature in new democracies. This chapter made clear that not only mass support but also effective functioning of the democratic institutions is crucial for democratic consolidation. Strengthening the actual power of democratic institutions remains a big challenge for the future of African democracies.

Notes

1. Delhey and Tobsch 2000.
2. Linz 1990.
3. In contrast, Przeworski 1991 and Di Palma 1990 do not believe that mass su port for democracy is decisive for consolidation. These scholars are exceptions, though; most researchers consider mass support as crucial for an effective democratic system.
4. Shortly after assuming office, he granted civil servants a 30 percent salary increase as complaints mounted following increases in prices for food, water, and electricity since March 2002.
5. See Mozaffar 1997 for more information.
6. See the following websites and webpages for more information: www.cidcm.umd.edu/inscr/polity/Mlil.htm and www.freedomhouse.org. Concerning the judiciary, note that local chiefs, in consultation with elders, decide the majority of disputes in rural areas.
7. See: www.afrobarometer.org/roundlc.html. The data from the second round (until 2004) have not yet been released.
8. The questions differ somewhat in the different countries. In Ghana, Mali, Nigeria, and Tanzania, the question is "How much do you trust the following institutions: the National Assembly?" The following four answers are possible: 1. "I do not trust them at all." 2. "I distrust them somewhat." 3. "I trust them somewhat." 4. "I trust them a lot." In Botswana, Lesotho, Malawi, Namibia, South Africa, Zambia, and Zimbabwe, the survey question is somewhat different, namely: "How much of the time can you trust parliament to do what is right? Is it: 1. Never, 2. Only some of the time, 3. Most of the time, or 4. Just about always." A comparable question was not asked in Uganda.
9. See Lipset 1959; Rostow 1960; Neubauer 1967; Dahl 1971; also Doorenspleet 2005.

10. Lipset 1959: 75.
11. Ibid., 83.
12. Neubauer 1967: 1007.
13. See Mishler and Rose 1993: 17.
14. Inglehart 1997; Inglehart 1990; Inglehart 1997; Dolton 1996.
15. See Almond and Verba 1963; Inglehart 1990; 1997.
16. Dahl 1994.
17. Almond and Verba 1963.
18. Inglehart 1990.
19. See Inglehart 1997: 173.
20. Lipset 1959.
21. Ibid., 84.
22. Putnam 1993: 167.
23. Ibid., 90.
24. Inglehart 1997: 188–194.
25. Two categories are excluded on the basis of the results of factor analysis: Women's organizations and other associations.
26. Lipset 1959.
27. Mishler and Rose 1993.
28. Ibid., 2.

Part II

6

Evolution of Parliament–Executive Relations in Zambia

Jotham C. Momba
Department of Political Science, University of Zambia,
Lusaka, Zambia

Introduction

The role of parliament is cardinal in democratic governance, and this importance should be viewed within the context of the need for separation of powers for the full realization of democracy. For a country like Zambia, this is even more imperative considering that the country emerged from a relatively authoritarian one-party system in which the functioning of the various arms of the state was obscured by the extensive powers of the party and the president.

Prior to the introduction of the one-party system, the Constitution provided for a President. It also vested legislative powers in a parliament that constitutionally consisted of the national assembly and the president, which translated into extensive powers for the president in relation to the National Assembly. The legislative body in this arrangement did not have the relative autonomy enjoyed by the legislature vis-à-vis the executive that it enjoys in presidential systems. Neither did it have the powers enjoyed by the legislative bodies in the parliamentary systems.

Following the Constitutional Review Commissions of 1991 and 1995, some changes toward strengthening the National Assembly were introduced. In the current constitution, the National Assembly has been given the power to ratify the appointment of a number of constitutional offices, and the parliamentary committee system has been strengthened in order to enhance the oversight role of the National Assembly. However, in spite of these and other reforms, the power relationship between the executive, particularly the president and the national assembly, has remained unchanged.

This dispensation that countries in transition experience the pains of political change, is even more imperative considering that the country emerged from a relatively authoritarian one-party system in which the functioning of the various arms of the state was obscured by the extensive powers of the party and the president. This is a point that was recognized by the Mwanakatwe Constitutional Review Commission, who in their Report observed:

> Most petitioners argued that concentration of power in any one person or one institution could be detrimental to democracy. Democratic governance presupposes full appreciation of the doctrine of the separation of powers. The Zambian people were particularly anxious that mechanisms should be put in place to ensure that an over-zealous and interventionist executive should have no capacity to interfere with the legislature and the judiciary branches. This underlies the petitioners' clear demands for the complete separation of powers.[1]

The principle of separation of powers in Zambia was recognized formally from as early as 1964, when the independence constitution was adopted. The purpose of this chapter is to examine the extent to which the Zambian parliament has effectively played the above roles and others expected of it in a democratic political environment. This, we shall do by examining the changing role of the National Assembly from 1964, when Zambia became a sovereign state, and, presently, passing through three Republics: the First Republic from 1964 to 1973, the Second Republic from 1973 to 1991, and the Third Republic from 1991 to date.

The "Hybrid" System and its Impact on the Role of Parliament: Independence Constitution

The independence Constitution provided for an executive president. It also vested legislative powers in parliament that constitutionally consisted of the national assembly and the president.[2] Although the constitution provided for some elements of the Westminster parliamentary system, it also had elements of a presidential system. The system provided for a president who would be directly elected[3] and whose term of office was not dependent on his ability to continue enjoying the support of the national assembly.

The national assembly was given several formal powers. Among these powers was the power to pass legislation. In order to become law, any legislation that was passed by the national assembly had to be assented to by the president. In the event of the President withholding his assent to any Bill, the national assembly had the power to return the same bill for assent to the president within six months if passed by a two-thirds majority of the Members of Parliament. Once the bill was resubmitted, the President had either to give his assent within 21 days or dissolve the national assembly and, by so doing, automatically terminate his term of office as well.

The national assembly was also given the power to elect the president in situations where the president-elect dies between the time the poll is taken and the swearing in of the new president, since at that time there was no vice-president to succeed the president. The national assembly also had the power to amend the Constitution by a two-thirds majority; the only exception was the amendment of Chapters III and VII and Sections 72(2) and 73 of the Constitution that dealt with fundamental human rights that, until 1969, could only be amended through a referendum.[4] The national assembly was also given the power to remove the President from his office for violation of the constitution or gross misconduct.

Despite the presidential features of the political system, the national assembly operated strictly along the lines of the Westminster parliamentary system. The relative freedom that the Members of Congress in the presidential system of the United States enjoy in legislative matters was not considered part of the Zambian legislative process. The national assembly did not have the power to ratify constitutional appointments that were made by the president. For example, the Zambian national assembly had no power to ratify the appointments of ministers, the judges, and the attorney general. On the other hand, because the system provided for an executive president who was not a member of the national assembly, the national assembly did not enjoy the kind of prestige that parliaments in other countries enjoyed, in that all major announcements affecting the country were made in the legislative body. In the case of Zambia, nearly all important announcements affecting the country were announced outside parliament. The various economic reforms were announced at either the United National Independence Party (UNIP) National Councils or other UNIP forums. Although the president was given the power to convene, to address, and to send messages to the national assembly at his discretion, he never used the opportunity availed to him through this prerogative to make major announcements in the national assembly.[5]

For a number of reasons, the national assembly during the first republic was not able to exercise these formal functions to the fullest. In both the first and second parliaments, UNIP had more than a two-thirds majority in parliament and hence the legislative process was, largely, a mere formality. On the other hand, the Members of Parliament from the ruling party rarely offered any input in the law-making process within the national assembly. The executive had a tight control of their Members of Parliament. UNIP Members of Parliament were expected to raise whatever concerns they had about any proposed bill in the UNIP parliamentary caucus meetings. The UNIP chief whip revealed this in the heat of a parliamentary debate when, in 1968, he told parliament that: "We have got various levels at which these problems are sorted out and discussed. And by the time we come here, we have more or less sorted out our differences on our side here."[6] This meant that the UNIP backbench Members of Parliament were not expected to contradict ministers in the national assembly.

The national assembly was also expected to play a watchdog role over the conduct and performance of the government. In performing this role, the Members of Parliament were expected to "keep the executive within limit." This function was performed by the opposition party, with limitation. As in the case of the process of law-making, the UNIP backbench Members of Parliament largely shied away from performing this role. As Tordoff and Molteno concluded, the role of the UNIP Members of Parliament for most of the first republic was "almost non-existent. They had a strong tendency not to attend and an even stronger tendency not to participate."[7]

The inability of the UNIP backbench Members of Parliament to play an active role in the national assembly was, therefore, largely the result of Kaunda exhorting the UNIP Members of Parliament to take a much more active role in the national assembly, including performing what the "weak opposition" was supposed to perform.[8] At the same time, his party took a very unfavorable view of the Members of Parliament who criticized the government in the national assembly. The case of a junior minister who was forced to resign both his parliamentary seat and ministerial office after he attacked the government in parliament is an example of such unfavorable reactions.[9] As indicated earlier, the Members of Parliament were expected to use the party parliamentary caucus meetings to raise whatever critical issues they wanted to raise against the government. Because of the attitude taken by UNIP, attendance by the UNIP Members of Parliament was very erratic and many of them never made regular contributions in the national house. One reason was that such contributions were largely in support and praise of government ministers.

The UNIP party leadership was able to ensure that its UNIP members in the national assembly conformed, largely through the effective use of the whip system and the extensive power of patronage at the hands of the president. This party's hold on their Members of Parliament was reinforced by the constitutional amendment of 1966, which under article 65(4) of the Constitution provided that a Member of Parliament who left the party on whose ticket he was elected would forfeit his seat. The introduction of this amendment followed the resignation of two Members of Parliament, one from the opposition African National Congress (ANC) and the other from the ruling party to form another political party, the United Party.

Despite the fact that the National Assembly played an insignificant role in the first national assembly, it played a useful role in the country. As pointed out by Gupta, the debates generated great public interest and the publicity given to its proceedings in daily newspapers provides an opportunity to the people to know what goes on in the higher echelons of the national administration.[10] More importantly, the national assembly played a representative role, as Members of Parliament were provided with a forum to articulate the interests of their constituents. In his article, "The Zambian National Assembly: Study of an African Legislature", Gupta (1965–1966) observes that the Members of Parliament brought to the notice of the government problems and grievances of their respective constituencies by raising questions and by use of motions.[11] However, despite the availability of this avenue, it seems that, with the exception of the white members who were elected on the reserved seats, many MPs did not utilize this facility to the fullest, particularly members of the ruling party. The white MPs used the national assembly to articulate the interests of their constituencies and of the white population in general.

The position of the ruling party constrained the extent to which the UNIP Members of Parliament could articulate the grievances of their constituencies. First, despite the occasional urging by the president for the UNIP MPs to participate more actively in the national assembly debates, the members were expected to use other avenues to resolve matters pertaining to their constituencies. They were expected to use the offices of the district governors, other party officials, and other government officials at the district level rather than raise such issues in the national assembly. More importantly, it was pointed out to them that the responsibility to represent the interests of the people was largely that of the party and the constituencies they represented belonged to the party. At the general conference of 1967, Kaunda made this point most explicit when addressing the delegates:

> As already pointed out, we emphasize the constituency belongs to the party. . . . A UNIP Member of Parliament is part and parcel of the whole,

and does not therefore carry out his own policies in the constituency. Only independent Members of Parliament can do that for that is what the people in that constituency will have chosen ... We believe that the people have a right to make claims from their government through their party. This they do naturally through the party leadership at all levels and that is why Members of Parliament go where the party sends them.[12]

Despite this, some UNIP Members of Parliament used occasions like this when they were passing a vote of thanks after the president's speech in the national assembly.

From the discussion of the independence constitution, the way it was interpreted and used by the executive and Kaunda in particular, it is clear that the executive–legislative relations in the first republic were very unbalanced in favor of the executive, particularly the presidency. The president's powers over the national assembly were further enhanced by the 1969 Constitutional Amendment Act, which gave the president power to extend a state of emergency without the need for renewal of such state of emergency by the national assembly.

The Role of Parliament under the One-Party System: UNIP Supremacy over State Institutions

The one-party Constitution incorporated all the constitutional provisions of the independence Constitution that created a very powerful presidency and a weak national assembly. The 1972 constitutional review commission chaired by the then vice president Mainza Chona, who established the one-party Constitution, made a number of recommendations that would have reduced some of the powers of the president and increased the powers and prestige of the national assembly. The attempts at reducing the powers of the president relative to other constitutional offices, particularly the national assembly, seems to have been a reflection of the suggestions of petitioners.[13]

The Commissioners recommended the creation of the position of Prime Minister, to be appointed by the president with the approval of the national assembly. It was also recommended that the power to appoint cabinet ministers and junior ministers should be vested in the prime minster, which he would do in consultation with the president. While the government accepted the creation of the position of prime minister, it rejected the recommendation that the appointment be subject to the approval of the national assembly, as it did the recommendation that the power to appoint ministers be vested in the prime minister. The significance of these proposals is that it would have greatly enhanced the accountability of the prime minister to the national assembly as well as the cabinet ministers and junior ministers since they would be appointed by him.

The Commission also recommended that while the president had the power to veto any bill, once such a vetoed bill had been referred back to the national assembly for further consideration and passed by a two-thirds majority, the president would be obliged to give his assent. The government rejected this, as well as the recommendation that all bills passed by the national assembly be assented to by the president within 21 days.

The government's rejection of the commission's proposals that would have lead to some redistribution of power between the executive and legislative meant, essentially, that power continued to be concentrated in the hands of the president and a continued weakness in the national assembly. This was one of the salient features of the one party as it was constituted in 1973. The powers and prestige of the assembly was eroded further by the principle of supremacy of the party organs over the state organs institutionalized during the second republic.

The principle of the supremacy of the party provided that the party's central committee was superior to the cabinet. Despite the provisions of the republican Constitution that gave it the supreme legislative powers, the national assembly was made subordinate to the party's national council of which all party functionaries at the district level and above and all Members of Parliament were members.

The supremacy of the national council over the national assembly essentially meant that the responsibility of the national assembly was to implement the resolutions of the national council. This created serious problems for the Members of Parliament because the republican constitution vested legislative powers in the national assembly. It was the national assembly that was the supreme legislative body in the land, and yet it was supposed to be accountable to the national council in terms of the party constitution. From the point of view of the party leadership, the national assembly was supposed to formalize the decisions of the national council by passing them into law.

In principle, the Members of Parliament in the second republic were free to speak and vote as they liked in the national assembly, the government had accepted the Chona commission recommendation that under the one-party system, "Members of Parliament were free to speak and vote as they liked on any issue in the national assembly."[14] However, in practice this was not the case. Members of Parliament were not expected to criticize the executive or government policies as these were considered party policies. Kaunda himself graphically spelt out the projected role of the national assembly in the one-party set-up when he reprimanded Members of Parliament who adopted independent postures in the national assembly. He referred to the Members of Parliament who criticized party policies as subversive. Underlying the national assembly's "rubber stamping" role, Kaunda outlined what he expected of the Members of Parliament in these terms:

> As Party members, Members of Parliament should at all times observe Party rules. They should also defend party policies in the House, instead of attacking them. Policies and decisions made by their National Council are expressions of the people's will . . . they are the wishes of the majority and therefore they should be respected. If any member of this council holds contrary view on any subject that is being discussed by the Council, he is free . . . to give his case. But once the Council has taken a decision on the matter, it is a duty of each one of us to respect that decision and defend or implement it. . . . . We must accept the majority view . . . even if we do not agree with it. If we don't then . . . we must resign our seats. . . . If the National Council decides that a certain action has to be taken it has got to be taken. . . . If it is legislative action that is needed to implement a policy decision on the National Council, the National Assembly as an Arm of the Party, must act accordingly, without question.[15]

During this time, more than during the first republic, the Members of Parliament were seen more as agents of the executive and the party in the sense that their role was seen by the party leadership as essentially to explain to the people the polices of the government.

The attempts by the party leadership to control the national assembly and their attempt to usurp its constitutional powers as the legislative body were greatly resented by both Members of Parliament and the public. The Members of Parliament regarded themselves as the true representatives of the people since they were the only ones that were generally considered to have been democratically elected. Thus, on several occasions, individual Members of Parliament ignored the party line in their debates in parliament. However, on several occasions, the central committee used its veto power to bar Members of Parliament who proved difficult from contesting subsequent elections. One such Member of Parliament was the former minister of finance who had been a Member of Parliament for Livingstone from 1973 to 1978 and was one of the critical Members of Parliament. The central committee vetoed him when he wanted to contest again in 1978.

In terms of the parliamentary electoral process, the 1973 Constitution provided for a two-stage method of electing Members of Parliament. The first was the primary election in which party leaders at district, ward, and branch levels formed themselves into electoral colleges to nominate three candidates among all the contestants to qualify and enter the second and final stage of the elections—the parliamentary elections in which all the qualified voters in the country participated. According to the 1973 Constitution, any card-carrying member of the party was eligible to contest parliamentary elections subject only to veto by the central committee. The Constitution was amended in 1978 and provided that only people who had been members of the party for at least five years prior to the nomination were eligible for election to Parliament. The provision for primary elections was subsequently abolished and they were last held in 1978. Thus, one distinct advantage that the system had over the multiparty system was that contesting parliamentary elections were more open than was the case in either the First or Third Republics.[16]

The result was that a larger number of people sought election to parliament during that period than at any other time. Furthermore, more people entered the political scene during this time than at any other time. The parliamentary elections themselves were highly competitive. Although candidates were subjected to formal campaign meetings conducted by the party officials, the actual campaigns, where enormous amounts of money was spent and where issues that mattered to the voters, including the suitability of each of the candidates, were discussed, took place outside these official campaign meetings. The party's control on who became a Member of Parliament after the vetoing process was over was severely limited. Hence, a number of party men lost to relatively new men. In fact, a number of political observers noted the role of the one party electoral system in this respect. For example, Bornwell Chikulo made the following observation:

> What has been the impact of the one party electoral system on the nature of political recruitment? To begin with, the introduction of primary election stage has increased the potential for a broader representation as candidature is open to all citizens registered as members of UNIP.[17]

The elimination of the primary elections in the electoral process after 1978 increased the potential that Chikulo referred to. One can venture to state that the parliamentary elections during the one-party system were sufficiently democratic by any standards.

The various interest groups also used the national assembly to articulate their interests during this period.[18] In particular, the business community used the national assembly to attack the government's "socialist" policies and to influence government to change its policies toward Rhodesia and Southern Africa in particular. Arthur Wina, a former minister of finance in the first republic, who seemed to have been one of the leaders of this group in 1978, made the following criticism of the party policies:

> Statements have been made by his Excellency Minister of Industry that Zambia welcomes investments from outside (and) this is the right decision

which must be followed.... I am worried that a series of counter statements from certain other levels in our country tend to spoil this effort.... It is not unusual to read from the Newspapers that some leading members of the Government addressed a visiting dignitary and took almost three quarters of the time congratulating that dignitary about the achievement of their system.[19]

Cherry Gertzel and Karen Eriksen also documented cases of Members of Parliament who were very critical of Government's "socialist" policies and its policies toward Southern Rhodesia and Southern Africa in general.[20]

Largely because of the use they put the national assembly in articulating their class interests, a large number of business people sought election to the national assembly. In fact, the largest number of people who participated successfully in the parliamentary elections during this period was businessmen. In their analysis of the rise of a capitalist class in Zambia, Carolyn Baylies and Morris Szeftel stated that there had been a tendency in the 1970s for those in the business sector to seek active participation in politics. They found that about 44 percent and more than 30 percent of the winners in the 1973 and 1978 parliamentary elections, respectively, had business interests of some kind.[21] Chikulo put the percentage of those with business interests elected to the 1978 parliament at 41 percent.[22]

Attempts at Reforms to Strength the Legislative and Watchdog Functions of the National Assembly, 1990–1995

Before coming to power, the Movement for Multiparty Democracy (MMD) expressed strong commitment to strong parliamentary control of the executive. In making their submission to the Mvunga Commission, the party made several important suggestions that were intended to strengthen legislative control over the executive and reduce some of the powers conferred on the President. Among some of the proposals made by the MMD was that the President of the country should be elected by the National Assembly and accountable to the House. It also suggested that the National Assembly should have power to scrutinize the conduct of Government officials.[23]

Largely because of the position the MMD took during the fight against the one-party system, particularly their belligerent position against the 1991 constitution, there were very high expectations after the party won the 1991 elections that major revisions of the constitution would be undertaken to change most of the "dictatorial" clauses of the constitution.

Among organizations that called for the urgent review of the constitution was the Law Association of Zambia that argued that "the current document contained flaws because it was drawn under duress"[24] and the Forum for the Democratic Process that attacked the Government for taking "lukewarm steps to revise the constitution," which it said was "a hindrance to the fledging democracy."[25] The general expectations of Zambians were best epitomized in an article to the *Weekly Post* by a University of Zambia Lecturer:

> Before assuming power, the MMD expressed its intention of replacing the current Republican Constitution with a more democratic one. This was because it regarded it as a document of convenience, the result of compromise between a UNIP one which favored a strong executive [President] and its own proposals aimed at preventing a recurrence of authoritarian rule experienced during the Second Republic.[26]

However, once in office, the MMD government was reluctant to make any significant constitutional changes. Although they accepted participation in the 1991 elections under the 1990 constitution under "protest," they moved very slowly toward making any significant constitutional reforms. In fact, within a year, the MMD leadership began to campaign for the retention of the extensive powers of the president. It was after some period of vacillation that the Government eventually appointed a constitutional review commission in 1993[27] and in its submission to the commission, the ruling party called for the establishment of a strong executive arguing that:

> We had the privilege of being in Government for three years now. Our considered position is that many of the provisions of the current constitution have proved to be adequate . . . we wish to reiterate that it is our considered view that the best system of government is presidential democracy.[28]

As in the case of 1972 and 1991, there was general consensus among the petitioners that the Constitution gave too much power to the president. A fact that greatly influenced the Commission on a number of important recommendations that would have strengthened the national assembly. Among the petitioners was the national party, then the third largest party in parliament that proposed that the national assembly elect the president so that the executive powers of the president are; "Controlled by deliberate checks and balances, which would be possible only if the president is answerable and accountable to the national assembly by having this body elect the incumbent."[29]

It was against the background of this and several other proposals from petitioners throughout the country that the 1993 constitutional review commission made a number of important recommendations to the government on restructuring the various organs of the state. Significantly, in writing their report, the commissioners stated as one of their guiding principles the need: to ensure effective checks and balances in the political system, the promotion of relative autonomy as well as upholding of the independence of all branches of government.[30]

Thus in attempting to strengthen the national assembly within the context of the need to provide effective "checks and balances," the commissioners made several recommendations. First, they proposed the creation of constitutionally established national assembly committees which, in their opinion, would "revitalize the national assembly and make it into the principal organ for checking and supervising the executive branch."[31] Second, the commission proposed that the national assembly should have power to pass a vote of no confidence in individual ministers and when such a vote has been passed, the affected ministers should be removed by the president.[32] The commissioners also recommended that the clause that provides for the president to appoint additional eight Members of Parliament should be abolished because "nominated members tend to give leverage on the executive to influence the composition of the legislature and would be hard to justify under the new dispensation."[33] The government rejected all these proposals. While in opposition, the MMD had opposed the nominated members' clause in 1991; the party rejected the commission's recommendation to abolish this provision when it was in Government.[34]

The commissioners also wanted to increase the number of constitutional offices that would be accounted to the national assembly and to measures intended at increasing this accountability. Among these was the creation of the position of parliamentary ombudsman in place of the current investigator-general. The commissioners recommended that this officer should come under and be appointed by the national assembly in consultation with judiciary service commission because:

> As originally conceived, the investigator-general plays the role of ombudsman whose main function is to protect the citizens from misadministration, petitioners did not think that any officer appointed by the executive, and accountable to the executive, could be expected to check effectively and control the executive. It was a contradiction in terms as it violated the notion that one power ought to be balanced by a different power.[35]

The government rejected this.

Parliament and the Executive Relationships in the Third Republic

The 1991 and 1995 efforts produced some constitutional changes toward strengthening the position of the national assembly, albeit without significantly changing the power relationships between the executive and the legislative body, as we shall see soon. In contrast to the situation prior to the third republic, the current Constitution gives the national assembly power to ratify presidential appointments to a number of constitutional offices such as that of the chief justice, attorney general, the chairman, and members of the electoral commission. Although these powers are largely formal as long as the ruling party commands a majority in the national assembly, there have been instances when some appointments were delayed because of some resistance in the national assembly. One such case involved the appointment of the same person to both positions of attorney general and solicitor general.

Another constitutional reform undertaken in the third republic is under Article 51: the Constitution provides that the cabinet shall be collectively accountable to the national assembly. This was understood to be the case in line with the British parliamentary convention before 1991, after that it was provided for in the constitution.

There were other provisions introduced in the current constitution. According to article 88 (6) (b) of the Constitution, the national assembly can dissolve itself. By so doing, they would also terminate the term of office of the president. The importance of this provision is more symbolic than practical, in the sense that at least the provision to dissolve the national assembly is not the exclusive prerogative of the president. However, the possibilities of the national assembly making such a move are very remote.

Comparatively speaking, the national assembly in the third republic was more active and has on several occasions exercised some of its constitutional powers with more success than was the case during the first republic. The government has also on several occasions been forced to withdraw government bills during or before the second reading due to the opposition from the Members of Parliament. Among such bills was the Lands Bill of 1994,[36] which had to be resubmitted with several provisions removed,[37] the Constitutional Officers (Emoluments) Bill of 1995, which sought to empower the president to specify the salaries of constitutional office holders by statutory instrument[38] and the State Security (Amendment) Bill of 1999.[39]

In 2001, amidst recriminations within the MMD, leading to the expulsion of 22 Members of Parliament from the party, a serious attempt was made to impeach former President Chiluba. About 65 Members of Parliament had petitioned the speaker of the national assembly to convene the national assembly for purposes of impeaching the president under Article 37 of the Constitution.[40] However, despite the fact that more than the required one-third of the Members of Parliament petitioned the speaker to convene the national assembly, he did not do so.[41]

The national assembly has been relatively active in its watchdog role in scrutinizing the conduct and performance of the executive, particularly in the past five years. This has been largely due to two factors. The first has been the result of internal conflicts within the ruling party; primarily over Chiluba's attempt to have the constitution changed to enable him to seek a third term and the conflict between the current president and his predecessor. The increase in the number and the relatively high quality of the opposition Members of Parliament after 2001 have been other contributing factors.

There have also been some reforms intended to strengthen the watchdog role of the national assembly in the form of the creation of department-oriented committees. They were introduced to reinforce the regular committees of the national assembly, the public accounts committee, committee on delegated legislation, committee on government assurances, and estimates committee. The department-oriented committees that cover all government ministries are: agriculture and lands; economic affairs and labor; communications, transport works and supply; energy, environment and tourism; health, community development and social welfare; information and broadcasting services; national security and foreign affairs; education, science and technology; local government, housing and chiefs affairs; legal, governance, human rights and gender matters; sport, youth and child affairs. These committees have been relatively active. The responsibilities of these are committees are: to study, report, and make appropriate recommendations on the mandate, management, and operations of the executive; to carry out detailed scrutiny of certain activities undertaken by the government; and to make, if necessary, recommendations on the need to review certain policies and/or certain existing legislation.[42]

The committees have made the public aware of the issues that their reports bring out and that they table before the national assembly.

These notable departures from a relatively dormant legislative body of the first republic, notwithstanding the current constitution, has not made any substantial alterations to the unbalanced power distribution between the executive, in particular the president, which has existed since 1964. The extensive powers that the president has been enjoying since 1964 have remained essentially unchanged despite the general sentiments against such powers that came out during the three previous constitutional review commissions. The extent of the powers enjoyed by the president over the national assembly were itemized in a paper presented to Professors' World

Peace Academy in Lusaka by a current cabinet minister, then an opposition Member of Parliament, Dr. Ludwig Sondashi. He summarizes these powers in the following terms:

> With regards to Parliamentary affairs, the President besides his powers to veto bills, and assenting to a bill for it to become law, he decides on the date, venue, program and the bills to come before the Legislature. He has power to appoint and remove the members of the Electoral Commission, permanent Human Rights Commission, the Anti-Corruption Commission . . . subject to certain powers in certain cases of ratification by the Legislature. . . . The president enjoys substantial powers to control public expenditure and he is the custodian of public moneys.[43]

Although the members from the ruling party have at times criticized some legislative pieces of their party, they have in the majority of cases given support to government legislative programs. In fact, almost all the bills that had been withdrawn were successfully reintroduced, including the highly controversial Lands Bill that was successfully resubmitted the following year. In any case, the more serious challenges by the Members of Parliament took place only under exceptional circumstances such as the cited case of the attempt to impeach the president, that happened amidst the crises over Chiluba's third-term bid or in the context of the current differences between the current president and his successor as has already been indicated.

As was the case in the first and second republics, the ruling party has not taken too kindly to Members of Parliament who have exercised independent stances in the national assembly. The ruling party and its president can and have used threats of expulsion to bring MPs that consistently defied the party to toe the party line. The position of the executive in this regard is strengthened by the retention of article 65(4) of the Constitution that provides for the expulsion of a Member of Parliament from the national assembly on either leaving or being expelled by the political party on whose ticket he/she was elected.[44] Moreover, through the party caucuses, they are able to get even the aggrieved Members of Parliament to support the government. The reaction of the then minister of finance to the criticism of some aspects of his 1998 budget shows an example of such threats and revealed the extent of the leaders' expectation of the behavior of the backbenchers from the ruling party. Censuring the behavior of such MPs, the late minister remarked: "We cannot have the MMD tearing itself apart. This document is a product of your part and should be your document as well. And if you are not happy with the budget, leave the party."[45]

In 1999, calls were made for the resignation of MMD Members of Parliament for taking positions that were unacceptable to the party leadership. The MP for Chipili in Luapula Province was one such MP who came under attack in 1999 for referring to Mr. Chiluba's 1999 speech at the opening of the national assembly as "hollow" and containing nothing. He was subsequently suspended with a view to expel him from the party.[46] The expulsion was never carried out.

Although the Members of Parliament have been relatively active in their role checking on the government, the national assembly in this role has remained relatively weak. In the period before the 2001 elections, this weakness manifested itself in several ways. The parliamentary scrutiny of the activities of the executive has not been as rigorous as it should be. The national assembly has done very little about the auditor general's reports and other parliamentary reports that have been very critical of government. The national assembly's weakness has also been revealed by its inability to respond in decisive ways to a series of crises that have faced the country. In countries with strong legislatures, allegations of gunrunning made in 1999 against some members of the executive that threatened the national security would have demanded and received satisfactory explanations. Unconventional executive actions such as the creation of what has been referred to as the "slush fund" with the approval of the MMD would not be allowed by strong legislatures.

The accountability of the cabinet to the national assembly, which was one of the reforms intended at strengthening the oversight role of the national assembly, is neutralized by the constitutional provision that "the cabinet shall be responsible for advising the President with respect to policy for the Government" in view of the fact that, constitutionally, the president is not bound by the advice from the Ministers and is expected to act in "his deliberated judgment."[47] Since the president is not answerable to the national assembly over matters on policy, Ministers may not see themselves as collectively accountable to the national assembly. This has, therefore, weakened the role of the legislature in holding the cabinet accountable to the national assembly on government policy.

Conclusion

From the preceding discussion, it is clear that the Zambian national assembly has gone through some major crises regarding its role. What seems to emerge is that while there seems to be some recognition of the importance of the legislative, once in office, members of the executive have attempted to control the legislative body. This attempt has been made in all three republics with varying degrees of success. In fact, judging from the nature of the debates that took place in the third republic, Members of Parliament played a critical role in both scrutinizing the conduct and performance of the executive and representing the views of their social and geographical constituencies more than was the case under the first and second republics. This was in spite of the institutional arrangements that formally made the national assembly a "rubber stamp" organ of the party's national council. Members of Parliament raised more questions during this period than at any other period.[48]

In general, however the Zambian experience indicates that the powers of the president in relation to those other state organs and office, including the national assembly, are enormous. In constitutional terms, the hybrid system that Zambia adopted in 1964 and which is still the preferred system does to a large measure disparate the powers of the president and the national assembly. Essentially, the effect of the hybrid system was engineered to give the president all the powers that go with presidential systems without a relative independence of legislature often associated with "pure" presidential systems. It likewise adopted from the parliamentary system a very strong whip associated with the Westminster parliamentary convention without giving the power to the Legislature to remove the Government from office.

The above observations, notwithstanding the fact that the National Assembly managed to force government to withdraw some bills and seriously threatened a president through the attempted impeachment, did indicate that, given the right conditions, the national assembly can also play its constitutional role effectively. An increased number of Members of Parliament from the opposition parties could be a pointer in that direction. Furthermore, the very existence of debates in the national assembly that are disseminated through the print and electronic media assists in highlighting and bringing to the fore a number of critical governance issues that affect the country, which otherwise would not be known and publicly debated.

Notes

1. Zambia, Government of the Republic of 1995b.
2. For details of the formal powers and functions vested, see Zambia, Government of the Republic of 1972. Although the legal definition of parliament is that of the national assembly and president, most literature in fact refers to the national assembly as parliament, and this is the general understanding as exemplified by the fact that even in Zambia, the members of the national assembly are officially referred to as Members of Parliament. Consequently,

the reference in this chapter to parliament would mean the national assembly. The two terms would be used interchangeably.
3. Although the president was directly elected, the election procedures provided that each candidate would indicate the president he or she supported in the elections, so that all the votes that a parliamentary candidate got were also the votes that the presidential candidate got in each of the constituencies. In this way, the presidential elections were tied to parliamentary elections.
4. This is by the 1972 edition of the Zambian Constitution. In The Referendum (Amendment) Act of 1969, the Government called for a referendums to end all referendums in relation to this section. Thereafter, the national assembly could amend any section in this Article.
5. For this unique blend of the presidential system and parliamentary system in Zambia and how it enhanced the powers of the President, see, among others: Simb Mubako 1970; Pettman 1974.
6. Debates 13, Feb. 14, 1968, 269.
7. For a detailed discussion of Parliament in the First Republic, see Tordoff and Molteno 1974: 235.
8. See, for example, Kaunda's comments in *Times of Zambia*, Mar. 22, 1969.
9. In his maiden speech, Mr. Jethro Mutti, the Member of Parliament for Livingston, claimed that the Zambian Ministers were the highest paid ministers in Africa and should give up their Mercedes-Benz cars. He was heavily criticized by the UNIP Members of Parliament, and subsequently offered his resignation—both his parliamentary seat and ministerial position. He was persuaded by Kaunda to rescind his decision to resign. For details of this episode, see Tordoff and Molteno 1974: 240.
10. Gupta 1965–1966.
11. Ibid.
12. United National Independence Party, Mulungushi 1967 Conference Proceedings.
13. Zambia, Government of the Republic of 1992: 10–14.
14. Ibid., 8–9.
15. Zambia, Government of the Republic of 1975: 23.
16. The principle of political parties presenting their official candidates tended to restrict the numbers of people in the elections and limited the role of the local people in the choice of their local Member of Parliament. In the study of political parties by Robert Mushota, it was found that a number of political parties in the 1996 parliamentary elections imposed parliamentary candidates on the local party structures. See Mushota 1997.
17. Chikulo 1970: 107.
18. See Momba 1993: 201–203.
19. Debates.
20. See Gertzel 1984; Eriksen 1978.
21. Baylies and Szeftel 1982: 201–202.
22. Chikulo 1970: 108.
23. For a summary of the MMD proposals, see 1994: 107–109. See also *National Mirror*, Feb. 11, 1991.
24. *Times of Zambia*, Mar. 1, 1992.

25. Ibid., July 9, 1993.
26. Ntalasha 1992.
27. *Times of Zambia*, Nov. 16, 1992.
28. *Post Newspaper*, Oct. 7, 1994.
29. Ibid. Nov. 8, 1994.
30. Zambia, Government of the Republic of 1995a: 115.
31. Ibid. 141.
32. Ibid. 117–118.
33. Ibid. 131.
34. Ibid. 69.
35. Ibid. 194–195.
36. *Times of Zambia*, Nov. 18, 1994.
37. For example, the provision providing for freehold land tenure was dropped. See *Times of Zambia*, June 16, 1995.
38. Ibid. Mar. 18, 1995. The main objection to this Bill was the fear that it would compromise the autonomy of the judges.
39. Debates 113, Aug. 24–31, 1999: col. 424.
40. *Times of Zambia*, Sep. 9, 1996.
41. According to Article 37(b) of the Constitution, "If notice is given to the Speaker of the national assembly signed by not less than one-third of the members of the national assembly of a motion alleging that the president has committed any violation of the constitution or gross misconduct and specifying the particulars of the allegations and proposing that a tribunal be established under this article to investigate those allegations, the Speaker shall; . . . if Parliament is not sitting (and not withstanding that it may be prorogued) summon the national assembly within 21 days of the notice and cause the motion to be considered at that meeting."
42. See Burnell 2003: 50.
43. Sondashi 1998: 1–2.
44. Zambia, Government of the Republic of Report of 1995: 130–131.
45. *Times of Zambia*, Feb. 12, 1998.
46. Ibid. Feb. 12, 1999.
47. See Burnell 2003 for a discussion of this contradiction.
48. Ibid.

7

Longitudinal View on Ghana's Parliamentary Practices

Kwame Boafo-Arthur

Department of Political Science,
University of Ghana Accra, Ghana

Introduction

This chapter addresses the development of parliamentary practices and hazards what may happen in light of what currently seems as an entrenchment of democratic governance in Ghana. This ambitious scheme cannot by any means claim to offer an exhaustive survey of cumulative events that in reality span a period of over 150 years when the Bond of 1844 that placed the coastal Fante states under British suzerainty was signed. I attempt only to scratch the surface and elucidate the struggle to control Ghana's legislature from the distant colonial past to the present.

The chapter is divided into five main parts. The first part tackles the struggles by the elite to have a say in not only the law-making process but also the administration of the country during the colonial period. The second part deals with parliamentary activities in the immediate post-independence era from March 1957 to the overthrow of Dr. Nkrumah on February 24, 1966. The third part deals with the short-lived Second and Third Republics, 1969–1972 and 1979–1981, respectively.

The fourth part covers the post 1990s rule of the National Democratic Congress (NDC) and the New Patriotic Party (NPP) governments respectively. In this section, more emphasis is placed on the structure and composition of the Fourth Republican parliament, parliamentary committees, and their powers as well as the relationship between the legislature and the executive.

Where appropriate, I attempt to compare and contrast the 1992 Constitution with the constitutions of 1969 and 1979, albeit not in greater detail. The analysis focuses on the uneasy relationship between legislature and executive, using historical events and case studies to illustrate the discrepancy between parliamentary theory and practice. The final part, which is also the conclusion, offers some prognosis on the future of parliamentary practices and the democratic future of Ghana.

From the Bond of 1844 to the 1948 Riots: The Colonial Legislative-executive Antecedence

Under the auspices of the Bond of 1844, the Fante states on the coastal belt of Ghana were placed firmly under British rule and control. However, effective administration of the nation including Ashanti by the British started in 1874 when the British defeated the Ashanti kingdom in the Sagrenti War. It marked the consolidation of British authority on the Gold Coast. In the first instance, the coastal belt was made a Crown Colony in 1874. Ashanti was declared a conquered territory and the Northern Territories were made British protectorates in 1901.[1] Through education and commerce, however, a coterie of elite anxious to have a say in the administration of the nation emerged. Lawyers, doctors, merchants, government clerks, and others who benefited from the educational system introduced by the British felt that they needed a say in the administration of the country.

The coastal belt had both Legislative Council and an Executive Council, which were the major law making and policy-making bodies in the colony respectively. It was unrepresentative in the sense that it was not an elected body and had its membership chosen and appointed by the Governor. Both official colonial officers and unofficial, private business interests dominated the Legislative Council. The dependence on a few Africans, normally the traditional rulers, proved effective in helping them to stamp their authority on the people.[2] This is because the people revered their traditional rulers and accorded the same respect even when the colonialists, to assure absolute subjugation, were using them as tools of indirect control. In reality, however, the British exercised Legislative power on the Gold Coast between 1850 and 1957.[3] It was, however, not until 1946 that the Ashanti Confederacy was placed under the jurisdiction of the Legislative Council.[4] The Bond of 1844, which became the basis for British jurisdiction on the Gold Coast, clearly spelled out the relations that were to exist between the coastal states and the British. Section A of the Bond states:

> Whereas power and jurisdiction have been exercised for and on behalf of Her Majesty the Queen of Great Britain and Ireland, within diverse

countries and places adjacent to her Majesty's forts and settlements on the Gold Coast; we, Chiefs of countries and places so referred to, adjacent to such forts and settlements, do hereby acknowledge that power and jurisdiction, and declare that the first objects of law are the protection of individuals and of property.[5]

It is interesting to note that only eight chiefs who were all in the present-day Central Region of Ghana signed the Bond. Between 1850 and 1865, the Gold Coast had its own legislative council or parliament made up of the Governor and no fewer than two other persons designated by Royal authority. The legislative council was to make "all such laws, institutions and ordinances as may from time to time be necessary for the peace, order and good government of our subjects and others within the said present or future forts and settlement in the Gold Coast."[6]

The role of the traditional chiefs was given a lease of life by the British colonial rulers. The introduction of indirect rule had the effect of shifting political power in the Colony to the British since the traditional rulers who were indirectly used as administrators were responsible to the Governor or District Commissioners (DCs). As pointed out by David Apter, "no traditional power existed beyond the sufferance of British tolerance."[7]

In the early eighteenth century, a Provisional Council was set up. The chiefs and the newly established Provisional Council served as the bridgehead through which the British administered the provinces. The central government was represented by the Governor and supported by the legislative council on which chiefs were represented together with elected representatives from the municipalities. Largely, chiefs became the locus of political power in the colony apart from the Governor and the DCs.

It must be stressed, however, that as far back as 1850, areas under British rule on the Gold Coast had executive and legislative councils. The snag was that members were appointed, not elected. The first African member of the legislative council was appointed in 1889 and by 1916 the legislative council was composed of 11 official and 10 unofficial members. In 1925, it was enlarged to include elected members. The Executive Council was also increased to include eight members and the membership never included any African.[8] However, the Legislative Council, which was now composed of 30 members, had nine Africans some of whom were elected through the Joint Provincial Council. Meanwhile, the activities of nationalist lawyers who were members of the Aborigines' Rights Protection Society (ARPS) and the National Congress of British West Africa (NCBWA) were opposed to the British and, in fact, Casely Hayford of the NCBWA reasoned, "anyone who sat on the Legislative Council was in effect a traitor."[9]

Legislative Changes after the Second World War

Rapid socio-political changes, however, took place on the Gold Coast after the Second World War with a tremendous impact on legislative engineering. The reasons are not hard to determine. The Gold Coast was seen as a model colony so the riots of 1948 shocked the sensibilities of the British administrators. Second, in 1951, the first experiment in representative governance had proved successful, and finally the upsurge of Ashanti nationalism, which led to agitation for a federal state, had faded. Therefore, by the arrival of Governor Allan Burns in 1942, the conditions were appropriate for "the introduction of a large measure of representative government."[10] In 1946, the Burns Constitution was introduced with 18 of the members being elected representatives. However, the riots of 1948, which was precipitated by the shooting of soldiers wanting to present a petition to the Governor, most probably led to the early demise of the constitution because the Watson Commission that was charged to investigate the causes of the riot recommended full responsible government for the Gold Coast. The Watson Commission recommended the creation of a Gold Coast Assembly with legislative functions and parliamentary status. The Coussey Committee of 1949 was set up to study the Watson report and advise on the way forward. Its recommendations included the reconstitution of the Executive Council as a ministerial body responsible to the legislature.

In 1950, however, the Arden-Clarke Constitution replaced the Burns Constitution of 1946 and set up a legislature of 104 members, 70 of whom were directly elected—33 from the colony, 18 from Ashanti, and 19 from the Northern Territories. This paved the way for the general election of 1951. Meanwhile, on the Gold Coast, nationalist activities had reached a fever pitch with the formation of the United Gold Coast Convention (UGCC) party on August 4, 1947 at Saltpond.[11]

The legislative council under the Arden-Clarke Constitution of 1950 was dissolved and the Gold Coast prepared for general election, which took place in February 1951. Although Nkrumah was in prison because of the Positive Action of 1950, he was allowed to stand election. The CPP won the election and the Governor invited Nkrumah to form the next government whereupon he was appointed the Leader of Government Business. From then to the time of independence, Nkrumah and the Governor worked intimately as a team. In 1952, following the visit of Mr. Olive Lyttleton, Nkrumah was appointed the first African Prime Minister.[12]

Under the Nkrumah Constitution of 1954, the Assembly was to be directly elected by secret ballot in single-member constituencies. The implication then is that, ultimately, administrative actions depended largely on instructions from Her Majesty. Without doubt, the African

Cabinet led by Nkrumah was ruling the country, but most instructions according to the constitutional instrument had the imprint of Britain. This was something that might not have pleased those in the legislative assembly. Nonetheless, since the Gold Coast was yet to be independent, nothing could be done about it. The new parliament met for the first time in 1954 and a detailed program to prepare the nation for self-rule was outlined. It included the reopening of "negotiations with the United Kingdom Government with a view to the achievement of independence" and "the speeding up of a policy of Africanization of the public service."[13]

The road to independence was itself strewn with political landmines. The CPP and the British tasted Ashanti nationalism with the emergence of the National Liberation Movement (NLM) that started agitating for a federation instead of the unitary government favored by the British and the CPP. Nkrumah invited the opposition leaders to the negotiating table by the end of 1954, but this was rejected in early 1955. In April 1955, a Select Committee of the legislative assembly was appointed to "examine the question of a federal system of government and the question of a Second Chamber for the Gold Coast. . . ."[14] On the basis of memoranda received, the Select Committee rejected federation and a second chamber for the country. When further attempts to draw the opposition to the negotiating table failed, the threat of secession was issued by the NLM. Baffuor Akoto, one of the firebrands of the NLM noted, "If upon the strength of these CPP Ministers' statements the United Kingdom Government granted the Gold Coast independence without a general agreement on the constitution, Ashanti also would separate herself from the rest of the country."[15]

A conference at Achimota to resolve the constitutional impasse failed. Consequently, the colonial government noted that since the Achimota Conference "had failed in providing the requisite agreement, there appeared to him [the Secretary of State] no alternative but to hold a general election."[16] The CPP was thus forced to call for election in 1956. The CPP won 71 out of the 104 seats and the path was paved for the granting of independence. Based on the elections, independence was granted to Ghana on March 6, 1957. The key question is what became of the country and its parliamentary institutions after the attainment of independence?

PPC Control over the Legislature, 1957–1966

Parliamentary practices call for political tolerance on the part of the political divide. Arguably, given the acrimonious relationship between the CPP and the UGCC and between Nkrumah and the leadership of the other parties, political tolerance was in short supply by the time of political independence. The failed call by Ashanti nationalists for a federation, the failed Achimota Conference to iron out differences, and the overwhelming electoral victory of the CPP in the snap 1956 elections were enough grounds for bitter political co-existence between the ruling CPP and the opposition parties. Added to this were Nkrumah's own views and perceptions of the opposition, which bordered on hatred, if nothingelse, for ideological reasons. The method hatched by Nkrumah at the onset of the nation's political journey after independence did not augur well for nation building and democratic governance. Nkrumah had stated in his autobiography that, given the "violent, waspish and malignant" nature of his political opponents, there was the need for a "temporary benevolent dictatorship."[17] Maybe the objective was to assure himself of absolute state control by the CPP, but the passage of the Deportation Act, the Emergency Powers Act, and the questionable Preventive Detention Act (PDA) of 1958[18] were meant to give totalitarian powers that he might have felt were needed by the young state to facilitate development. "More than any other action of the CPP, the Act poured scorn on the party that led the country to independence."[19]

More significantly, the deportations as argued by Austin happened to be the prelude to a series of measures with the objective of silencing political opponents. There were those designed to deprive the opposition of their regional support, such as the Political Parties Restriction Bill or Avoidance of Discrimination Act in December 1957, which outlawed the existence of parties on a regional, tribal, or religious basis. Some chiefs that were pro-CPP such as Bechem were upgraded and those that were anti-CPP such as Duayaw Nkwanta were downgraded.

The CPP assumed total power at the expense of the opposition through crafty political organization by turning the Trades Union Congress (TUC) and the Farmers' Council (FC) into wings or branches of the party. The opposition parties had to come together to form the United Party to offer opposition to Nkrumah and the CPP in the National Assembly. Meanwhile, earlier in November 1958, 38 leading opposition members were detained under the PDA.

In 1960, a republican constitution was introduced that transformed the 1951–1957 structure of government into a presidential one with the concentration of power in Nkrumah's hands. That probably was the undoing of the CPP itself. Its contest with the colonial government ended, the struggles with the NLM in 1954 was history, and the political competition with the UP after 1957 was no contest since the CPP had overwhelming majority and most of their leading members were either in detention or exile. With the opposition decimated by the PDA and the vast presidential powers conferred on Nkrumah by the 1960 constitution, the CPP "turned on itself."[20] Many top-level CPP officials and ministers were purged. Yet, the government wanted to introduce the Criminal Code (Amendment) Bill with the objective of establishing a Special Criminal Division of the High Court from which there would be no appeal. Mr. K. A. Gbedemah who was Nkrumah's finance minister attacked the bill in parliament starting with the PDA and drawing attention to the number of people jailed, without trial, under this bill. Soon after this spirited opposition to the Criminal Code Amendment Bill, Gbedemah left the country into exile. To think that Gbedemah feared for his life and left the country, being a henchman of Nkrumah and a co-architect of the independence of Ghana, tells volumes about the politics of the period and how parliament had been turned into a one-sided circus dancing to the tunes of the executive. The CPP was bereft of its early leaders by the end of 1961.

The failed attempt on Nkrumah's life on August 1, 1962 at Kulungugu was yet another opportunity for Nkrumah to cut to shreds the independence of the judiciary having successfully made parliament act at his disposal. The acquittal of three prominent CPP men in the Kulungugu trial—Tawia Adamafio, Ako Adjei, and Coffie Crabbe was enough to earn the Chief Justice, Sir Arku Korsah, the sack. On December 23, 1963, the National Assembly in a special session passed the Law of Criminal Procedure (Amendment No. 2) Act that empowered the president to quash any decisions of the special court; and the decisions were declared of no effect on December 25, 1963. By the end of the year, Nkrumah sought amendments to the Constitution; one was to invest him with the power to dismiss a judge of the High Court at any time for reasons that appear sufficient; and the second was to create a one-party state in Ghana. A referendum on a one-party state was held in January 1964 with an overwhelming support for the proposals.

Subordinating the police, civil service, judiciary, and the universities to party control on top of declaring a one-party state were not the best means to nurture a nascent democratic country. Ghana thus failed to become a beacon of light in democratic governance to Africa during the First Republic. It would seem to appear that given the trend of events with regard to daily constriction of human liberties, the military intervention of 1966 that ousted Nkrumah and the CPP from power was a necessary evil. The question is whether the successor civilian regimes after the military interregnums fared better in terms of parliamentary democracy.

Parliamentary Practices during the Second and Third Republics

Without doubt, the mode of governance of Nkrumah and the numerous laws aimed at stifling the opposition took its toll on democratic governance.

Ghana became a one-party state and, with that, individual liberties were virtually non-existent; many people could not comment freely on issues especially when it was against the government. The military government that followed the overthrow of Nkrumah in 1966, the National Liberation Council (NLC), promised the restoration of liberties that had been trampled upon by the CPP government; however, the casualties of the military regime were the constitution and the National Assembly. The Establishment Proclamation that came into effect on February 26, 1966 suspended the 1960 constitution and paragraph 2 (2) (d) of the Establishment Proclamation noted, "The National Assembly elected under the said Constitution of the Republic of Ghana is dissolved."[21] Unlike the subsequent military regimes, the NLC was unequivocal in declaring its non-political ambitions. It stated among other things that it had "no ambition what so ever to rule the country indefinitely."[22] It announced its intention to appoint a Constitutional Reform Commission to produce a Draft Constitution. The regime did not hesitate to prepare the country for constitutional rule. After general elections in 1969, the Progress Party (PP) led by Prof. K. A. Busia won 105 out of the 140 seats assembly to form the next civilian government of the country.

The government did not commence on a bright note. The military government proscribed the CPP and prevented the party from contesting the election. The National Alliance of Liberals (NAL), led by Mr. K. A. Gbedemah won 29 seats and thus became the de facto opposition leader. He was, however, disqualified from taking his seat in the National Assembly on the wings of the controversial Article 71 (2) (b) (ii) of the 1969 Constitution which states, among otherthings, that no person shall be qualified to be a member of the Assembly who has been adjudged or otherwise declared "by the report of a Commission of Inquiry to be incompetent to hold public office or that while being a public officer he acquired assets unlawfully, or defrauded the State, or misused or abused his office or willfully acted in a manner prejudicial to the interests of the State."[23] By then the government had eroded most of its support base within a very short time. This compelled Dennis Austin to comment, "With remarkable fortitude . . . the Progress Party government engaged in battle with each section of its supporters."[24]

Ethnicity was another problem that bedeviled the Second Republican parliament. The ruling party never won a seat in the Volta Region, the home region of the Ewe ethnic group, and this became a big problem for the government, as it appeared the government was predominantly an Akan government even though it won massively in all regions with the exception of the Volta Region. Parliament was clearly polarized along ethnic lines and proclivity toward ethnic exclusiveness is dangerous to democratic governance and even parliamentary work and ethics. However, in comparison with the First Republic, the country enjoyed all the freedoms enshrined in the constitution of 1969.

In terms of parliamentary practices, the Second Republic was a Westminster-type of government where the party with majority seats in parliament formed the government and all ministers were Members of Parliament. The Second Republic adhered to the tenets of the constitution. The basic freedoms of the people as enshrined in Article 12 (a–c) of the 1969 Constitution were respected. However, the lopsided nature of parliament did not help in lively debates as the opposition parties, even after coming together to form the Justice Party, took undue advantage in fruitless walkouts from parliament on flimsy grounds. The January 13, 1972 coup equally deprived the nation of the chance to see the blossoming of liberal democracy under the Premiership of one of its staunchest advocates in Africa, Dr. K. A. Busia.

The military had a long rule from 1972 to 1979 when another general election was held under the auspices of the Armed Forces Revolutionary Council (AFRC). The Peoples' National Party (PNP) led by Dr. Hilla Limann won to form the government of the Third Republic. The 1979 Constitution conferred on the country the executive presidential type of the United States of America but with a single chamber. It meant that the president, the vice-president, and Ministers of State were not Members of Parliament. As aptly noted by Ayensu and Darkwa, the most lasting highlight of the Third Republic was the parliamentary rejection of the government's budget. This was unprecedented in the history of the country. It was rejected on the grounds that "it fails to deal with the fundamental and urgent economic problems confronting the country."

The minority amendment called upon the government to take immediate and realistic steps to tackle these pressing problems. The amendment was supported by a vote of 54 to 51 and the House unanimously accepted a revised budget, which was presented later. It must be stated that the system in operation was the best for the country. The political climate was more propitious for competitive politics than the earlier republics. "For instance, the opposition group cut across the ethnic spectrum unlike under the Second Republic, and most members were seasoned politicians who were presumably well aware of the demands of responsible opposition."[25] The government had a very slim majority in parliament and this led to lively debates over issues. The fact that the minority could force the rejection of the budget pointed to a vibrant parliament that had only the interest of the nation at stake as opposed to partisan and parochial party interests.

Just like the Second Republic, the Third Republican parliament did not last its four-year term as it was overthrown by Flt. Lt. Jerry John Rawlings, the former Chairman of the AFRC, on December 31, 1981. Rawlings formed the Provisional National Defense Council (PNDC) and, for eleven years, the country was under the firm rule of the military. However, unanticipated changes in the global system, tacit pressure from development partners, and sporadic agitations by civic groups led to the break up or the metamorphosis of many dictatorial one-party or military regimes in Africa including the Provisional National Defense Council (PNDC) of Ghana. The vice-like hold of the PNDC on Ghanaian politics for 11 years was loosened and the country was ushered once again into a democratic system of government. The PNDC was politically astute enough to form its own party—the National Democratic Congress (NDC)—to hand over power to itself after winning contentious presidential and parliamentary elections in November/December 1992.[26]

I discuss below the structure, functions, and nature of the parliament of the Fourth Republic as well as the relationship between the legislature and the executive. Along the lines, I attempt a brief comparison of aspects of the legislature under the 1969, 1979, and the 1992 Constitutions.

The Fourth Republican Parliament

Under the 1992 Constitution, Ghana is a unitary state with a uni-cameral legislature. The 1969 and 1979 Constitutions provided the same unicameral legislature with slight differences. Whereas the 1969 Constitution prescribed the Westminster or parliamentary type of government, the 1979 Constitution prescribed a presidential type of government with an executive presidency. Under the 1969 Constitution, the Prime Minister and his Ministers who formed the Executive were all Members of Parliament. The president was vested with executive authority and in the performance of his functions acts "in accordance with the advice of Cabinet or a Minister acting under the general authority of Cabinet." The president was also enjoined to consult any other person or authority.[27] In the case of the 1979 Constitution, Ministers of State were appointed with the prior approval of parliament from among persons who are qualified to be elected as Members of Parliament, and a Member of Parliament appointed as a Minister of State was obliged to resign from parliament in accordance with Article 65 (1) and (2). However, the 1992 constitution is a hybrid of the Westminster and presidential types because there is an executive presidency whilst the constitution states in Article 78 (1) that "the majority of Ministers of State shall be appointed from among Members of Parliament." Thus in the current dispensation there is a fusion of the Executive and the Legislature, to a large extent, because, unlike Article 65 (2) of the 1979 Constitution, ministers appointed by the president under the 1992 Constitution do not resign their parliamentary seats.

The Structure of Parliament[28]

Under the 1992 Constitution, the first three parliaments were composed of 200 members elected from 200 constituencies in the ten regions of the country. This is in accordance with Article 93 (1) of the Constitution. However, the fourth parliament of the Fourth Republic sworn in on January 7, 2005 is composed of 230 members by virtue of the Representation of the People Parliamentary Constituencies Instrument, 2004 (C.I. 46) which increased constituencies and by implication parliamentary seats by 30. Under both the 1969 and 1979 Constitutions, however, the national assembly or parliament was composed of no fewer than 140 members as per Articles 70 and 75 respectively.

Officers of the House

According to Article 95 (1) of the 1992 Constitution, "there shall be a Speaker of Parliament who shall be elected by the members of Parliament from among persons who are members of Parliament or who are qualified to be elected as members of Parliament." Article 95 (3) states, "No business shall be transacted in Parliament other than an election to the office of the Speaker, at any time when the office of the Speaker is vacant." Until the election of Speaker is conducted, the Clerk of Parliament shall act as the Chairman to the House. In fact, the Speaker is the third in command after the President and the Vice-President.

Under the speaker are two Deputy Speakers known as the First and Second Deputy Speakers who, according to Article 96 (1) (a) and (b) respectively, shall be elected by Members of Parliament from among the Members of Parliament; and both shall not be members of the same political party. The appointment of two Deputy Speakers contrasts with what pertained under the 1969 and 1979 Constitutions where there was only one Deputy Speaker.[29] Under the 1992 Constitution, the election of the Speaker and his two Deputies shall be by secret ballot in accordance with Article 104 (4). However, during the tenure of the first three Parliaments the Speaker and the two Deputy Speakers were not elected by secret ballot. Rather, it was through consensus by the majority and the minority parties in parliament. The term of the Speaker is coterminous with the life of parliament and in the first parliament Mr. Justice D. F. Annan had two terms of four years each. The Speaker of the third parliament, Mr. Peter Ala Adjetey, was not elected for the fourth parliament because a new person, Mr. Ebenezer Sekyi Hughes, who was a member of the Council of State, was proposed by the majority party. Surprisingly, the minority NDC party rooted for Mr. Ala Adjetey who incidentally was a former chairman of the ruling NPP before he became the Speaker, when the NPP won the 2000 general elections. It emerged later that the majority and the minority parties had reached consensus on Mr. Sekyi Hughes but the minority reneged on the consensual agreement reached earlier when the time for the election of the Speaker was due. Thus, for the first time since the fourth Republican parliament commenced, Members of Parliament had to vote by secret ballot in the House for the Speaker. At the end of the voting the majority nominee, Mr. Ebenezer Sekyi Hughes, got the nod with 134 to 96 votes for Mr. Peter Ala Adjetey the former Speaker. There was a consensus by parliamentarians on the First Deputy Speaker, Mr. Freddie Blay, who is a member of the Convention Peoples Party (CPP). However, because the minority did not stick to the consensus reached with the majority in the case of the election of the Speaker, the majority proposed Hon. Alhaji Malik Alhassan Yakubu of the NPP for the position of Second Deputy Speaker while the minority proposed Hon. Kenneth Dzirasah, who was the First Deputy Speaker of Parliament for two terms during the NDC period and also the Second Deputy Speaker when the NPP came to power. But in the secret ballot which followed, the majority candidate won by 135 votes to 94.

Composition of Parliament

The composition of Parliament by political parties since the Fourth Republic is illustrated in table 7.1.

There have been by-elections since the beginning of the Fourth Republic and the outcomes affected the numerical strength of parties in parliament. In the first parliament, there were four by-elections, three of

Table 7.1 Political Parties Represented in Post-1990s Parliaments, Ghana

Party	First Parliament (1993)	Second Parliament (1997)	Third Parliament (2001)	Fourth Parliament (2004)
NDC	189	132	92	94
*NCP	8	—	—	—
PNC	—	1	3	4
NPP	—	62	100	128
CPP	—	—	1	3
EGLE	1	—	—	—
*PCP	—	5	—	—
Independent	2	—	4	1
TOTAL	200	200	200	230

* Boycotted the elections where no representation is indicated.

which were won by the NDC and one by an independent candidate. There were two by-elections in the second parliament, which was split between the NDC and the NPP. During the third parliament, there were seven by-elections including three seats previously held by the NDC, and they were all won by the NPP. The NPP and other smaller parties not in alliance with the NDC boycotted the 1992 parliamentary elections and were therefore not represented in parliament. Since the end of the first parliament two parties that had had representation in parliament—the National Convention Party (NCP) and the Peoples Convention Party (PCP)—became defunct.

Functions of Parliament

It is trite to state that parliament embodies the will of the people because parliamentarians who represent the 230 constituencies of the country try to highlight the developmental needs of their constituents. However, the fundamental function of parliament is law-making, but in Ghana, as in several other democratic polities, there are other functions apart from legislating. Financial control of public funds, for instance, is vested in parliament. The whole of Chapter 13 of the 1992 Constitution spells out unambiguously such financial duties of Parliament. Chapter 13 of the 1992 Constitution is a replication of Chapters 13 and 11 of the 1979 and 1969 Constitutions respectively. However, all references are to the 1992 Constitution.

Article 174 makes it clear that without parliamentary authorization no tax can be imposed by the government. Under Article 178, no monies can be withdrawn from the Consolidated Fund without the authority of parliament except monies directly charged to the Fund. The power and duty to monitor public expenditure is also vested in parliament and parliament is enjoined to act promptly on the Auditor-General's Reports for this purpose. Various articles of the Constitution delineate other financial powers invested in parliament. Article 181 underlines the power of parliament to authorize the granting or receiving of loans; Article 184 deals with the parliamentary function of monitoring Ghana's foreign exchange receipts and payments or transfers; Parliaments authorizes tax waiver, or exemption, or variation on the strength of Article 174; and Article 187 (15) states clearly that "the accounts of the office of the Auditor-General shall be audited and reported upon by an auditor appointed by Parliament."[30]

Parliament also exercises oversight of the Executive through scrutiny of policy measures and executive conduct through its Committees, summoning Ministers to answer questions in parliament and censuring Ministers.

In addition, it approves or disapproves presidential nominees for Ministerial appointments, Chief Justice and other Justices of the Supreme Court as well as the Members of the Council of State and other public offices specified by law.

Parliamentary Committees and their Powers

A lot of parliamentary work is done at the committee level where inter-party rivalries are largely muted. Work at the Committee level is very challenging for parliamentarians "because it demands powers of reasoning and analysis rather than the display of rhetorical and debating skills, which are the most widely advertised aspects of parliamentary activity."[31]

There are two main committees in the House—Standing Committees as stated under Order 151 (2) and Select Committees as outlined under Order 152. According to Order 151 (1) of the Standing Orders of the Parliament of Ghana, there is also the Committee of Selection composed of the Speaker and not more than nineteen Members of Parliament. The Committee of Selection according to Order 151 (2) prepares and reports to parliament lists of Chairmen, Vice-Chairmen, and Members to constitute the Standing Committee of the House as well as the sixteen Select Committees. This is in line with Article 110 (1) of the 1992 Constitution, which states "parliament may, by standing orders, regulate its own procedures." The Committee of Selection does the same for the 16 Select Committees. The Standing Committees of the House comprise the following: (a) the Standing Orders Committee; (b) the Business Committee; (c) the Public Accounts Committee; (e) the Subsidiary Legislation Committee; (f) the House Committee; (g) the Finance Committee; (h) the Appointments Committee; (i) the Committee on Members Holding Offices of Profit; (j) the Committee on Government Assurance; and (k) the Committee on Gender and Children. In effect, the Standing Committees of the House deal with in-house procedural matters.

The 16 Select Committees reflect as much as possible the various ministries that the president may create. The committees are as follows: (a) the Committee on Food, Agriculture, and Cocoa Affairs; (b) the Committee on Lands and Forestry; (c) the Committee on Health; (d) the Committee on Constitutional, Legal and Parliamentary Affairs; (e) the Committee on Works and Housing; (f) the Committee on Local Government and Rural Development; (g) the Committee on Communication; (h) the Committee on Foreign Affairs; (i) the Committee on Employment, Social Welfare, and State Enterprises; (j) the Committee on Defence and Interior; (k) the Committee on Trade, Industry, and Tourism; (l) the Committee on

Environment, Science, and Technology; (m) the Committee on Education; (n) the Committee on Youth, Sports, and Culture; (o) the Committee on Mines and Energy; and (p) the Committee on Roads and Transport.

According to Article 103 (3) of the Constitution, the functions of parliamentary Committees shall include the investigation and inquiry into the activities and administration of ministries and departments as may be determined by parliament. Proposals for legislation may be consequential outcomes of such investigations and inquiries. And in line with Order 153 (1) and (2), a Member of Parliament shall serve on at least one Standing Committee and no Member shall serve on more than three Standing Committees except the Deputy Speakers and the Majority and Minority leaders in parliament. Membership of the Committees, according to Article 103 (5) of the Constitution and Order 154 shall, as much as possible, reflect the different shades of opinion in parliament.

The general powers of each Committee is in accordance with Article 103 (6) of the 1992 Constitution and includes such powers, rights, and privileges as vested in the High Court of Justice or as Justice of the High Court at a trial in respect of: (a) enforcing the attendance of witnesses and examining them on oath, affirmation or otherwise; (b) compelling production of documents; and (c) the issue of a commission or request to examine witnesses abroad.

In sum, the parliament of the fourth Republic differs from those of the second and the third Republics in that the structure and essence of the current parliament is a fusion of the Second and Third Republican parliaments. As noted, even though a majority of Ministers are drawn from parliament, they still retain their seats and form part of the Executive. In fact, there is even a Minister for Parliamentary Affairs who is seen as an effective link between the Legislature and the Executive, apart from the Ministers who are also Members of parliament. Thus the Executive has a strong foothold in the Parliament of the fourth Republic unlike in the third Republic under the 1979 Constitution where ministers were appointed mainly from outside parliament and those appointed from parliament were obliged to resign their membership before they could assume ministerial responsibilities. The Second Republic under the 1969 Constitution was a pure British or Westminster model where the leader of the party with the largest number of seats becomes the Prime Minister and all Ministers were appointed from parliament.

The nature of the Fourth parliament appears to have been influenced greatly by the nation's experiences under both the parliamentary and presidential systems of government. It must be conceded that unanticipated military interventions did not allow both systems to blossom and flower. Nonetheless, the Committee of Constitutional Experts and the Consultative

Assembly set up by the PNDC government were convinced that the future democratic development of Ghana would be enhanced by the hybrid system as it currently pertains. Brief highlights of the fourth Republican parliaments are discussed in the next section.

Interrogating Parliamentary Practices

There were several highlights of the first parliament of the fourth Republic. The most outstanding was the passage of the Value Added Tax (VAT) in 1995 and the demonstration it engendered. An amorphous political pressure group known as the Alliance for Change led by members of the opposition who boycotted the parliamentary election in 1992 organized a protest march against the tax. The government allowed a wing of its party—the Association of the Committee for the Defense of the Revolution (ACDR)—to attack the demonstrators, leading to the death of four of them through gunshots. That was the lowest point in the government as it demonstrated the lowest level of governmental tolerance of political opposition. Parliamentary reactions to the killing were very feeble because it was dominated by the NDC and those who attacked the demonstrators were members of the ACDR. No one was caught and charged with the killings, which remain a blot on the NDC government.

In a way, the opposition outside parliament never allowed the government to have its own way in everything as they took several issues to court for interpretation, which the government lost. Thus, though outside Parliament, opposition activities prevented what would have amounted to "electoral dictatorship" given the fact that Parliament was under the absolute control of the NDC.

An important innovation of the 1993–1997 parliament was the institution of the End of Session Public Forum whereby, at the end of each parliamentary session, parliament publicly gave an account of its activities and the public was allowed to ask questions.

The opposition parties that boycotted the parliamentary election in 1992 participated in the elections of 1996. Even though the opposition in parliament was numerically disadvantaged, as table 7.1 clearly depicts, they successfully kept the government on its toes. What became clear was the gradual tolerance and respect shown by the ruling party and its leader, former President Rawlings, to the opposition parties. In congratulating them for being represented in parliament, he said:

> Let us all, no matter our differing opinions and party loyalties, work towards our common goal, which is the prosperity and well-being of all Ghanaians. Mr. Speaker, in the pursuit of this goal, let us put aside ethnic, religious and

other aspects of our human diversity. The common purpose that unites all of us, who genuinely seek the equitable development of our country, is far greater than the differences that can only divide us if we allow them to do so.[32]

A significant development at the very onset of the second parliament of the fourth Republic was whether Ministers of States in the previous government were to be vetted in accordance with Articles 78 (1) and 79 (1) of the Constitution or only newly appointed Ministers were to be vetted by the Appointments Committee of Parliament. This was because the NDC retained power after the 1996 general elections and some of the Ministers were renominated. The view of the NDC majority was that Ministers and Deputy Ministers who had been duly vetted and appointed during the first term need not be vetted for the second term. The NPP minority felt that the "retention" of Ministers was alien to our law and the Constitution. On February 14, 1997 the NDC-dominated House resolved that "if a person has been appointed a Minister or Deputy Minister with the approval of parliament and as an incumbent Minister or Deputy Minister, he is retained by the president, it shall not be necessary for parliament to give another approval for such Minister or Deputy Minister."[33] The minority NPP was dissatisfied with this resolution and the Minority leader, Mr. J. H. Mensah, filed a suit at the Supreme Court for a true and proper interpretation of certain provisions of the 1992 Constitution. On May 28, 1997, the Supreme Court ruled on the matter. On the question of prior approval of retained Ministers, the Supreme Court declared, "Every presidential nominee for ministerial appointment, whether retained or new, requires the prior approval of parliament." The court therefore upheld the contention by the Minority group that by the combined effects of Articles 58 (1), (2) and (4), 78 (1) and (2), and 79 (1) and (2), 97 (1), 100 (1) and 113 (1) of the 1992 Constitution, presidential, parliamentary, and ministerial terms were coterminous. The implication was that the tenure of ministers of state expires with that of the president and parliament. Consequently, ministerial nominees of a new parliament require prior approval by the relevant parliamentary committee.

The court, however, decided by a majority decision that "prior approval" is not a term of the Article. That is to say, "prior approval" does not connote "consideration and vetting" and the courts have no powers to question how parliament exercises its powers of approval. The precedent has been set as the court went on to state that a newly inaugurated parliament might not have all its committees in place to undertake the delicate job of vetting. However, on July 8, 1997 a compromise resolution entitled "Procedure for the Approval of Retained Ministers," which was passed by consensus, had the effect of vetting nominees in line with the rules of the House and stressed that prior approval is not a term of art.[34] The key resolution under the procedure adopted by consensus was as follows: (a) that the Resolution of February 14, 1997 is hereby reviewed; (b) that any person nominated by the president for reappointment as minister or deputy minister shall have prior approval by parliament in accordance with rules of the House; and that (c) that prior approval is not a term of art.

The beauty of parliamentary debates and the will to strengthen parliamentary procedures to stand the test of time were brought to the fore even though it took the Supreme Court to interpret and rule on the relevant constitutional articles.

There was an unprecedented governmental turnover through the ballot in the 2000 elections. For the first time in the history of Ghana a sitting government was democratically changed after the landmark election with the defeat of the NDC by the NPP at the polls. The new parliament had more than 60 percent new faces as the outgoing ruling party had its parliamentary representation drastically reduced (see the table 7.1). As a result of losing some by-elections, the NDC ended the third parliament with 89 seats while the NPP benefited from the by-elections and ended with 103 seats.

Admittedly, parliamentary structures and procedures were strengthened during the third parliament. The change of government was good for the nation as it demonstrated that there is always an alternative to a sitting government not through the barrel of the gun but through democratic elections. Many old parliamentarians retained their seats and debates in the House demonstrated maturity. Important issues that were hotly debated in the House during the third parliament included the dual citizenship bill, setting up the National Reconciliation Commission, International Financial Corporation (IFC) loan, the CNTCI loan, and the National Health Insurance levy bill. The minority NDC, for instance, walked out on occasions in the case of the NRC and the National Health Insurance levy bills. The walkouts notwithstanding, the two bills were passed into law.

In December 2004, the NPP under President Kufuor won a second term of four years in office. On January 13, 2005 the Speaker referred to the Appointments Committee presidential nominees for the second term of President Kufuor's administration. The procedure adopted by the Committee is not only a pointer to the growing maturity of parliament but also the essence of relying on established principles or precedents that would enhance not only parliamentary procedures but also democratic governance. The Committee, therefore, recalled the debates on re-nominated Ministers in February 1997 in tandem with Articles 78 (1), 79 (1) and 256 of the Constitution that provide that no person shall be appointed a Minister or Deputy Minister without prior parliamentary approval. In addition, the Committee relied on Order 172 (2) of the Standing Orders of Parliament that enjoins the Appointment Committee to recommend to parliament for approval or otherwise persons nominated by the President for appointment as Ministers and Deputy Ministers as well as the Supreme Court decision of May 28, 1997 on the question of prior approval of retained Ministers.[35] Thus the principle laid in the *J. H. Mensah v. The Attorney General*'s ruling in favour of prior approval of ministers by parliament has become an important precedent for vetting of ministers in Ghana. It is a plus to Shana's democratic system that what was initially perceived by the then ruling NDC as "mischievous" when the NPP sought interpretation from the Supreme Court on the issue of retained ministers has enhanced our parliamentary procedures. The vetting of presidential nominees has now become an important exercise in the Ghanaian parliament. It is meant to find out about the integrity and competence of those appointed, to examine the records of retained ministers whilst in office, and to allow the electorate to make input in the selection of Ministers through memoranda on nominees if necessary.

To be sure, the vetting process cannot be compared to what pertains in the US in terms of intensity and time taken. As pointed out by Mr. Alban Bagbin, the NDC Minority parliamentary leader and a ranking member of the Appointments Committee, Ghanaians are not used to the vetting process and the parameters are not well defined. The public must therefore appreciate the work the parliamentary Appointments Committee has done so far.[36] In the end the appointments of three ministers were put on hold by the Committee pending further investigations on issues raised in memoranda by some people and seemingly unsatisfactory answers given to some questions asked by the Committee.

It has become apparent that sensitivity to public opinion has gradually become a hallmark of the ruling NPP. To avert unnecessary national tension and accusations of manipulation of the Electoral Commission, the government dropped a controversial proposal to set up a procurement agency specifically for the electoral body. Again, the government had to give in when opposition parties vehemently protested against the Representation of the Peoples (Amendment) Bill that would have allowed Ghanaian citizens, apart from those in the Embassies and High Commissions, to vote in the 2004 elections.

Parliamentary Democracy's Prospects

With the successful conduct of the December 2004 elections and the inauguration of the fourth parliament of the fourth Republic democracy appears to be on course in Ghana. With each election, parliament is strengthened as past experiences inform actions and enhance parliamentary procedures. However, the sustained strength of parliament to enable it carry out its constitutional mandate depends on how Ghanaians accept in principle and in practice the importance of parliamentary work to national democratic development and how the House is equipped for its arduous tasks. It trite to state that parliament is one of the arms of government and whether the nation develops or equitable laws are made or the norms of parliamentary democracy are upheld depends on whether parliament is given free rein to carry out its mandated functions. However, there are contentious provisions in the 1992 Constitution that combine to deprive parliament of maximum commitment by all parliamentarians to legislative work in the House. The concept of separation of powers was meant to save the populace from executive high-handedness. The dictum that "power corrupts and absolute power corrupts absolutely" further supports the argument for separation of powers.

Article 78 (1) enjoins the president to appoint the majority of ministers of state from among Members of Parliament (MPs). Clause 2 of the same Article states, "The President shall appoint such numbers of Ministers of State as may be necessary for the efficient running of the State." This requirement, in my view, is unambiguously frustrating the work of parliament in several ways. The combination of parliamentary and ministerial duties appears to have been at the expense of parliamentary work.

The Constitution has no ceiling whatsoever on the number of Ministers to be appointed by the government in power. Clause 2 of Article 78 states: "The President shall appoint such number of Ministers of State as may be necessary for the efficient running of the State." Arguably, every government picks the best material for ministerial appointments. As such, picking the majority of ministers from parliament is unduly restrictive and combining ministerial responsibilities and parliamentary or legislative duties becomes Herculean to many. The nation becomes the loser as it is deprived, in some instances, of the presence of experienced parliamentarians whose inputs into bill-making and parliamentary debates do not only enliven parliament but also ensures that the nation gets the best from her elected legislators.

In conclusion, the commendable strides Ghana has made in democratic governance and the maturity parliament keeps demonstrating in its approach to parliamentary work seems not to be doubt. For sure, limitations are engendered by the hybrid nature of the governmental system being operated with specific reference to the appointment of the majority of ministers from parliament. Ministerial responsibilities are onerous and the same applies to parliamentary responsibilities. Thus legislators who are also part of the executive have to embark on serious balancing act by combining ministerial responsibilities with parliamentary duties. Naturally, much attention may be focused on one of the functions than the other thereby making it difficult, in my view, for the nation to derive maximum benefit from the expertise of ministers cum legislators. In principle, both responsibilities are being performed but in reality much could have been derived from full time legislators or full time Ministers of State than what pertains. Democratic governance is on course as tremendous strides have been made by the various arms of government especially the legislature. No one can deny the fact that a lot remains to be done in the area of strengthened parliamentary staff, parliamentary offices, and training of new parliamentarians. In the light of the foregoing, I believe majority of Ghanaians will agree with the assertion that a strengthened parliament with functional committee system, to a large extent, holds the key to national efforts to ensure governmental accountability, transparency, and democratic consolidation.

Notes

1. Apter 1955: 119.
2. Osei 1999: 23.
3. Ayensu K.B. and Darkwa 1999: xi.
4. Apter 1995: 119.
5. Cited in Ayensu and Darkwa 1999: 3.
6. Ibid., 5–6.
7. Apter 1995: 133.
8. These were the governor, colonial secretary, the Chief Commissioner of Ashanti, the Chief Commissioner of the Northern Territories, the attorney-general, the financial secretary, the director of medical services, and the secretary for native affairs. Incidentally, what amounted to a Cabinet was fully composed of foreigners.
9. Apter 1995: 133.
10. Price 1975: 50.
11. The leading members of the Convention were A.G. Grant as Chairman; R.S. Blay, vice-president; J. B. Danquah, vice-president; R.A. Awoonor Williams, treasurer; W. E. Ofori Atta; E. A. Akufo Addo; J. W. de Graft Johnson; Obetsibi Lamptey. Later John Tsiboe and Cobina Kessie were added from Kumasi.
12. Price 1975: 54.
13. Dennis Austin, Politics in Ghana 251.
14. Ibid., 297.
15. Ibid., 306.
16. Ibid., 308.
17. Ibid., 371.

18. In August 1957, the Deportation Act was passed and applied to the deportation of Alhaji Othman Larden and Alhaji Ahmadu Baba, a Nigerian by birth, who was an influential leader of the large Muslim community in Kumasi. He was opposed to Nkrumah. It was also used to deport Bankole Timothy, a Sierra Leone journalist working for the *Daily Graphic*. In 1958, the PDA was passed first to muzzle the opposition but later muzzled the CPP as well.
19. Ayensu and Darkwa 1999: 39.
20. Ibid., 402.
21. National Advisory Committee, Establishment Proclamation, The Rebirth of Ghana: The End of Tyranny, Feb. 26, 1966.
22. Ibid., 29.
23. Ghana, Government of 1969.
24. Cited in Goldworthy, 1973: 11.
25. Boafo-Arthur 1993: 234.
26. See The New Patriotic Party n.d. which chronicles the alleged electoral malpractices perpetrated by the PNDC government to favor the NDC in the Presidential election of 1992.
27. Apart from the Prime Minister and the Cabinet, the President, under the 1969 Constitution could also consult the Council of State. See Articles 37 (1), 38 (1), and 53 (1) of the 1969 Constitution of the Republic of Ghana.
28. Very useful information in this section was drawn from Ghana, Parliament of n.d.; Ghana Parliament of 2000.
29. See Article 74 (2) of the 1969 Constitution and Article 83 (b) of the 1979 Constitution of the Republic of Ghana.
30. See Ghana, Parliament of 2004.
31. Boateng 1996.
32. Cited in Ayensu and Darkwa 1999: 117.
33. Ghana, Parliament of 2005: 3.
34. Rex Owusu-Ansah 2003–2004.
35. See Ghana, Parliament of 2005.
36. *Daily Guide*, Jan. 29, 2005.

8

People, Party, Politics, and Parliament: Government and Governance in Namibia

Henning Melber

The Nordic Africa Institute, Uppsala, Sweden

Introduction

The transition to independence negotiated and implemented for Namibia under the initiative of the United Nations was a process of controlled change. As a result of the negotiated settlement, the national liberation movement South West African People's Organization (SWAPO of Namibia) reconstituted itself into the dominant political party. It now controls the government, cabinet, and parliament paving the way to firm political hegemony without abandoning the structural legacy of settler colonialism both in terms of continued socio-economic discrepancies and with regard to the limits in profound changes toward a truly democratic political culture. Moreover, there are lasting structural and psychological effects resulting from the colonial legacy remaining in effect during the post-colonial era of social transformation.[1]

Decolonization and Democracy

SWAPO's armed liberation struggle, launched in the mid-1960s, had a major impact on the course of decolonization, but Namibian independence was as much the result of a negotiated settlement, which finally after the end of the Cold War period was also guided by the strategic interests of the two power blocks. The mandate implemented by the United Nations Transitional Assistance Group (UNTAG) under UN Security Council Resolution 435 (1978) provided the supervision of free and fair general elections for a constitutive assembly among all parties registered under the transitional authority composed jointly by the South African Administrator General and the United Nations Special Representative competing for votes in the country. Those in competition, on the other side, were not operating from a basis of equal opportunities. While the one side (South African allies) could rely on massive support from the colonial power, the other side (SWAPO) had the privilege of being the only recognized representative of the Namibian people internationally. The possibility of any similar support to other forces not aligned to the two sides was eliminated by the factual constraints imposed upon them since the increased polarization emerging since the 1970s.

The anti-colonial struggle was about national liberation, and in pursuance of this goal (which also translates into the seizure of political power for the organized liberation movement), "SWAPO was above all a pragmatic organization."[2] In that sense, sovereignty was defined as political independence in a state under a government representing the majority of the people, who were so far excluded from full participation in society through the imposed apartheid system. The power of definition concerning the post-colonial system of political governance was exercised during this process mainly by the national liberation movement in interaction with the international system represented by a variety of competing actors under the polarized conditions of superpower rivalry during the 1970s and 1980s. The agenda was shaped by the aim to establish a formally legitimate and internationally recognized sovereign Namibian state. Throughout the 1970s and 1980s, the liberation struggle was understood and perceived foremost as the right to self-determination. Once achieved, the task to formulate and adopt further specifications were left to those policy-makers who emerged as representatives of the Namibian electorate as a result of free and fair general elections. It was, therefore, not democratization, which was the priority on the agenda for Namibia, but decolonization.[3] Notwithstanding this priority, the Republic of Namibia, as proclaimed on March 21, 1990, resembled all formal aspects of a democratic political system. This in itself can be regarded as a positive surprise given the legacy of more than a century of authoritarian and discriminatory structures on which the colonial society had based its minority rule. A rule which was prepared to accept as an integral part of its nature the systematic violation of basic human rights to exclude the majority from meaningful and fair participation in the socio-economic and political spheres.

Democracy at Independence

The constitutional democracy that was formally institutionalized as a last preliminary step toward formal sovereignty of the Republic of Namibia confirmed in its contents as well as the drafting procedures, a negotiated compromise. Since the constitutional document had to be adopted by a two-third majority among the elected 72 members of the constitutional assembly, none of the parties involved in the process of negotiations had the power to impose a unilateral decision upon the other interest groups represented in the constituent assembly. SWAPO, with 41 seats (57 percent of the votes) had missed the two-third majority. The DTA (Democratic Turnhalle Alliance) with its 21 seats (28 percent of the votes) failed to represent a powerful opposition. In this constellation, both parties preferred a negotiated settlement to continued conflict. The unfolding process has been qualified as "an impressive example of successful bargaining by opposing political elites in a transitional democratic context."[4] There is evidence to confirm the hypothesis advocated by Dobell[5] that the negotiated settlement in Namibia resembled aspects of an "elite pact." The constitutional negotiations were the final chapter of a decolonization process "closely supervised by international forces, and facilitated by a 'transitional pact,' " that, "alongside at least an instrumental commitment to democracy on the part of opposing forces, has surely also made a difference."[6] The negotiated settlement started under United Nations supervision, continued to acknowledge the externally defined rules of the game while the parties involved were "eager to seize the reins of power."[7] The pragmatic give-and-take approach is documented by Namibia's first Head of State, who states plainly in his biography, "we agreed without argument that Namibia would be a multiparty democracy with an independent judiciary and a strong bill of rights."[8] Similar views, stressing the consensus among the main parties, were presented by both the then leader of the DTA and Namibia's first Foreign Minister (since August 2002, the Prime Minister) during a conference among relevant actors and directly involved stakeholders in the transition, recalling the Namibian decolonization process.[9] And a local politician involved in the drafting process explained to Dobell,[10] "everybody wanted to be seen as a democrat during these negotiations."

The package, which paved the way for a sovereign Namibia under a SWAPO government, implied a socio-economic and political regulatory framework emerging as a compromise between antagonistic social forces. It was an independence process under UN auspices, which has "profoundly influenced the form of the new Namibian democracy."[11] The constitutional rooting of formal political liberties and human rights secured a "yardstick for good governance."[12] To that extent, it offers a meaningful impact as a tool contributing toward a process of democratization. The *Grundnorm* introduced, however, still required societal acceptance. Testing the essence against some features of social reality, a law professor at the University of Namibia observed a "discrepancy between the acclamation of the Constitution as the symbol of liberation and independence, and the translation of the Constitution into daily life."[13] The Under-Secretary for Legal Affairs at the Ministry of Foreign Affairs had another important warning to offer. "To instill democratic and human rights values," he pointed out, "is not enough, however; we also need to insist that institutions themselves become more democratic." It is an irony, he continued, "that although we have a widely admired Constitution, the organizations which are supposed to provide the officials who will protect this constitution, namely our political parties, are the most undemocratic institutions in the country."[14]

Political Hegemony under SWAPO

The most striking phenomenon in terms of political development during Namibia's first decade of independence has been the constant gain and consolidation of political power and control by the former liberation movement. From election to election during the first ten years, it managed to add further strength to its dominant role. SWAPO had originally failed to obtain the aspired two-third majority votes in the elections for the Constituent Assembly in November 1989. With a marked decline of overall votes and an almost constant numerical support base, it managed to grasp exclusive control over the parliamentary decision-making process with the national elections in December 1994, which it maintained and consolidated since that time (see table 8.1).

Over the first decade, another characteristic feature emerged, whereupon no numerically meaningful opposition party could firmly establish itself as a relevant political factor. In stark contrast to this sober fact, is the strong reaction provoked by the founding of the Congress of Democrats (CoD) as a new political party in early 1999. Many observers originally expected the CoD to attract a meaningful number of frustrated SWAPO followers, thereby challenging the two-third majority of the previous liberation movement, from which ranks some of the CoD activists defected. Instead, the CoD mainly split the number of votes among the opposition parties and established itself as the second strongest political factor only by a marginally higher number of votes than (and at the expenses of) the "traditional" opposition party, DTA.[15] Opposition parties never managed to obtain enough weight to challenge the factual dominance of SWAPO seriously.

Table 8.1 Election Results, 1989–1999 for Namibia's Largest Political Parties

Election	Votes	SWAPO	DTA	UDF	CoD
1989 Constituent	687,787	384,567 (56.90%)	191,532 (28.34%)	37,874 (5.60%)	0.00 0.00
1992 Regional	381,041	256,778 (68.76%)	103,359 (27.68%)	9,285 (2.49%)	0.00 0.00
1992 Local	128,973	73,736 (58.02%)	42,278 (33.26%)	7,473 (5.88%)	0.00 0.00 0.00
1994 National	497,499 (73.89%)	361,800 (20.78%)	101,748 (2.72%)	13,309	0.00 0.00 0.00
1998 Local	6,3545 (60.35%)	37,954 (23.91%)	15,039 (6.66%)	4,191	0.00 0.00
1999 National	536,036	408,174 (76.15%)	50,824 (9.48%)	15,685 (2.93%)	53,289 (9.94%)

Source: Keulder (1998: 63) and official figures by Directorate of Elections for 1999.

During the first decade of Namibian Independence a political system emerged, which displayed tendencies toward a factual one-party state under increasingly autocratic rule. As if to illustrate the point, SWAPO conducted its election campaign during 1999 with a brochure in which it states, "saving democracy, or more appropriately saving the opposition, is the latest version of Europe's burden to civilize the natives."[16] Based on its reputation as the liberating force and in the absence of serious political alternatives, SWAPO managed to entrench firmly political dominance also by means of obtaining a continuously higher proportion of votes in a legitimate way.[17] In contrast, an increasingly repressive atmosphere during the election campaign in late 1999 might be perceived as a "lack of consolidation of Namibian democracy."[18] The far-reaching mandate encouraged the misperception that the government is supposed to serve the party and that the state is the property of the government.[19]

The parliamentary and presidential elections on November 15 and 16, 2004 provided the so-far latest results to illustrate the overwhelming dominance of the party in power. The way in which party political office bearers as public servants abused their access to state owned facilities during the campaign confirmed once again the existing misperception equating the party with government and government with the state.[20] Out of a record number of 838,447 ballots (some 85 percent of close to one million registered voters) SWAPO again secured above 75 percent of the valid votes and 55 out of the 72 seats in the National Assembly from March 2005 onward.

During the fourth legislative period, parliamentarians will represent seven different parties (previously five) with six of them sharing 17 seats. Opposition parties were more divided than ever before, while the different party programs showed little to no substantive alternatives. The CoD maintained the second rank within the party landscape despite a decline from seven to five seats. The DTA continued its steady decline and has four from previously seven seats left. The Herero based National Unity Democratic Organisation (NUDO) separated from the ranks of the DTA and obtained three seats of its own. The United Democratic Front (UDF)—another ethnically oriented interest group rooted in the Damara communities—consolidated its position by increasing its seats from two to three. The Republican Party (RP), supported mainly by members of the white minority, campaigned like NUDO for the first time outside of the DTA and gained one seat. The Monitor Action Group (MAG), representing the most conservative white element in post-colonial Namibia, surprisingly managed to keep its one seat.

Numerous minor irregularities and inconsistencies in the electoral procedures, discrepancies in the voters' list, and the casting and counting of votes, as well as an undue delay in announcing the election results, however, provoked a subsequent legal intervention by the CoD and RP. They filed a court application to enforce insight into documents the Electoral Commission of Namibia (ECN) refused to grant. The High Court ruled in favor of the application. Based on the evidence collected, CoD and RP contested the election results in the High Court. They claimed that they had discovered an array of failures to comply with the Electoral Act and discrepancies between voting figures and results as well as a series of other irregularities.[21] As a result, they asked for a new election or alternatively a recount of the votes. This was opposed by the ECN. A ruling by the court was pending at the time of writing. Whatever the result of this hitherto unprecedented controversy over election results in Namibia might be for the first time the image of unreserved democratic practices has been seriously tarnished and any doubts were cast over Namibia's democratic principles and practices.

While a slogan in the days of the liberation struggle claimed that "SWAPO is the people," the adjusted slogan for today might be that "SWAPO is the government and the government is the state." This tendency toward abuse of state power fails to acknowledge and hence disrespects the relevant difference between a formal democratic legitimacy (through the number of votes obtained in a free and fair general election) and the moral and ethical dimensions and responsibilities of such legitimacy. As a result, also in Namibia, "the state often uses democracy to perpetuate hegemony rather than to advance rights, liberty and democracy."[22] Several examples of recent years offer empiric evidence to substantiate the case in point. They confirm the suspicion that "the adoption of non-democratic measures is often justified against the backdrop of achieving 'national' objectives through a democratic mandate." [23] The contested results of the last parliamentary and presidential elections of November 2004 are a particular case in point. The degree of dominance by SWAPO seems to be more of interest to the party than the legitimacy of its mandate beyond any doubt also within the ranks of politically dissenting citizens. The suspicions created over the irregularities witnessed will have a lasting effect, no matter what the High Court is ultimately going to rule.

Namibia's Bi-cameral System

As Kaakunga concludes,[24] Namibia's Constitution seeks to reconcile a strong central executive (with a president having substantive executive powers) with the devolution of power to the nationally elected Members of Parliament and the regionally elected members of the National Council as a second chamber. During the initial stages of the drafting process of Namibia's Constitution, the elected members of the constituent assembly were in disagreement over the structures and the divisions of power in the new democratic system to be established. While SWAPO favored a strong executive president with almost unlimited powers and a single parliament elected on the basis of popular vote and proportional representation, most of the smaller parties advocated the establishment of two chambers and a more symbolically representative head of state with markedly less executive functions.[25] At the end, the compromise negotiated and agreed resulted in a President with fairly far-reaching executive competence, a law-making national assembly (parliament) and complementing regionally elected political bodies (regional councils), which in turn elected from each of the electoral regions two representatives to the national council as a second chamber with mainly advisory and consultative functions. As a precondition agreed upon, a Delimitation Commission would first submit proposals for redrafted regions on a non-apartheid basis, which then would be the constituencies for the regional councils to be elected. This was the compromise to overcome the reservations from SWAPO in the light of the distorting regional structures as a product of the apartheid era. Having its main support base in the densely populated northern region of former Ovamboland, the party was afraid that such a second chamber based on regional elections would offer the political parties previously in support of the "divide and rule" under "separate development" an opportunity to obtain more political weight than the proportional figures country wide would provide for.

Established in September 1990, the Delimitation Commission reviewed the existing territorial and administrative legal realities on a regional basis with the aim to revise the apartheid structures of so-called separate development introduced and consolidated since the early 1960s. In July 1991, the Commission submitted a report to Cabinet, suggesting 13 regions with six to ten electoral districts (according to the population density). Cabinet adopted the proposals in September 1991. The national assembly adopted end of August 1992 the necessary legislature to pave the way for implementing the institutions provided for in the Constitution, by passing the Regional Councils Act, the Local Authorities Act, and the Electoral Act respectively.[26] The subsequent first local and regional elections in the independent Republic of Namibia took place between November 30 and December 2, 1992 and were honored by the voters with more than 80 percent participation. Despite its original lack of confidence in the own popularity throughout the country, SWAPO managed to secure a regional dominance almost everywhere. The party obtained an absolute majority in 9 out of the 13 regions and as a result controlled the National Council with 19 out of 26 seats (the remaining seven seats occupied by the DTA) from the beginning with a two-third majority: "Thus, while SWAPO had initially (before 1992) feared, and the DTA had hoped, that the National Council would be dominated by opposition party members, these concerns and aspirations were clearly not borne out."[27]

The last regional elections took place on November 29 and 30, 2004 and confirmed the overwhelming dominance of SWAPO with another landslide victory. With more than half (53.5 percent) of the almost one million registered voters turnout was markedly less than in the national elections only a few days earlier. The party collected 96 of the 107 constituencies and increased its seats in the 13 regional councils from 80 percent to 90 percent. Notwithstanding this increasing monopoly over political affairs in both houses, the National Council gained over the years profile as a complementing body, which managed to add reputation and provided policy debate to Namibia's democracy by acting as another visible platform and forum in its own right, though only limited competences and influence. After its original consolidation phase, the National Council even challenged the supreme role of the parliament to seek recognition as a body with equal power and rights. Given the overall dominance of the one and same party in both houses, the issue was resolved by means of an internal arrangement, which offered the members of the national council not more influence and power but certainly higher reputation and status.[28]

Interestingly enough, a series of intrigues and power struggles accompanied the nomination of the SWAPO candidates on the ground prior to the 2004 elections. The most prominent victim was the previous

Chairperson of the National Council, who failed to continue his career. These in-fights seem to indicate that in contrast to its original minor role, the regional councils and in particular the national council have gained both reputation and impact in policy-making and seem to offer a more attractive political career (and possibly means of exercising influence) than during the initial stages. This confirms recent trends, which suggest that members of the national council have become far more active in shaping the official political discourse and left behind the image of a mere rubber-stamping institution. On several occasions has the national council in the law-making process started to resume responsibilities, which contributed to the reform of submissions before ultimately passed as acts by the national assembly. The continued hierarchy between the two chambers, with clear ultimate responsibilities vested in the national assembly, however, remains uncontested. However, the stigma of being "only" a regional or national councilor has clearly faded and been replaced by more acknowledged and respected (self-) images. With the growing one-party tendency in both houses, however, the supportive role of the national council to plural democratic dialogue (even within the same party due to different functions and roles of the representatives) might be reduced again.

The Role of the Legislature

The national assembly (parliament) was established in terms of Article 44 of the Constitution as the highest law-making body of the Republic of Namibia "with the power to pass laws with the assent of the President."[29] As Article 45 stipulates, "members of the National Assembly shall be representative of all the people and shall in performance of their duties be guided by the objectives of this Constitution, by the public interest and by their conscience." [30] It consists of 72 elected members. Article 46 (1) (b) allows for a maximum of six additional members appointed by the president "by virtue of their special expertise, status, skill or experience." They have no vote "and shall not be taken into account for the purpose of determining any specific majorities that are required under this Constitution or any other law."[31] The parliamentarians are elected every five years on a proportional representation system basis. They are voted into office from lists submitted by political parties admitted to stand for elections by the Directorate of Elections. Under Article 133, the Constituent Assembly elected under UN supervision in November 1989 constituted the independent Republic's first National Assembly "and its term of office and that of the President shall be deemed to have begun from the date of Independence." Subsequently, the term in office ends after five-year cycles on that date (March 21), when the newly elected members in the parliamentary and presidential elections (normally at the end of the preceding year—1994, 1999, and again in 2004) individually swear or solemnly affirm "to uphold and defend the Constitution and laws of the Republic of Namibia to the best of my ability."

Article 35 (1) rules that Ministers are appointed by the president from Members of the national assembly or in the case of Deputy Ministers from either members of the national assembly or the national council (Article 37). In both cases, Members of Parliament include those appointed by the president under Article 46 (1) (b). Given the current size of the cabinet with some 40 Ministers and Deputy Ministers, almost all SWAPO-MPs are members of cabinet or tasked to attend cabinet meetings on behalf of their Ministers. There is a constitutional obligation for members of the cabinet to be accountable to both the president and the National Assembly (Article 41). Given that almost half of the Members of Parliament are at the same time a minister or deputy minister, the division of power in the interest of checks and balances is hardly maintained. Furthermore, parliamentarians who at the same time are executing responsibilities as ministers or deputy ministers seem not empowered to represent the voters to the fullest capacity. Hence, most SWAPO-MPs are as (deputy) ministers, accountable to themselves and the president. This is an assemblage, which is at best, a double-edged sword. The separation of powers as emphasized by Kaakunga[32] is under the given circumstances, more "wishful thinking" than practical reality. SWAPO-MPs in most instances take the floor during parliamentary debates in their function as Ministers or Deputy Ministers appointed by the president, instead of as parliamentarians representing the voters. This blurs the borderline between different responsibilities and competences and ultimately weakens the national assembly, which also has far too limited capacity to undertake any meaningful work within parliamentary standing committees on issues of public interest.

In a critical assessment of the relationship emerging between parliament and cabinet during the first legislature period after Independence, Bukurura concludes: "Parliament consciously or unconsciously gave room to the executive to become strong because that was considered desirable." [33] With reference to an explanatory statement by the Speaker of parliament, he identified the irreconcilable beliefs that a) under the given circumstances of the new independence, a strong executive would be a good thing and that b) the executive once consolidated would relinquish the "borrowed" strength at a later stage to parliament. As he concludes, both assumptions were problematic and pivotal to the institutional relationship. As a result,

> the executive has been very alert to the leeway it commands from a more than "sympathetic" Parliament. Put differently, it is parliamentary deference

to the executive that has bolstered executive strength. Parliament, therefore, has lost the initiative. As a result, it is the executive itself, and not Parliament that will ultimately decide, at its own pace and on its own terms, when the time is right to grant political space to Parliament.[34]

It therefore comes as little surprise that the National Assembly has not participated in the major challenges the Namibian state has so far been confronted with for debate (less so for decision-making). The Constitution was changed for the first time in 1998. Despite strong objections from most other political parties and within the public sphere, SWAPO's politically elected representatives in both houses (the National Assembly and the National Council) adopted with the required two-third majority the constitutional modification allowing its president a third term as Head of State.[35] By doing so, the SWAPO MPs merely executed a decision made at the SWAPO Congress. From a formal point of view, such policy intervention is legitimate and based on the mandate received through general elections by secret vote of all citizens registered. Such a move, however, despite its formal legitimacy, ignores all cautions that it might be perceived as the wrong signal. During August of the same year (1998), the country joined a war in the Democratic Republic of Congo as a result of a personally ordered intervention by the Head of State. He is constitutionally entitled by the power vested in his office to such a far-reaching single-handed initiative in the protection of the national security interest. Nevertheless, its execution in this particular case posed the question if this was indeed necessitated by the stipulated urgent state of emergency. After all, it happened in total ignorance of the need for any consultation among the elected political office bearers (and hence representatives of the people). Neither the Cabinet nor the Parliament was considered with the matter.

A year later, in August 1999, the failure of nation building with regard to the Caprivi region became evident by an armed attempt for secession, which failed miserably but provoked a massive repressive response by the state authorities in the region and led to a new stage of national chauvinism.[36] Once again, parliament was only rudimentarily involved in the issues at stake. While in recess, the president used the authority vested in his office to proclaim for the first time in the history of the Namibian Republic a state of emergency. Since it was lifted before 30 days lapsed, the national assembly was not even involved in this far-reaching decision, as it has only to authorize a further extension after 30 days.[37] From the end of 1999 onward, Namibian army forces were involved in military conflict with UNITA until its collapse after the death of Savimbi. It turned parts of Namibia's own border areas into a low-key war-zone with high sacrifices for the local civilian population.[38] Parliament again played if at all only a minor role not even in the decision-making process, but at best in the subsequent efforts to justify and legitimize the policy decided by the Head of State and implemented upon his instructions.

Critical voices on these and other issues, not necessarily disputing the options pursued but questioning the procedures in the decision-making process were labeled as unpatriotic elements. Loyalty to Namibia is equated with loyalty to SWAPO's policy and in particular the party's president. Dissenting views are marginalized. Nation-building efforts take place at the expense of minorities. Gay-bashing and xenophobic sentiments bordering on racism are among the repertoire of the highest political office bearers, including statements during parliamentary debates from members of the August house.[39] The independence of the judiciary is openly questioned when it makes unpopular decisions not in favor of the government's political will. Party officials, including MPs and Ministers, articulate repeatedly unconstitutional demands without being corrected by the leadership.

Public Perceptions of Democracy, Government, and Governance

Namibia's political culture reveals more than a decade after independence some less-comforting features. A survey conducted at the turn of the century among six African countries[40] ranks Namibia last in terms of public awareness of democracy. A summary of the report concludes with reference to Namibia and Nigeria, "the consolidation of democracy is a distant prospect in both these countries." [41] In a follow-up survey among 11 African countries, the preference for democracy among Namibians has declined during 2002–2003 from close to 60 to just above 50 percent and ranks second last, only followed by Lesotho, where support for democracy actually increased considerably.[42] While some 70 percent among the interviewed Namibians considered the political system in the original 1999–2001 survey as a full democracy or with minor problems only, the observations point in 2002–2003 with a decline to just below 60 percent to a loss of such legitimacy.[43] As pointed out in a related survey elsewhere, in both countries (Namibia and Lesotho), "one fifth of the population is willing to flirt with non-democratic alternatives." [44]

An earlier survey by the Helen Suzman Foundation among six Southern African states produced another sobering result: Namibia was the only country in which a large majority would not accept defeat of its party. It diagnosed "a complete collapse of confidence in the future" while finally "not much more than one third of respondents felt confident of democracy's future." [45] Another empirical survey reveals "that not all Namibians have a clear understanding of the concept of democracy, and that not all Namibians share the same understanding of that concept." [46] The most recent survey among Namibians aged 18 to 32 concludes: "Namibia does not have sufficient young Democrats to make the consolidation of democracy a foregone conclusion." [47] Instead, there is a strong correlation between the degree of support for public institutions and the affiliation to the party in political power, suggesting a sharp divide along partisan lines between "us" (SWAPO) and "them" (non-SWAPO).[48] Given the SWAPO dominance, the result of the factual one-party dominance is actually a relatively positive approval rate among Namibians in contrast to other countries with less clear political affinities among the population.

Comparatively speaking, the country's political performance rated well in a series of national public-attitude surveys on democracy, markets, and civil society in Africa undertaken during August/September 2003 with 1,200 respondents. In the 15-country study, Namibia has together with Ghana and Kenya the "most satisfied democrats." [49] However, while results show the highest trust in the president (approval rate of 91 percent compared to a mean rate of 70 percent among all countries), there is visibly less support for institutions and the lowest esteem among all countries for the political opposition. While on average, 19 percent of respondents in the 15 countries held the view that the president should be able to serve as many terms in office as he wishes, Namibian respondents ranked with 29 percent agreement (second highest to Mozambique). With 45 percent (mean: 19 percent) by far the highest proportion among all 15 countries agreed that the president should pass without worrying about what the national assembly thinks. This corresponds with the lowest approval rate of 36 percent (in contrast to a mean 61 percent among all countries) to the statement that members of the National Assembly represent the people and should therefore make laws even if the president does not agree.[50]

On the basis of such empiric evidence, the ambiguous conclusion offered by Keulder, Nord and Emminghaus seems to be a fair—though at the same time worrying—reflection of both the strength and weakness of Namibia's relatively young and not-yet-consolidated state of democracy. As they maintain based on their findings, the country's single-dominant-party system based on overwhelming electoral support for SWAPO

> must be regarded as being a significant source of stability in the current democratic system. Support for the ruling party translates into support for institutions, and that is what will prevent a crisis of legitimacy during the founding years of a young democracy. The negative effect associated with this, however, is that the future of the democracy is placed in the hands of the ruling elite.[51]

Limits of Parliamentary Democracy

John Saul[52] proposes as a result of this sobering reality to question decolonization as "Liberation without Democracy." The track records of the liberation movements with regard to their internal practices during the wars of liberation as well as their lack of democratic virtues and respect toward the protection of human rights once in power are far from positive examples.[53] Fighting against unjust systems of oppression, rooted in totalitarian colonial rule of a minority, did not protect them from resorting to internal oppression of the worst kind.[54] The result of such constraints is at best restricted permissiveness and hardly any receptive attitude toward criticism, especially when articulated within a public discourse. Nonconformity is associated with disloyalty if not betrayal. The marginalization if not elimination of dissent hence limits the capacity to reproduce the political system through constant modifications based on corrective innovations to the benefit of the public interest and subsequently their own credibility and legitimacy. The circle of political office-bearers tends to be restricted to those comrades who gained reputation and respect for the display of personality structures of a command-and-obey system, but not for their democratic convictions as independent-minded, autonomous individuals.

The result is a ruling new political elite operating from commanding heights shaped in and based upon the particular context of the post-apartheid societies by selective narratives and memories related to the war(s) of liberation. It constructs or invents new traditions to establish an exclusive post-colonial legitimacy under the sole authority of one particular agency of social forces.[55] The (self-) mystification of the liberators plays an essential role in this fabrication of legitimacy. Tendencies to autocratic rule and toward the subordination of the state under the party, as well as politically motivated social and material favors as a reward system for loyalty or disadvantages as a form of coercion in cases of dissent are obvious techniques. The political rulers' penchant for self-enrichment with the help of a rent- or sinecure-capitalism goes with the exercise of comprehensive controls to secure the continuance of their rule. Development policies "are conceived and developed in an authoritarian manner, which limits people's space and undermines their participation in the decision-making process."[56] The "national interest" serves the purpose "to justify all kinds of authoritarian practice" to allow that " 'anti-national' or 'unpatriotic' can be defined basically as any group that resists the power of the ruling elite of the day."[57] Such selective mechanisms of the exercise and retention of power have much in common with the commando structures that emerged during the days of the liberation struggle, especially in exile.

Similar mechanisms can be seen in many other societies around the world that are regarded as democratic states. That power corrupts is by no means a solely African truism. Nor that giving up power—even in democratically anchored and regulated conditions with a long tradition—is difficult for many once they had a taste of it. This has been labeled in the African context as "repressive reversal" with reference to earlier processes of decolonization. They resulted under new nationalist governments in an effort to refute challenges to their policies in "the transformation of the discursive realm from being civic and cosmopolitan to becoming parochial and local." [58] It is interesting to note in this context of the analysis presented by Alexis de Tocqueville (1805–1859). His critical retrospective on the shortcomings of the French Revolution (the first volume published in 1856) reflects the degree of frustration provoked by the restoration of power structures under Louis Napoleon after his *coup d'état* in 1851. Tocqueville's studies on the old state and the revolution (*L'ancien régime et la révolution*), provide relevant insights beyond the particular case.[59] He argues that the French revolutionaries in the process of implementing the structures of the new system maintained the mentalities, habits, even the ideas of the old state while using them to destroy it. And they took the rubble of the old state to establish the foundation of the new society. To understand the revolution and its achievement, he concludes, one has to forget about the current society but has to interrogate the buried one. His ultimate reasoning ends in the suggestion that freedom has been replaced by another repression: revolutionaries in the process of securing, establishing, and consolidating their power base sacrificed the declared ideals and substantive issues they were fighting for in the name of the same revolution.

For parliaments to be part of the problem or part of the solution, will, most likely, depend on the balance of power(s) in the given constellation. For the time being, the questions are still valid, with which Mbahuurua ended some reflections on occasion of ten years of Namibian independence, "To what extent does the executive support other political institutions as viable democratic elements? Or, put differently, is the executive in Namibia democracy-promoting or democracy restraining?" [60] In critically taking stock of the potential and constraints of Constitutionalism as a negotiated result of the anti-colonial liberation struggle and its controlled transition toward legitimate majority rule based on at least formally democratic principles, Bukurura suggests "that certain practices in liberation struggles compromised and in some ways continue to play a part in respect of pluralism and diversity of views after independence." [61] Some of the lessons learned in this process may themselves "not be favorable to the furtherance of diversity, political pluralism, and respect for, and sustenance of, a human rights culture." [62] The challenge therefore lies in the

8. Nujoma 2001: 424. The specific (meaning selective) narrative of Sam Nujoma is both enlightening and sobering as his particular perception corresponds to his pragmatism in terms of socio-political ideology (or actually lack thereof). Hence a critical assessment of his "memoirs" concludes, "that Nujoma has little understanding of, or commitment to, democratic values. A reading of *Where Others Wavered* (Nujoma 2001) will bring no comfort to those concerned about the future of democracy in Namibia today" (Saunders 2003: 98).
9. cf. Weiland and Braham 1994.
10. Dobell 1998: 101.
11. Saunders 2001: 10.
12. Erasmus 2000: 98.
13. Hinz 2001: 91.
14. Pickering 1995: 107.
15. The 2,465 votes (0.46 percent) that the CoD obtained over the DTA proved beyond a doubt that, despite the same number of seats in the National Assembly, the CoD qualifies as the official opposition. Notwithstanding this fact, attempts were initiated to construct bypassing arrangements. The DTA and the UDF were prepared to assist SWAPO in this effort by entering a parliamentary coalition, which was used to award them the status as official opposition. Common sense finds it difficult to see any justification or rationale for such acrobatics, which ultimately take place at the expense of the legitimacy and credibility of the representatives of the political system in Namibia. Furthermore, such an arrangement made two opposition parties active collaborators in anti-democratic tricks exercised by the majority party in government.
16. SWAPO Party Department of Information and Publicity 1999: 24.
17. See among the numerous reports on the different elections, i.e. Commonwealth Secretariat 1995; Glover 2000; Keulder 1998 and 1999; Keulder, Nord and Emminghaus 2000; Kössler 1993; Lodge 1999 and 2000; Simon 2000; Soiri 2001; Weiland 1995.
18. Glover 2000: 147. On this basis, the strong reaction by SWAPO to the newly established CoD is even more disturbing. While this could have been interpreted prior to the 1999 elections as a sign of uncertainty and lack of self-confidence on behalf of the party's leadership and activists, the ongoing almost paranoid dimension of a witch hunt even after the election results displayed features of an irrationality that might be explained only in psycho-analytical categories. This applies also to the election post-mortems conducted by SWAPO's party organ "Namibia Today" and the continued smear campaigns and character assassinations it pursued since then unabated and with ever-increasing vigor against anyone perceived to be in open or public disagreement with the official party line.
19. This equation is supported in the analytical contributions by Chris Tapscott, Heribert Weiland, and Andre du Pisani at the conference, Namibia after Nine Years: Past and Future, as published in Forum for the Future (1999). See also Kössler and Melber 2001; Tapscott 1995 and 2001; Weiland 1999.

abuses, viewing the goal of Namibian independence as of greater importance. In particular, SWAPO had to be seen as morally superior to the South African security forces. This contributed to an environment in which human rights violators continued to act with impunity." For a detailed account by one of the victims of the mid-1970s wave of internal repression, see Nathanael 2002. For an overview of the issue of the "ex-detainees" and its treatment in particular in the Namibian Parliament, see Saul and Leys 2003.
55. See Kriger 1995 and Werbner 1998 for Zimbabwe; Melber 2003a for Namibia.
56. Salih 1999: 163.
57. Harrison 2001: 391.
58. Hyden and Okigbo 2002: 38.
59. Cf. Erdheim 1991.
60. Mbahuurua 2002: 61.
61. Bukurura 2003: 44.
62. Ibid.
63. Ibid., 45.

9

Parliament and Dominant Party System in Ethiopia

Kassahun Berhanu
Political Science and International Relations,
Addis Ababa University, Ethiopia

Introduction

This chapter reviews the mode and manner of instituting the Ethiopian legislature under three successive regimes: Emperor Haileselassie, the Dergue (one-party dictatorship), and Ethiopia People's Revolutionary Democratic Front (EPRDF). It also attempts to identify similarities and differences in respect to the organization and mode of operation of the Ethiopian legislature, and the roles it played in undertaking oversight and control functions. I undertook this effort in order to explore whether democratic governance has even been the defining element of Ethiopian polity in the different political systems in question. To this end, the workings of the Ethiopian parliament will be examined in terms of its changing roles under autocracy (a no-party imperial rule), the Dergue, and EPRDF (a multiparty system characterized by an overwhelming dominance of a single party). It is, however, observed that in all historical periods the Ethiopian has operated under the shadow of a one- or dominant-party system neither of which is conducive to vibrant democratic governance legislative process and outcomes.

Blending Parliament with Mainstream Locus of Power

This section deals with the processes involved in the creation of a "modern" legislative body as a major component of the political system under successive regimes in Ethiopia. The unfolding of internal and external dynamics caused the need for adopting non-traditional means and ways of administration through creating legislative institutions. Moves in this direction were presumed to lend aspects of modernity while at the same time serving as a basis for legitimacy of political regimes that presided over the Ethiopian state at varying times.

Genesis of a "Modern" Parliamentary System under Imperial Rule

After his accession to absolute power by assuming the throne, Haileselassie introduced the first "modern" constitution as a feature of the Ethiopian political scene in 1931. The Constitution provided for a bi-cameral law-making body and endorsed Haileselassie's quest for assuming uncontested executive, legislative, and judicial power. Such omnipotence of the Emperor as a custodian of legitimacy and exercise of public authority was stipulated in the different provisions of the Constitution, which read as follows:

- The territory of Ethiopia, in its entirety, is, from one end to the other, subject to the government of His Majesty, the Emperor. All the natives of Ethiopia [as] subjects of the Empire form together the Ethiopian nation (Art. 1)
- In the Ethiopian Empire, supreme power rests in the hands of the Emperor (Art. 6).
- The Emperor shall lay down the organization and the regulations of all administrative departments. It is his right also to appoint and dismiss the officers of the army, as well as civil officials, and to decide as to their respective charges and salaries (Art. 11).
- The Emperor has legally the right to negotiate and to sign all kinds of treaties (Art. 14).

Article 31 of the Constitution empowered the Emperor to appoint members of the upper chamber of parliament (the senate) from among the ranks of the aristocracy and persons that have allegedly a proven record of serving the state in high-ranking civilian and military positions. This was immediately expressed by the Emperor's appointment of the first twenty-five senators notably from the ruling houses of Amhara and Tigray, among others. Article 32 stipulated that members of the lower chamber of parliament (House of Deputies) were not to be elected by the nobility and landed gentry through an indirect electoral mechanism. It was declared that this practice would persist "until the people of Ethiopia become" capable of directly electing their representatives. According to Yacob,[1] the criterion of eligibility for serving in the House of Deputies is anchored in the fact that the designated representative should be affirmed as someone who is loyal to the Emperor, a patriot, a devotedly religious person, and firm in character.

Haileselassie's reform measures and centralization drives were temporarily halted because of the Italian Fascist invasion and occupation of the country that lasted between 1936 and 1941. After the termination of Italian rule in East Africa at the height of the World War in 1941, Haileselassie was restored to power. His return did not initially signal the regaining of his pre-war omnipotence owing to conditionality imposed on some aspects of his previous jurisdiction by the British Military Administration (BMA). The resurgence of attitudes and dispositions against centralized rule facilitated by the invasion and the subsequent dismantling of Haileselassie's Government on the one hand, and the rebellious mood then prevalent among influential leaders of the resistance on the other, posed threats to the resumption of absolute control at first. Such and similar impediments were, however, short lived and their removal was soon effected through a combination of approaches ranging from appeasement and cracking upon the possible blocs of opposition by way of using both diplomatic and administrative measures.

Following the restoration of Ethiopian sovereignty in 1941, the 1931 Constitution and the pre-war parliament were reinstituted. Provincial administration was restructured into 12 provinces each of which embraced 20 electoral districts. All persons who paid taxes, who held *rist* (property in land), and all notables were given the right to vote.[2] Each electoral district sent its representatives to the administrative capital of the province where in the presence of the provincial governor, an ecclesiastical dignitary, a representative of the Ministry of Interior, and a sworn official of records were selected to represent the province in the Chamber of Deputies.[3]

Once firmly entrenched in power, Haileselassie's first move was to reassert his absolute authority by administering a deadly blow to the dispersed pockets of power that had taken advantage of his five-year absence to resurface. Levine identifies three innovations of the regime in the post-1941 period.[4] These were the reestablishment of the standing army under the control of the centre, the introduction of a new fiscal system under the Ministry of Finance, and reorganization of provincial administration—all detrimental to regional power centers anchored on ascriptive and traditional claims and aspirations. Asmelash argues that these accomplishments provided the Emperor with power and prestige to a degree unprecedented before.[5] Immediately after the country's liberation in 1941, the administrative machinery of the Ethiopian state was completely overhauled.[6]

The retention of the Emperor's loyal entourage and court camarilla in key positions of the post-war government rendered the regime to pose as a bastion of authority and influence to be reckoned with.

Now that every thing is put in place according to the wishes of the Emperor, subsequent measures aimed at consolidating central rule began to unravel persistently. The first in the series of such moves was articulated by the enactment of the Imperial Ethiopian Government (IEG) Decree No. 1 of 1942 (IEG 1942) providing for the establishment of provincial administration and specifying on institutions, officials and their role, jurisdiction and competence, accountability, composition of councils and commissions, etc. The Emperor presided over all administrative jurisdictions through the Ministry of Interior empowered to supervise governors at the various levels of the provincial administrative hierarchy. The central ministries (Finance, Justice, etc.) were required to field their representatives accordingly and public duties were to be disposed under the coordination and supervision of governors posing as the henchmen of the central government.

A number of developments, which transpired in the decade and a half that accompanied the liberation of Ethiopia both within the country and abroad, necessitated infusing new elements in the workings of the imperial government. This culminated in constitutional reform, which led to changes in the mode and manner of conducting elections and constituting the legislature. In addition to the changing political climate of the early 1950s in the sub-region characterized by national liberation struggles in the non-self-governing territories of the sub-region, Eritrea's federation with Ethiopia in 1952 clearly exposed the inadequacies of the 1931 Constitution. It is to be noted that the 1931 Constitution contrasted unfavorably with the liberal Constitution granted to Eritrea by the United Nations. Moreover, the Emperor's government was criticized from several quarters for its reluctance to adopt a liberal constitution that allows sets of freedoms and liberties for its citizens. Thus, the need for a new liberal constitution that was envisaged to induce Eritrea to be more close to the "motherland" began to be increasingly felt. Speaking in retrospect in April 1961, a few months after the foiled coup staged by the Imperial Guard, the Emperor summarized the reasons that led to the enactment of the Revised Constitution as follows:

> As our Empire grew and flourished, it became apparent that the Constitution of [1931] no longer responded adequately to the needs of our people. Accordingly, in 1955 ... We promulgated the Revised Constitution. ... In it, provision was made for our people to enjoy direct representation in the business of government. The division of power

among us, our Ministers acting collectively and individually and our Parliament, was solidified and acquired permanent institutional form.[7]

Markakis and Asmelash assert that two of the basic motives that inspired constitutional reform in 1955 were the same ones that had inspired the experiment of 1931, namely, the Emperor's concern for international image and continued centralization of his authority in a more subtle form.[8] Save for the sanctioning of a bi-cameral legislature (the Chamber of Deputies and the Senate), to whose lower house deputies could be elected by the eligible electorate, and professing respect for such rights and freedoms as speech, press, association, and assembly, the Revised Constitution has left the fundamental structures of the central government intact.

The 1955 Revised Constitution was an improvement on its predecessor (the 1931 Constitution). It maintained the incontestable position of the Emperor in the legislative, judicial, and executive branches of government as stipulated in Article 27, which affirmed his omnipotence in the following words:

> The Emperor determines the organization, powers and duties of all ministries [and] executive departments and the administrations of the Government and appoints, promotes, transfers, suspends and dismisses the officials of the same.

Article 96 (b) of the 1955 Constitution sanctioned that elections to the Chamber of Deputies were to be conducted on the basis of direct universal suffrage in rural and urban constituencies. A candidate running for a seat in the lower chamber was required to be "a *bona fide* resident and owner of property in his electoral district." The eligibility criterion based on property ownership automatically disqualified the rural and urban poor that comprised the bulk of the population, thereby ensuring the entrenchment of the propertied classes in the legislative organ of government. Notwithstanding this, however, the 1955 constitutional reform brought about a situation where participation in elections on the part of the public as voters and candidates considerably increased.

According to the National Election Board of the Imperial Government (1973), the number of candidates, registered voters, those who went to the polls on election dates, and elected candidates steadily grew between 1957[9] and 1973 from about 3.7 million in 1957 to about 7.3 in 1973.[10]

Despite this, however, Yacob argued that the general increase in the number of candidates, registered voters, or the number of seats could not imply representation of the interests of the rural or urban poor.[11] The role of the poor and non-propertied sections of society was limited to legitimating the perpetuation of an oppressive system through voting for candidates favored by the status quo. The same Yacob stated that:

> The constitutional provisions as well as the electoral laws made it easy for rural elites and landlords to stand as candidates. Indeed, they were readily able to satisfy the criteria of ownership of immovable property (land ownership), loyalty to the imperial government and had rudimentary education. They used their informal family and class ties to get their nominations supported and further accepted by election officials. They had no problem of paying the registration fee or the legally required deposits with the Electoral Board. . . . It was very difficult, if not impossible, for the common people even to get candidacy in an electoral contest.[12]

Clapham argued that the 1955 Revised Constitution was more comprehensive than the 1931 version.[13] It further developed the centralizing and the modernizing themes of the 1931 Constitution, albeit in a subtle manner, and defined the empire as a fief under the sovereignty of the Ethiopian Crown. It pre-empted and neutralized the ramifications of the Federal Act that defined the relationship between Eritrea and Ethiopia thereby bringing the former closely within the bounds of the latter. At face value, the Revised Constitution appeared to have broadened and strengthened the base of the three branches of government and the Emperor. In fact, however, the ever-present omnipotence of the Emperor essentially remained unaffected. The Emperor received a pre-eminent place as a sovereign and head of state. Markakis summed up the situation by stating that parliament [the senate in particular] served such purposes as providing a place of honorable retirement for the nobility by creating a means of associating the still widely influential nobility with the already initiated centralizing and modernizing drives of the regime.[14]

The Ethiopian Legislature in the Post-Revolution Years, 1987–1991

The outbreak of the revolutionary process that terminated the *ancien régime* in 1974 was initiated by a combination of factors emphasizing a set of claims and demands, which Haileselassie's government neither wanted to tackle nor was capable of addressing. Students, workers, civil servants, and other sections of the population rose in protest by hinting at the various forms of injustice and malpractice under which the country and its people have suffered. In the process, the military and the security forces that used to serve the regime as instruments for suppressing the popular will in the past joined this constituency of discontent.

Among plethora of demands and claims, one could cite the major ones like the nationality question, religious equality, land to the tiller, improved working conditions and remuneration for workers, constitutional reform, reorganization of the state, etc. In effect, these were directed towards putting an end to the status quo. Posing as the better-organized and armed detachment of the mass movement, the military assumed power by creating a committee (Dergue) composed of junior and non-commissioned officers as its representatives. This culminated in the establishment of the "Provisional Military Administrative Council" (PMAC), alias Dergue. Owing to pressures from the various radical sections of society and thinking that it was expedient to catch up with the revolutionary tide calling for fundamental reforms on basic issues of popular concern, the Dergue set out to take several measures presumed to be in accord with legitimate popular aspirations in the context of changed situations.

Immediately upon its control of the Ethiopian state, the Dergue suspended both parliament and the Constitution of the imperial regime. This was undertaken by declaring its intention of ruling by decree until such time that conditions are ripe for enacting a new constitution that would form the legal basis for a popularly elected government. It was after over a decade of military rule that the Dergue claimed to have managed to form a monolithic party of a Leninist type, namely, the Worker's Party of Ethiopia (WPE), in 1985. This was accompanied by such events as the inauguration of a self-styled civilian constitutional government designated as the People's Democratic Republic of Ethiopia (PDRE) whose legitimacy was grounded in a new constitution—the Constitution of the PDRE.

The process of drafting the PDRE Constitution was closely controlled and monitored by the leadership of the military regime and the Worker's Party at the helm of both presided the same personalities. Educated and experienced individuals from various institutions, including institutions of higher learning in the country were entrusted with the task of drafting the new constitution and producing a draft document in line with the guidelines and directives received from the wielders of power in the government and the party, notably the military strongman Mengistu Hailemariam. Moreover, the experts were further required to justify and publicly defend the various provisions of the draft.[15]

Members of the Constitution Drafting Commission (CDC) appointed by the Dergue in 1986 included the experts who produced the draft document, Central Committee members of WPE, high-ranking government officials, leaders of client mass-organizations and professional associations closely associated with WPE, and widely known public figures and religious leaders. Most of the 354 members of the CDC did not possess the knowledge and experience for deliberating and debating on a constitutional document, nor did they have the mandate from their respective "constituencies" to undertake such a task. They were deliberately handpicked for the sole purpose of serving as smokescreen by way of portraying the entire process relating to the venture as having induced the active participation of wide sections of society. The Drafting Commission convened three sessions to deliberate on the contents of the draft, which was eventually submitted to the Central Committee of the Workers Party of Ethiopia for approval. The party leadership subjected the draft to scrutiny for ideological and policy conformity and decided that it be presented to the people for "enrichment" through public discussion at forums organized for the purpose.[16]

According to an official document (PDRE 1987), the draft was translated and published in 14 local languages of which two million copies were distributed across the different parts of the country. It was claimed that over 12 million eligible citizens of voting-age took part in the public discussions facilitated by 1,250,000 coordinators in 25,000 forums.

The Central Committee endorsed the final version of the Constitution at its 5th Plenary Session of September 7, 1986, and decided that this be ratified by a popular referendum, which was expedited by a Referendum Commission comprising 61 members headed by the Secretary General of WPE and the military Head of State, Mengistu Hailemariam. In the different parts of the country, Referendum Committees spearheaded by the henchmen of the regime were set up at regional, provincial, district, and polling station levels to monitor and coordinate the exercise. The Referendum was held in February 1987 in 25,000 polling stations. It was reported that 14,035,718 people or 96 percent of the registered voters went to the polls. Of these 81 percent were reported as having voted in support of the Draft Constitution while 18 percent did not.[17]

The promulgation of Proclamation No. 314/1987 provided for the establishment of a National Electoral Commission (NEC) charged with the task of coordinating and overseeing elections to the National Parliament (Shengo). According to Article 64 of this Proclamation, candidates for seats in the National Parliament (Shengo) were to be drawn primarily from among the ranks of WPE members, WPE-affiliated mass organizations and trade unions, and the military and security establishments that were firmly under the grip of the party. Eight hundred and thirty-five electoral constituencies were designated where each was determined based on a population size of 75,000 for the rural areas and 15,000 for urban areas. Party committees determined eligibility to candidacy, and those that qualified to run in the elections were introduced to the electorate during meetings conducted in the forums created for the purpose. The electorate went to the polls on June 14, 1987 to endorse the only candidate for the one-seat constituency. According to Yacob the winners were actually known before the ballots were cast.[18] The electorate was mobilized to perform the ritual of electing the already selected candidates. Out of the 15,166,463 registered, 87.7 percent cast their votes.[19] On June 14, 1987, national elections were held from dawn to dusk in 812 constituencies throughout the country, and the same number of representatives was endorsed/elected.[20]

One issue of interest worth mentioning here is the "election" of candidates to the national and regional legislatures. The PDRE Constitution empowers the Workers Party of Ethiopia (WPE), the pro-government mass organizations and the units of the "Revolutionary" Armed Forces to present candidates for the elections. The assumption is that these establishments represent the masses of the people and thus the exercise could qualify as a popular venture. The climax of such a mockery was that, in most cases, three candidates (resembling identical triplets) approved by the WPE were initially presented to run in each constituency. When the election date approached, two of these were dropped and only one was made to appear before the potential voters. In addition, many candidates are reported to have run in the localities where they have never set foot before. It is in this manner that the "People's Democratic Republic" came to life.

Consequently, a uni-cameral legislature (Shengo) with a membership size of 813 persons was inaugurated on September 9, 1987. The designers of the representation structure of the PDRE Parliament carefully worked out mechanisms for a balanced representation of diverse social groups. According to official sources,[21] the process was purposively designed to include members, supporters, and sympathizers of the ruling party (WPE) from the different sections of Ethiopian society. Taking into account such parameters as occupation, education, and age and gender composition accomplished this arrangement. Accordingly, the profile of deputies in terms of occupation was peasants (36.5 percent), workers in the industrial, manufacturing, and service sectors (12 percent), service members from different army units (12.9 percent), full-time party activists (8.5 percent), and party members and supporters in the civil service (27.3 percent). Women comprised 6.4 percent of the total number of the elected deputies.

Proclamation No. 1 of 1987 that officiated the Constitution of the Peoples Democratic Republic of Ethiopia (PDRE) is of interest for understanding developments with regard to the situation of local government since the mid-1970s. Alleged to have supplanted military rule with a popularly elected constitutional government, this legal document contains a number of provisions that relate to local administration. Article 59 affirms the unitary nature of the Ethiopian state under whose jurisdiction came the administrative and newly designated autonomous regions. Article 61 stipulated the possible existence of as many administrative units as necessary under autonomous regions whose boundary and level of hierarchy "shall be determined by law." The national legislature of the PDRE (Shengo) depicted as the highest organ of state power was authorized (Article 63 part 2 a, b, and c) to establish administrative and autonomous regions, determine their boundary, level of hierarchy and accountability, and source of revenue and enact proclamations by which they are administered. Among the duties of the Council of Ministers of the Central Government, supervising the work of the executive committees of the Shengos of administrative and autonomous regions (Article 92 part 3) was included.

While Article 65 of the PDRE Constitution ensured representation of nationalities in the central legislature, Article 95 stipulated that the highest organ of state power of an administrative or autonomous region to be the regional legislature (Shengo). The Constitution lists down the duties of this body (cf. Article 97, parts 1–9) which include implementing laws, decisions, and directives of the state, determine social and economic plans and budget of the region subject to approval by the national legislature, elect judges of the regional courts, etc.

Subsequently, 5 autonomous and 24 administrative regions were established under the unitary structure of the PDRE on the basis of Proclamation No. 14, 1987.[22] It is interesting to note here that the five autonomous regions that were accorded autonomous status by this act were trouble spots marked for intensification of insurgent activities. These were the Ogaden, Assab, Tigrai, Eritrea, and Dire-Dawa. This affirms the primacy of political considerations once again influencing decisions pertaining to local government.

The Provisional Military Administrative Council (PMAC) inaugurated the PDRE with the aim of pre-empting critics and remains in power alleging that it has formed a constitutionally elected civilian government. A bogus constitution and a rubber-stamp legislature came into being to serve as smokescreen that was designed by disguising the military composition and the dictatorial nature of the regime. In essence, what has actually taken place was the dropping of the military ranks and uniforms of the top leadership and the rank and file in favor of civilian suits and party uniforms.

The PDRE Constitution of 1987 has affirmed the unitary nature of the state under whose jurisdiction came all administrative and autonomous regions. The national legislature was empowered to create and abolish local government units with the prerogative of sanctioning their existence or otherwise, determining their responsibility and source of revenue and enacting rules governing their mode of operation. Further, supervision of the performance of executive committees of the legislatures of the regions was made to fall under the jurisdiction of the Council of Ministers of the central government. The surprising thing in this regard is that all these decisions were reached at without consulting let alone actively involving, the people.

The National Shengo convened once a year for regular sessions. The 24-member Council of State, chaired by the Head-of-State and the General Secretary of Central Committee of WPE, carried out its activities in between the regular sessions. There were seven Commissions headed by party leaders and nine sections headed by Ministers without portfolio. They carry out the tasks of the State Council, hence of the National Parliament (Shengo).

The State Council (the executive) was theoretically the most powerful institution that functioned on behalf of the rubber-stamp legislative body. It was a club of the most powerful persons coming from the top and influential personalities in the WPE: 9 Full and 3 Alternate Politbureau members, 9 Full and 2 Alternate Central Committee members, and 1 ordinary party member with considerable influence. Of these, 11 were the top members of the Dergue's Executive Committee while eight were top civilian officials. Party-affiliated mass organizations like the Revolutionary Ethiopian Women Association (REWA), Ethiopian Peasants' Association (EPA), Revolutionary Ethiopia Youth Association (REYA), Ethiopian Teachers' Association (ETA), and Ethiopian Trade Union were all represented in the Council of State by their respective top leaderships.[23]

Tessema and Zekarias stated that notwithstanding this, however, the functions of unified state power under the PDRE Constitution was divided on paper between the National Shengo, the Council of State, the President of the Republic, and Shengos of Administrative and Autonomous Regions.[24] Theoretically, the National Shengo was the most important organ of state entrusted with the task of discharging significant functions of the state. For example, Article 3 (2) of the Constitution stipulated that "working people exercise their power through the National *Shengo* and Local *Shengos* they establish by election," and that "the authority of other organs of state shall derive from these organs of state power."

In the final analysis, the key governing institutions, including the legislature (Shengo) of the PDRE remained ineffective and impotent in the face of the overwhelming presence of the WPE, and notably the strongman who behaved as a typical despot. In the light of this, the PDRE Parliament was destined to count its final days without playing any meaningful legal and legitimate role in the form of oversight and censure of executive practices and malpractices. In roughly three years of their existence, the legislatures at the national and sub-national levels (Shengos) did not register a single instance of censuring and criticizing executive actions, opposing proposed bills, and scrutinizing performances of line departments.

Parliament under EPRDF Rule, Post–1991

The post-1991 Ethiopian legislature has its roots in the Transitional Period Charter that served as an interim constitution between July 1991 and August 1995. Following the overthrow of the military dictatorship, transitional parliament, namely, the Council of Representatives (COR) was formed as a supreme organ of power for the transition period. The incumbent Constitution, which is designated as the "Constitution of the Federal Democratic Republic of Ethiopia," was promulgated in August 1995 (FDRE, Proclamation 1/1995). Article 53 of the FDRE Constitution provided for the establishment of a federal bi-cameral parliament in the form of the House of Peoples' Representatives (HPR) and the House of the Federation (HOF) posing as the lower and upper chambers respectively.

Article 54 of the Constitution stipulates that members of HPR be elected for a five-year term on the basis of universal suffrage and by direct, fair, and free elections held in secret ballot. Accordingly, members shall be elected from among candidates in each electoral district by a plurality of votes cast. Members of HPR shall not exceed 550 of which at least 20 seats are reserved for minority nationalities. HPR is vested with a wide range of legislative powers concerning land and natural resources, inter-state commerce and foreign trade, transport and communication, nationality and immigration, labor, and political and civil rights. It is also empowered to enact labor, commercial, and penal codes and determine the organization of national defense, and security and police forces. It can declare a state of emergency in conformity with Article 93 of the Constitution and can proclaim a state of war on the basis of recommendations of the Council of Ministers (Article 54/9). General policies and strategies relating to issues of economic and social development, fiscal and monetary matters, international agreements, and appointment of ministers, federal judges, commissioners, etc., cannot take effect without the approval of HPR.

Articles 61–63 of the Constitution deal with various matters pertaining to the House of Federation (HOF) with regard to membership, powers and functions, and immunity of members. Article 61/1 and 2 stipulates that HOF is "composed of representatives of Nations, Nationalities and Peoples" whereby each of these is represented in the House by at least one member. The Constitution also provided that "each nation and nationality shall be represented by one additional representative for each one million of its population." Members of HOF are elected either by the State

Councils or by the peoples of the regions directly. The House of Federation is vested with a number of powers and functions (FDRE Constitution, Article 62). These include, *inter alia*, the power of judicial review (interpreting the Constitution), organizing the Council of Constitutional Inquiry, deciding on issues of self-determination, arbitrating, litigations and disputes that may arise between national/regional states. Also amongst its roles is instructing the Federal Government to intervene in instances when any one regional state threatens the constitutional order, and determining "division of revenues derived from joint, and federal and state tax sources, and subsidies that the federal Government may provide to the states."

National/Regional State Legislatures (State Councils) are bi-cameral. In the same manner as at the federal level, Article 50 of the Constitution allows national/regional states to organize legislative, executive, and judicial branches of government. Members of State Councils are elected by the people of their respective regions and run for seats as party and/or individual candidates. State Councils are the highest organs of authority in the national/regional states. They are dually accountable to the people of their respective regions and the House of Peoples' Representatives. All the powers that are not expressly given to the Federal Government alone or given concurrently to the Federal Government and the States are reserved to the Regional States (Article 52/1). Whereas such matters relating to economic policy and finance, foreign affairs, and national defense and security, among others, fall under the jurisdiction and competence of the Federal Government, others are reserved for the regional states. These include establishing different levels of state administration, enacting and executing state constitutions and other laws, formulating economic and social development policies of their regions, administering land and other natural resources in accordance with federal laws, levying and collecting taxes and duties on own revenue sources, establishing and administering state police forces, and maintaining public order and peace within the states. Most of the aforementioned powers and functions of national/regional states take practical effect on the proviso that approval is obtained from state councils in line with the provisions of the Federal Constitution. Article 50/8 stipulates that "States shall respect the powers of the Federal Government [and] the Federal Government shall likewise respect the power of the States" as provided for in the Constitution.

Post-1991 Ethiopia has embarked on a political dispensation anchored in a federal arrangement that accorded primacy to national "self-determination." This explains the need for instituting a federal bi-cameral legislature, the upper house of which is composed of "representatives of nations and nationalities." Establishment of bi-cameral state legislatures is meant to allow for local self-rule expressed in political devolution. Given that national/regional states are represented in the HOF of the Federal Legislature, forming bi-cameral state legislatures in the regions is found to be superfluous. It is worthy to note, however, that unbecoming behaviors and acts of national/regional governments and state councils can be checked and censured in instances when human rights violations and threatening of the constitutional order unfold in any one state. In such cases, the intervention of the Federal Government could be prompted on the basis of joint decision of both houses or the request of the HOF to this effect.

The role of the Ethiopian parliament in monitoring and implementing laws and policies is either totally absent or negligible at best. Parliament periodically deliberates on concerns associated with such things as prevalent poverty, corruption, and human right abuse in the country. Depending on the preferences of the executive, these led to enacting legislation on pertinent matters. HOR listens to reports of different agencies under the executive. In instances where irregularities and defaults characterizing the actions and behaviors of government agencies under the executive branch are uncovered, HOF hardly urges the executive to account for irregularities and measures taken on defaulter officials and institutions. Progress made in this regard is below satisfactory thereby necessitating improvement in checking and controlling abuse through more rigorous scrutiny and oversight.

For example, the parliamentary Budget and Finance Committee is legally empowered to participate actively in the budget process. However, its involvement is limited to endorsing government budget proposal of the Ministry of Finance and Economic Development. Given that the Budget and Finance Committee and other parliamentary bodies are not involved in the budget process from the start, they lack information for determining whether budget requests of the executive are appropriate or otherwise. This is one area that calls for improvement by seeking means and ways that could ensure active participation of parliament in the budget process and other oversight functions. In the absence of clarity and pertinent information resulting from lack of active involvement in the workings of government, parliament is left with no option other than endorsing reports and requests of the executive as presented.

It should be noted, however, that there are 12 parliamentary committees that are entrusted with the responsibility of controlling and monitoring the activities and performance of executive departments and agencies that fall under their respective jurisdiction and competence. One problem that Parliamentary Committees encounter in this regard relates to inadequacies in getting expert advice and opinion on matters that require technocratic skills in specialized knowledge. Such state of affairs persist unabated due to inadequate capacity characterizing the educational level and experience of legislators and unattractive incentive schemes available for experts who could have filled this gap by way of providing their services.

Parliamentary Dependence on Party Politics and Electoral Systems

Constitutional principles and political rhetoric aside, an important factor that sheds light with regard to the nature of the present regime in Ethiopia is its structure of dominance and the relegation of official multiparty system into a somewhat loosely conceived "dominant one-party" political system. Regarding the emergence of the EPRDF as a dominant party, there appear to be two contending views. While some argue that the establishment of a federal system of government along ethnic lines was intended to consolidate EPRDF's dominant position in Ethiopian politics,[25] others contend that the dominance of the EPRDF was an outcome of the federalization of the Ethiopia along ethnic lines.[26] Leaving aside these assertions, one could undoubtedly observe the dominant position of the EPRDF in the political life of the country in the post-Dergue period. The EPRDF ostensibly controls almost all of the regions through its member and affiliate organizations. Moreover, the EPRDF continues to control the security apparatus and the bureaucracy, which are crucial for maintaining and perpetuating its dominance. The miniscule role of opposition parties in the political life of the country also helped EPRDF to entrench itself staunchly as a dominant political organization commanding considerable organizational strength.

Popular sovereignty and representation of the people through democratic elections anchored in popular participation are among the fundamental principles enshrined in the 1995 Federal Constitution (Art. 8). There are, therefore, several institutions of political representation in today's Ethiopia. Legislative organs, at both the federal and regional levels could be considered as structures of political representation. Moreover, *Woreda, Kebele,* and in the case of the "Southern Nations, Nationalities and Peoples' Region (SNNPR) zones have their own elected councils.

The federal legislature is bi-cameral, and is composed of the House of Peoples' Representatives (hereafter HPR) and the House of Federation (hereafter HF). At the regional level, there exist elected bi-cameral legislative councils. The HPR is responsible for making laws and could be considered as the highest decision-making organ of the Federal Government. The HF serves as a constitutional court and deals, among others, with disputes that arise between regional states, issues of self-determination, and sources and appropriation of revenue between the Federal entity and its constituent parts.

The HPR has 547 seats. According to Article 54/1 of the FDRE Constitution, its members are directly elected for a five-year term from constituencies[27] (regular and special) throughout the country. The HPR has twelve specialized committees, which largely follow the organization of the executive branch of government.[28] These committees assist the HPR in the legislative process by organizing public discussions on draft bills and follow-up how the activities of federal ministries and agencies are performed. As the majority of the seats (87.9 percent) in the current HPR are controlled by the EPRDF, it dominates all of the standing committees of the House. The HPR will be in session for about eight months beginning from October to July each year. While in secession, the HPR regularly meets in accordance with the order of business it has set (FDRE Constitution Art. 58).

Regarding procedures for endorsement of legislation, the HPR approved a legislative procedure in October 1995. This procedure lists in detail the steps to be followed when legislation is initiated and ratified. Accordingly, members of the HPR and the Council of Ministers could propose a bill. When members of the HPR propose a bill, they need to secure endorsement signatures of at least twenty members of the HPR. After first reading by the HPR, a proposed bill will be submitted to the appropriate committee. The committees review the case, and if necessary organize public discussion and present their recommendations to the HPR at one of its sessions. After deliberations are made, the HPR makes decision by voting on the bill. The role of the HPR in initiating bills by its own initiative is so far very limited. Thus, the HPR is largely confined to approving bills proposed by the Council of Ministers (the Executive). Even in approving bills proposed by the executive, the role of the HPR in modifying what has been proposed is limited.

EPRDF's dominance in the HPR and its party discipline, which requires its members of parliament to support steadfastly proposed bills of the executive without much scrutiny and debate undermine the legislature's capacity to check any excess committed by the executive. Thus, the performance of the HPR in checking the executive is generally very low. So far, no member of the Council of Ministers has been censured by the HPR, even if the executive admits rampant corruption and malpractices within the government. Lack of experience in parliamentary procedures on the part of most of its members also weakens the HPR in carrying out its tasks. This problem is further compounded by the inability of the government to provide necessary facilities such as offices, means of transportation and communication, and others for the use of the deputies.

Like other parliamentary systems, the leader of the party or a coalition of parties, which controls the majority of seats at the HPR, establishes the Federal Executive (FDRE Constitution, Art. 73/2). The Prime Minister, who is vested in the highest executive powers of the federal government, is elected from among members of the HPR. There is no any limitation on the number of terms a given individual serves as a Prime Minister. The Prime Minister appoints ministers of the Federal Government (cabinet members) with the approval of the HPR from the two houses, and from among individuals who are presumed to possess the required qualifications. Such individuals are appointed even if they are not members of the legislature (Art. 74/2). This seems to have been intended to open up the opportunity for using the expertise of individuals who may not be interested to join partisan politics.

The president, who serves as a titular head of state, is also nominated by the HPR and elected by a two-thirds majority vote of the joint session of the HPR and the HF. The tenure of the president is for six years and is limited by a maximum of two terms. Any person elected from either of the houses is required to vacate his/her seat (FDRE Constitution Art. 70). Given this, any individual aspiring to assume the position of head of state needs the support of the EPRDF owing to the latter's heavy presence in both chambers of Parliament.

The HF can be regarded as a "council of nationalities", and is in principle composed of representatives of all ethnic groups. Accordingly, it is provided in the Constitution that at least one representative will represent each ethnic group in the HF. Moreover, additional one representative will be included for each one million population of a given ethnic group seeking representation in HF (FDRE Constitution Art. 61/2). Presently, only sixty-one ethnic groups are represented in the HF. This indicates that some of the ethnic groups of the country from among the estimated eighty-five are not yet represented. According to the FDRE Constitution, councils of regional states either elect members of this house by themselves or hold elections to have the representatives elected by the people of the regions directly.

Regardless of the official and formal facades that portray the Ethiopian Legislature as an institution that came into being because of liberal reforms and attendant arrangements, one can justifiably argue that its existence and mode of operation is a function of power relations closely associated with the workings of party politics and electoral systems. As could be gathered from the presentations in the preceding chapters, the Ethiopian Parliament has consistently depicted a feature of dependence on mainstream centers of power to which it is inextricably linked. This has been the common denominator of parliaments under the three successive regimes of Emperor Haileselassie, the Dergue and the EPRDF. In all cases, political factors and considerations have undermined the role of parliaments as bodies that failed to foster mechanisms of checks and balances that are pivotal in checking and controlling the mode of operation of the executive. The only distinction that could be discerned relates to context and form within which each of the legislatures existed and operated under the three political systems in question.

One can conclude from the foregoing discussion that successive Ethiopian Legislatures have increasingly been subservient to the wielders of power, notably the political executives. This has been the hallmark of parliaments under the three regimes of the last several decades: imperial rule, military rule, EPRDF. In spite of relative improvements in some spheres under the latter, however, the role of the legislature in exercising checks and balances and undertaking oversight functions still remains lamentable. In this connection, a few examples that support this assertion could be cited.

A case in point relates to what has transpired following the rift between the top leadership of the ruling political Front (EPRDF). Some members of the faction that is opposed to the incumbent Prime Minister and his associates on issues relating to the Ethio-Eritrean Conflict a few years ago were charged with corruption offenses and apprehended. These were denied release on bail as a result of a new legislation to this effect. The executive rushed a draft bill that prohibits individuals suspected of committing corruption, which was promptly approved by HPR with immediate effect. This move contravened the universally accepted principle of law that emphasizes presumption of innocence until proven guilty. Another case that could be raised to substantiate subservience of the incumbent Ethiopian Legislature to the Executive is associated with parliamentary endorsement of the "Five Point Peace Plan" regarding Ethio-Eritrean relations, which the Executive presented to Parliament in December 2004. In less than 24 hours following the adoption of the "Peace Plan" by the Council of Ministers, HPR was hastily convened to deliberate and approve the proposal. The fact is that at least non-EPRDF members of the House received the proposal document on camera at the very time when the Prime Minister started addressing Parliament on the very issue of the Plan. Despite pleadings by some legislators to be given time to consult their constituencies on the matter, the Executive managed to get the support of the overwhelming majority (most of whom are EPRDF deputies) in getting the proposal approved.

Conclusions

The widely accepted indicators used for determining whether the entrenchment of the governance realm marks a given political system relate to such pointers as legitimacy, participation, transparency, accountability, and the rule of law. Undoubtedly, the Ethiopian political system is signified by several improvements in a wide array of fields since the early 1990s. When compared to the past, particularly the era of military dictatorship, a relatively significant betterment in socio-economic and political terms poses as the hallmark of the Ethiopian body politic of the post-1991 years. Suffice to cite the legal recognition accorded to such matters like respect for democratic and human rights and civil liberties. It is also worthy to note that periodic elections were constitutionally sanctioned as the source of regime legitimacy, and have repeatedly taken place in the last ten years. These and a number of other reform measures resulted in the proliferation of several political parties, civil society organizations, and professional societies, among others.

Notwithstanding these, however, several of the basic ingredients that could have qualified the system to be noted for entrenching the governance realm appear to be lacking still. In a number of cases, limitations emanating from a host of shortcomings have rendered democratic constitutional and other legal principles ineffective to a major degree. Incompatibilities that surfaced between official pledges/rhetoric and the vigor of actual practice increasingly undermined efforts towards inaugurating the governance realm as a way of life in Ethiopia.

The incumbent Ethiopian parliament is marked with several shortcomings that do not allow it to perform its assigned duties as listed in the Federal Constitution. Several drawbacks underpin the performance of the Ethiopian legislature. There is lack of clear definition regarding working relationships between the two chambers as well as highly limited experience and exposure on the part of legislators as regards the workings of a federal system and legislative processes and parliamentary functions. It also suffers from lack of a sense of purpose and commitment affecting the disposition of several legislators who accord primacy to party loyalty and self-interest even at the expense of the general/"national" interest.

Many parliamentarians in Ethiopia have low levels of education and work experience in the public sphere. Their impression of how a "modern" legislative organ should operate is minimal. In addition, several view their position solely as a means of earning their bread and butter and an opportunity for escaping the painstaking elements and hurdles of rural life. Given the overarching presence and considerable prowess of the ruling Front, the overwhelming majority of the deputies managed to win their seats as a result of their allegiance to the EPRDF, which firmly controls the three branches of government. The urges of political loyalty and party discipline, therefore, often induce legislators to rubber-stamp decisions and policies presented by the Executive. Evidently, during its entire tenure, the Executive faced no threat and challenge worth mentioning in getting draft laws of its preference approved. The significant under-representation of opposition parties in Parliament created a favorable condition for the Executive to bypass easily censure and scrutiny in the legislative body.

In conclusion, the Ethiopian parliament is largely a legitimizing agent of the status quo, serving the dominant party (i.e. EPRDF) operating under the shadow of a dominant executive. In the circumstances, parliament is an organ of government rather than an instrument of governance influencing and changing the course of public policy. The fact that a single dominant party controls the legislature, coupled with the absence of an effective opposition, also meant that the legislature's effectiveness in exercising its oversight responsibility over the executive is highly negligible. Prevalent state of affairs, therefore, prompts one to raise questions regarding the legislature's effectiveness in serving as a counterweight to the dominant executive and in articulating public concerns by posing as a genuine representative body.

Notes

1. Yacob 1997.
2. Perham 1948.
3. Ibid.
4. Levine 1965: 179–180.
5. Asmelash 1987: 37.
6. Clapham 1969: 9.
7. Quoted in *Ethiopia Observer* 1961: 5/2.
8. Markakis and Asmelash 1967.
9. The first election following the promulgation of the Revised Constitution took place in 1957.
10. Electoral Board, 1973, Register of the Election Process of the 5th National Electron of Deputies.
11. Yacob 1997.
12. Ibid.
13. Clapham 1969: 40.
14. Markakis 1974: 104.
15. Yacob 1997.
16. Ibid.
17. PDRE 1987.
18. Yacob 1997.
19. PDRE 1987.
20. Ibid.
21. PDRE 1987.
22. PMAC 1987.

23. Ibid.
24. Tessema and Zekarias 1997.
25. Ottaway 1995.
26. Andrias Eshete quoted by Basta-Fleiner 2000.
27. Two types of constituencies are used for electing members of the House of Peoples' Representatives. In regular constituencies, which largely follow the geographic jurisdiction of the Woreda administration, there is one constituency per 100,000 inhabitants. Special Constituencies (numbering about 22) are established for minority nationalities whose constituencies are designated as "special woredas."
28. The standing committees of the House of Peoples' Representatives include: Pastoralist Affairs; Social Affairs; Capacity Building Affairs; Information and Cultural Affairs; Women Affairs; Budget and Finance; Legal and Administrative Affairs; Rural Development Affairs; Infrastructure Affairs; Trade and Industry Affairs; and Foreign, and Security and Defense Affairs.

10

Parliament as Machinery for Political System Control: The Inner Workings of Bunge, Tanzania

Vibeke Wang

Chr. Michelsen Institute, Bergen, Norway

Introduction

Based on the assumption that Africa's democratic consolidation is better served by an autonomous and influential parliament[1] capable of holding the executive accountable, this chapter contrasts the accountability function of Tanzania's post-1990s parliament with that of the one-party Tanzanian legislature. It analyses the internal functions of the multiparty Bunge (parliament) with particular reference to the committee system and party groups' contribution to parliament's ability to perform its accountability function. Accountability here refers to a two-dimensional concept that broadly embraces both answerability—the requirement to inform, explain, and justify—and enforceability, the capacity of accounting agencies (here parliament) to impose sanctions.[2] The empirical focus is on the transition from an essentially rubber-stamp Tanzanian parliament under the 1965–1992 one-party regime to what ideally should be a strengthened parliament with the gradual and formal restructuring to democratic rule from 1992 onward.[3] More specifically, the chapter inquires into the political role of the national assembly in Tanzania and examines critically to what extent it plays a significant role in holding the executive arm of government accountable.

The parliamentary committee system and party groups are often seen as the loci of power in legislatures.[4] Party and committees are strongly linked and a common assumption is that the more important the parties are, the less important the committees, and vice versa.[5] The inner workings and structuring of parliament are significant for its ability to influence policy outcomes and also for its ability to hold the executive accountable. This is underscored by what can be taken to lie at the heart of new institutionalism, i.e. the belief that policies are shaped by the institution through which they are processed.[6] Based on a distinction several authors have made between factors located in the external and internal environment of a legislature, the anticipation is that the internal variables can reinforce the Tanzanian parliament's accountability function but not determine it.[7] Still, the internal legislative features reveal to what extent the legislature has a standalone impact on the policy process, since internal factors are presumed to affect the allocation of legislative power.

Transition from One-party State to Multiparty Democracy

Tanzania (former Tanganyika) gained its independence from British rule in 1961. Shortly after, the National Executive Committee (NEC) of the ruling party, the Tanganyika African National Union (TANU; later renamed Chama Cha Mapinduzi) decided to transform the country into a one-party state. In the years to come, the party and the government were at times indistinguishable.[8] The political powers were centralized in the executive who had an almost exclusive monopoly of power and authority.[9]

The 1977 constitutional changes in Tanzania carried over the doctrine of party supremacy that was laid down in the 1965 Interim Constitution. Parliament now found itself relegated to a simple committee of the ruling party CCM.[10] Under this provision, parliamentarians were integrated into the party structure and both collectively and individually bound to abide by party resolutions and policies. Nyerere was both the chair of the party and the president, as well as the chair of the Central Committee (CC) and the NEC–in practice, the two most powerful party organs, with the NEC as the real powerhouse.[11] Parliament had no leader to represent it in the CC of the party and neither did it have representatives in the NEC.[12] As asserted by Pinkney,[13] there was never much doubt about parliament's subordination to the ruling party in theory or in practice, describing the MPs as "below-stairs" members of the political household.

The opening up of the political and economic process began slowly in the mid-1980s. President Nyerere, who had ruled the country since independence, stepped down in 1985 and Ali Hassan Mwinyi took over. His presidency coincided with a severe economic downturn and increasing pressure from Western donors to start economic and political liberalization. Against the backdrop of this, Tanzania implemented economic reforms in 1986, and this was followed by political transformation. The national assembly on May 7, 1992 repealed the one-party clause in the constitution formally separating the ruling party CCM from the government and adopted a multiparty system on July 1. The Bunge's position in the political system was *de jure* strengthened by restoring its status as a sovereign body. Further, it was empowered to approve or disapprove the presidential appointee for the office of the prime minister; it can pass a vote of no confidence in the prime minister, and impeach the president under certain specified circumstances (1977 Constitution, Art. 51(2), 53A, 46A). Moreover, the 1977 Constitution was amended to ensure a majority of directly elected single constituency members (Art. 66(1)).

In terms of party composition of parliament, the CCM, chaired by President Mkapa, held an overwhelming majority in both the 1995 (78.1 percent of the seats) and 2000 (87.73 percent of the seats[14]) multiparty union parliaments. As Van Cranenburgh foretold, "the superior organizational, material and symbolic resources of the governing party are likely to result in the emergence of a dominant party system."[15] Most of the opposition parties lack a comprehensive political program; they are conflict ridden, centered on individuals, have a narrow social base, and are urban biased.[16] The electoral system is based on the first-past-the-post principle and contributes to reducing the number of seats the already weak opposition gets in the Bunge.[17] In the same way, President Mkapa, who is now in his second and last term of office, has won the presidential elections with a large margin.

Regime transition took place under the guidance of the CCM. This management from above has given the leadership of the ruling party the opportunity to control the process and decide the rules of the game. The result has been little commitment to ensure progress toward democratic consolidation other than holding regular multiparty elections.[18] The system still vests tremendous powers in the executive, and lacks the checks and balances that a strong parliament could provide,[19] a problem that remains one of the greatest challenges to deepened democracy in Tanzania.

The Committee System

As Shaw observes, "parliamentary committee change—in particular through structural differentiation—is happening in the First World. So, too, is change—particularly the development of parliamentary committee infrastructure—happening in the Third World."[20] Strong committees must be valued as a minimal necessary condition for effective parliamentary influence in the policy-making process. Whether they are sufficient is, however, not as evident.[21]

The Bunge comprises 13 standing committees after the introduction of multiparty politics outnumbering the eight that existed during the one-party system. Moreover, eight departmental committees were established in January 2001 to look into the government estimates. These are permanent in nature, but meet less frequently than the standing committees. As a result, the standing committee system has been extended generating more favorable conditions for parliament to act independently in the policy process.

Under the parliamentary Standing Orders, the one-party Bunge was in principle permitted to establish select committees, but Kjekshus suggests that the government's stand seemed to be that no special policy-making forum was necessary outside the strict framework of the party.[22] The use of select committees can now be seen as a real supplement to the established system of standing committees and have been formed on a number of occasions.[23] Quasi-judicial "probe" committees were established both in relation to the Organization of Islamic Conference (OIC) issue,[24] as well as in relation to cases that have ended with the resignation of ministers. While only one ministerial resignation prior to 1992 possibly (and only partly) resulted from parliamentary pressure,[25] the frequency of ministerial resignations increased in the period from 1990 to 2002. During this time-span, three ministers lost their positions and in all three cases, parliament has been at least part of the reason for the outcome of the matters. In April 1993, the tourism minister, Abubakar Yusuf Mgumia, lost his place in government due to a scandal related to the leasing of Loliondo Game Controlled Area in Ngorongoro to an army brigadier from the United Arab Emirates for exploitation as a private hunting area.[26] A parliamentary select committee investigated the deal and the sacking of the minister could be seen as a partial admittance of wrongdoing on the side of the government. Some of the reason for this admittance was parliamentary pressure. In November 1996, finance minister Simon Mbilinyi left office over tax exemptions improperly granted by junior officials.[27] A select committee was formed to look into the matter and in its report, the committee concluded that the finance minister should be held accountable for the granting of exemptions where they were not due.[28] At the time, the resignation was proclaimed as a sign of increased transparency and accountability; however, it has later been claimed that Mbilinyi who had a reputation for competence, was ousted from cabinet because of frictions within the party.[29] The most recent resignation took place in November 2001 when the minister for Industries and Trade Iddi Simba, resigned from the government the day preceding the debate of a "probe" committee report into the "Simba Sugar Scandal" involving improprieties in the issuance of licenses to companies and the registration of importers. The resignation followed intense pressure on him as well as on the government, from MPs and the public at large.[30] The day before Simba announced his resignation, it was reported that MPs from the CCM had threatened to initiate a vote of no confidence against Prime Minister Frederick Sumaye if the government failed to force Simba to resign.[31] There are, in other words, signs of the post-1992 Bunge being able to impose accountability in a few controversial cases, which has led to ministerial resignations and involved the formation of a select committee. These must be seen as politically significant cases where parliamentary undertakings have been unpopular with the government, and where the pressure exerted by parliament to a certain extent has resulted in outcomes that have been adverse to government interests. In such cases, it looks as if the Bunge has been able to impose both answerability and enforceability. The "Simba Sugar Scandal" stands out as perhaps the greatest parliamentary triumph so far. Seemingly, in cases where parliament *in combination* with other forces, for instance the media or party frictions, exerts pressure, parliament may be the last straw. It is, however, a problem that, requests for establishment of select committees are frequently turned down by the Speaker's Office. The reason given is most often lack of resources.[32]

A distinguishing characteristic of the organizational structures at the center of Tanzanian one-party politics was that it was not always clear who was responsible for what.[33] There existed comparatively more ministries than standing committees and the committee structure was not specifically set out to parallel that of the bureaucracy. As Kjekshus maintains, except for the Public Accounts Committee (PAC), the position of the committees was not clearly defined.[34] There was a crosscut of administrative structure, and thus it was not always easy to identify the different areas of responsibility of ministers, making oversight of specific policy areas largely insurmountable.

Most of the multiparty committees are organized according to policy subjects and are set out to shadow one or more government ministries. Notwithstanding they are still too few in number to replicate effectively the current 19 government ministries. The administrative structure of the state apparatus has also become more clearly defined. The civil service has been slimmed down, and there are many ongoing attempts to enhance its efficiency and its professionalism.[35]

The scope of committee jurisdiction also relies on the goodwill of the Speaker of parliament. According to the standing orders, any committee may seek the speaker's permission for additional responsibilities but the speaker is not bound to consider such requests.[36] In 1998, for instance, the speaker turned down the petition of the committee to deliberate on a case of police brutality.[37] Additionally, the standing orders bestow upon the LCAC the right to scrutinize any act contravening the constitution but can only embark on this at the request of the speaker.[38] The speaker is in this way given an enormous amount of leverage over the workings of the parliament. The current speaker, Pius Msekwa, is a CCM ex-officio, and in the capacity of this, a member of the party's National Executive Committee (NEC). Accordingly, he is subject to party directions with regard to the way he runs his office and the proceedings in parliament.[39]

Committee Composition

In terms of committee composition, the formal procedures under multipartyism are quite similar to those of the single-party parliament. As during the one-party era, the standing committee membership lasted for one year in the 1995–2000 period and the committee members were free to select their own chair once a year—a practice that led to discontinuities in parliamentary business and restricted the building of expertise.[40] The rotation of standing committee memberships has been extended to 2.5 years in the 2000–2005 parliament thus establishing more favorable, if not ideal, conditions for acquiring experience and expertise. The multiparty committee members are assigned to the committees, by the speaker in proportion to party strength, gender, region, individual preferences, and expertise.[41] This is in contrast to the widespread practice of parties determining, or at least having the upper hand in determining, the assignment of their party delegation to the committees.[42] The membership of the newly established departmental committees last for the entire tenure (five years) of parliament.

During the one-party era, the Tanzanian MPs were inhibited by lack of skills necessary to analyze government bills.[43] They lacked expertise in legislative matters to the extent that they were unable to wield influence through committee review of proposed legislation.[44] As pointed out by an administrative top official, "Members of the Finance Committee and parliament do not have the education to understand these things."[45] Mgaywa describes a number of the MPs as distressed by the highly technical language of the estimates and accounting reports.[46] The budget documents and debates were labeled as both "extremely boring" and "rather tedious" by some MPs.

The number of MPs with higher degrees has increased in recent years. Thus, the ability of MPs to subject bills to thorough scrutiny is better than during the one-party era. A high-ranking government official put it this way:

> The content of a glass of water is a reflection of where the water has been drawn. It is the electorate who choose. The result does not necessarily reflect what I would like to see. However, we have come a long way. You can see the graph going up in terms of quality. The MPs are more educated and many do have the skills of reading between the lines.[47]

Despite this improvement to the better, a lot remains to be done. The National Framework on Good Governance from 1999, for instance, recognizes that for the Bunge to perform its functions effectively, the quality of the MPs needs to improve further.

Partisanship in Committees

The prevailing legislative norms during the one-party era was that an MP should not publicly oppose a policy decision made in the NEC and that criticism or opposition to government policy should solely be expressed in party discussions or within the assembly.[48] There is no evidence of the MPs speaking more freely in the privacy of the committees, quite the opposite. Hopkins, after having interviewed three chairs, asserted that none was particularly aggressive, or saw the committee as his most important legislative task.[49] The one chair that to some extent could be seen as assertive was expelled and lost his party membership in 1968. His findings are supported by Mgaywa who asserts that party policy could only be criticized in internal party meetings, and not at all in the Bunge.[50]

The party discipline at the committee level is somewhat more relaxed after multipartyism. Control over the committees by the party leadership is less strong, and the committee members are allowed to speak more freely.[51] The speaker underlines that because the committees meet behind closed doors (in camera), they operate on a non-partisan basis ensuring "a rational examination of issues and all viable alternatives."[52] As an MP from the opposition asserts, "In the committee we look at an issue as itself . . . so the party is not so important at the committee level."[53] All the same, there is always some element of party discipline involved, also in the committees, and particularly in matters considered to be important. A CCM chair confided that "they [the committees] could be even stronger if it was not for the party provision that the party caucus can go around and tell you 'please soften up' otherwise our committees would function in a very, very effective way."[54] Mmuya substantiates this when he makes it clear that the "CCM is in control of parliamentary affairs all through, from the committee to the full parliament stage."[55] On several occasions, party caucus meetings have been called when there has been major opposition to a government bill at the committee level, so as to impose party discipline. Hence, the MPs are not freed from observing the party lines even in the committees. As was pointed out by another CCM chair, "You have three levels here. The fierce discussions at the party caucus, some discussions at the parliamentary committee level and not much in the plenary."[56] Thus, the crucial debates take place primarily within the CCM party caucus. In the Bunge, however, the most vigorous discussions now are confined largely to the committees. This also implies that the Bunge has become more committee oriented. There has been a shift away from the plenary toward the committees.

Legislative Impact

The standing committees' impact on legislative viscosity[57] was minute during the one-party era. The fact remains that legislation was seldom altered by the committees [58] and was largely dealt with on a cursory basis.[59] The committees had no power to amend legislation; they could only recommend changes to be made. Moreover, as the committees did not have any sanctions at their disposal to enforce compliance with their requests or recommendations, the result was a situation where the government's will prevailed in practically all legislative matters. Although more or less the same formal requirements apply under multipartyism, there is today a more extensive committee system and the MPs' capacity and opportunity to analyze proposed legislation has improved. The actual work in parliament now commences at the committee stage. The speaker has asserted that parliamentary committees' comments and recommendations frequently effect amendments in proposed bills.[60] His view is supported by both opposition MPs and ruling party MPs, who all conveyed relative contentment with the way the standing committees operated. Ordinarily, the impression was that the government took into account and frequently complied with the recommendations made by the committees.[61] This is a considerable improvement in light of the rather discouraging committee performance during the one-party era. Notwithstanding committee oversight is still adversely affected by a lack of institutionalized possibilities for communicating dissatisfaction with the executive in a manner that entails real political costs.[62] In addition there are problems with funding and getting bills on time.[63] Some committees are now allowed to conduct public hearings. But, as the speaker asserts,[64] because of scarce funding this is only applicable to a few selected bills of particular importance or interest and the speaker authorizes the use of the mechanism.

One should not ignore the possibility of great latent authority being exercised by parliament, but there are no indications of this being the case during the one-party era. That the government systematically abstained from introducing legislation due to resistance in the one-party Bunge is highly unlikely. The position of the NEC vis-à-vis the Bunge was far too unbalanced for this to be a reality. To quote one member of the NEC[65] when asked about whether the NEC or parliament had more influence on the way government was run: "It is hard to say. Legally, I suppose, the national assembly is, but in fact, I think the NEC. . . . If MPs are not careful, the Party can discipline them. And they'll have to recall their decisions since the Party has control over them." In addition, the one-party parliament's authority was called into question a number of times. Two instances are particularly illustrative of this. In 1982, President Nyerere imposed new tax measures in his New Year message without the formal approval of parliament.[66] Similarly, the rehabilitation of the Bank of Tanzania was embarked on without informing or seeking the obligatory prior consent of parliament.[67]

The situation under the multiparty Bunge may have changed a little bit—a slight strengthening of the latent authority can be traced. Particularly, some of the most experienced CCM MPs emphasize that there have been occasions where the government has decided not to introduce legislation, or have withdrawn legislation, because it has sensed that the opposition in parliament has been substantial. In the case of the latter, legislation is most commonly withdrawn at the committee stage, before it has reached the committee of the whole House.

In February 2003, for instance, the government shelved a bill aiming to privatize the National Microfinance Bank (NMB) while it was still being discussed in the standing committee on Finance and Economic Affairs. The withdrawal of the bill came at a time where there were clear indications that the NMB bill would have been rejected in parliament.[68] A parliamentary draftsperson refers to the Public Service Act and the Regional and Local Administration Act as other examples.[69] All of these have been enacted at a later stage in a revised form. There have also been one or two instances of bills being withdrawn in the plenary, as a result of governmental refusal to incorporate committee recommendations. The government resolution that sought to empower the Minister of Finance to write off debts, losses, and lost properties occasioned by civil servants amounting to TSh 10 billion annually is a rare example of this.[70] Such demonstrations of parliamentary strength to date are, however, still the exception rather than the rule.

The government obviously takes into consideration a potential opposition in parliament when a bill *has* been introduced. The response a bill receives at the committee stage seems to be of some importance, and, occasionally, a bill has even been withdrawn after having reached the plenary. All the same, that the government should refrain from introducing legislation, which it anticipates is going to generate opposition in the multiparty parliament on a regular basis, is not very likely. In cases which are of great importance the government imposes party discipline, and it will have its way. Even so, parliament is reckoned with, and parliamentary opposition is not taken lightly. Although the meetings of the party caucus of the ruling party to some degree are used to decide whether legislation should be introduced at all, the likelihood of *important* legislation being stopped *before* it reaches parliament is minute. From the statements made by the MPs interviewed, it is reasonable to believe that this happens only in extraordinary circumstances and no one could point to specific cases. What *is* certain is that in really important cases, the government prevails. There was a general consensus in relation to this among the MPs interviewed as well as observers of parliament.[71]

Enhanced Party Discipline in the Bunge

The one-party MPs represented the government in their constituencies rather than their constituencies in the Bunge[72]; although some of the literature puts a greater emphasis on representing the party rather than the government.[73] This constituency-oriented role was largely in accordance with official expectations, which stipulated that the predominant role of the MP was to legitimize government and party decisions in the constituency.[74] Then came the furtherance of the interests and views of his/her constituents.[75] The MPs' role perception was reinforced by the sanctions the party could apply to those MPs who were perceived to act too independently in their constituency. The NEC had the power to screen candidates for election to the national assembly and in 1967 the NEC was given the power to expel party members who, for instance, publicly uttered criticism. Expulsion from the party carried with it automatic loss of your parliamentary seat. Losing your membership of the party and your seat in the Bunge were real threats if you did not live up to the "rules of employment." This was confirmed in 1968 when seven MPs were expelled from the party and lost their seats in parliament. The expulsions came "for having grossly violated the Party creed both in their attitudes and in their actions, and for showing a very clear opposition to the party and its policies."[76] Similarly, seven MPs from Zanzibar were stripped of their party membership and also their parliamentary seats in 1988, allegedly for sabotaging the party and destabilizing the Union.[77]

The MPs could not publicly utter criticism of a policy decision made in the NEC of the party, and criticism was further limited to opposition on practical grounds and not on the principle of ideology. Hence, Tanzanian one-party MPs generally confined themselves to discussing safe, parochial issues.[78] These could, on the other hand, be discussed fiercely and "embarrassing" questions could be raised.[79] Representation, in this way, took place within the strict framework stipulated by party rules, but within this framework, the MPs had a relatively free scope.

Party discipline is still considerable under multipartyism, and may in certain respects be considered as even stronger than before. Tightened party discipline is particularly evident in voting, but also when considering the vitality of debate taking place in the plenary of the Bunge. The one-party constituency-oriented role, which was mainly based on promoting the party, has, however, largely been substituted by a local orientation centering on clientelism. The main sources of this transformation are the effects of decentralization and the liberalization of the economy. An orientation toward the district is now essential and just as important as having the right party connections and a central position within the party structures as the competitiveness of politics has become fiercer.[80] Key local politicians are increasingly found to play the role of broker in their home communities, establishing links between the groups of clients and a patron, i.e. the MP.[81] The MPs are elected at the district level where they as opposed to the situation during the one-party system and are dependent on building a solid base of local following to win the election. This has considerably altered the MPs' outlook on representation. Significantly, the NEC of the CCM can still re-rank or nullify people's preferences, but it does so in a more transparent and careful manner.[82] As the primary elections within the CCM are more open and competitive and the level of formal party funding has been scaled down, the incentive for "buying" and bribing the electorate have been strengthened. The importance of cultivating political and personal ties with the constituency is naturally also reflected in the focus of the MPs in the Bunge. At times when party discipline is somewhat relaxed, the MPs often express a local outlook. Question hour is seen as the MPs prime opportunity to prove to his/her constituents that s/he is working hard to promote their interests. When in the Bunge the MPs work is, however, most of the time marked by strong party discipline.

The Vigorousness of Debate

The debates in the plenary have dampened after the introduction of a multiparty system. There are indications that the debates in the one-party full House were vigorous and lively relative to those taking place in the multiparty assembly. When responding to a question concerning the main difference between the one-party and multiparty Bunge, a majority of the MPs, as well as other observers of parliament, noted that the debates in the one-party plenary were more vital than the multiparty debates.

An explanation is that debates are now more concealed from the public, since they, to a large extent, take place in the privacy of the committees and the party caucus (especially the CCM party caucus) instead of in the plenary. Hence, when discussions take place in the plenary, issues have often already been decided on. An additional explanation is that the MPs now also to a large extent are forced to comply with the party line on issues which earlier would have been considered of lesser importance and could have been discussed more freely. As will be seen below, strong party discipline is enforced through various channels, and the available mechanisms of sanction are considerable.

The Whip System

With the advent of a multiparty system, a whip system based on the British model was introduced to maintain discipline. Both the ruling party and the opposition have a parliamentary whip whose function is to co-ordinate the parties' activities in the Bunge and to ensure discipline among the party members.[83] The three-line whip signals that the MPs have to toe the party line. The whip system can also be lifted in certain cases, so as to allow the MPs to vote according to their conviction. It has, however, been a trend that most cases in Tanzania are considered so important by the ruling party CCM that the three-line whip is applied.

Furthermore, after the introduction of multipartyism, you have the added factor of an opposition in parliament, which has stimulated an increased feeling of having to stand together. This is despite the fact that the CCM so far has had an overwhelming majority in parliament. Higher civil servants, administrative officers in the Bunge as well as the MPs time and again underlined that one of the main tasks of the CCM MPs is to toe the party line. The speaker of parliament eagerly underscores the weight a multiparty system puts on party discipline. When elaborating on the topic, he states, "It is misleading to talk about free expression in the national assembly by the MPs."[84] A senior CCM MP puts it this way:

> Today, you have a multiparty system and now we are strictly under the guidance of the party. We are now bounded together to protect ourselves against the other political parties. There is the fear that if we do not work together, the party will be forced to collapse or the government will be forced to

collapse. So the debates are not as strong as they used to be in the past, and the voting also, you have to vote for the party all the time.[85]

This system dictates a role for the CCM MPs where the party is the center of attention when in session. The ruling party largely considers that legislation not passed is an embarrassment and a sign of weakness; thus, party discipline is imposed in most matters. The opposition is not as organized and to a greater extent allow voting according to own conviction.[86] A further moderator on the MPs' freedom to act according to their personal preference has been the extensive use of the party caucus. Not surprisingly, it is the ruling party, which draws on this forum to impose discipline.

The Party Caucus

Since 1992, the party caucuses have been held whenever there have been major policy issues in the Bunge.[87] The CCM party caucus has developed into a formidable mechanism of control. Its organization is still far superior compared to the other party groups and has been actively used on several occasions.[88] A member of the opposition maintained that:

> Whatever argument comes up, the government always calls the caucus of the ruling party. Within the caucus, they come to some kind of consensus and since whatever decision is made in the House against the government is embarrassing . . . they hide and smooth out all these things in the party committee.[89]

One of the most experienced CCM MPs expressed it like this when commenting on the controversial privatization of the state-owned national electricity company TANESCO:

> The president immediately called a party caucus and imposed party discipline. He said something like "it is I who pass your names for the next election." He used a really humiliating tone and reduced the House to rubber stamp. The CCM MPs later spoke up and said that this was unfair because we are supposed to question the government.[90]

The strength of the party caucus is closely related to the mechanisms of sanction at the party's disposal. Subilaga simply states, "The MPs' responsibility is primarily with the party."[91] The president himself has on several occasions, and recently in relation to the privatization of public enterprises in Tanzania, made it clear in meetings of the CCM party caucus that MPs opposing particular pieces of legislation in the Bunge will not be able to stand for re-election. It should also be recalled that the committee work is affected by the party discipline. Most of the CCM MPs interviewed as well as members of academia pointed to the level of party discipline as a debilitating factor, severely restraining the MPs in their work.

Crossing the Floor

According to Tanzanian electoral law, you are required to be a member of a political party to stand for election (and to become a minister). Hence, independent candidates are banned—a situation applying to both the multiparty and the one-party systems. Because of this, the MPs cannot remain independent in parliament, and neither is it possible for them to cross the floor. This provides the parties with an effective disciplinary mechanism. Expulsion from the party in practice means that you have to resign your parliamentary seat and, for many, would equal losing one's livelihood. Since there is a lot at stake for an MP, the incentive for acting according to the party line is strong. The remuneration of MPs is relatively generous with attractive fringe benefits. It has been suggested that the executive "buys" the MPs, including the opposition. For instance, loans for expensive cars to all the MPs, irrespective of party, may have functioned to ensure the MPs' loyalty.[92] Regardless of the effect of the latter, the outcome is that, as asserted by a CCM MP, "you get MPs and ministers that are easily disciplined by the party and its chairman."[93]

Conclusion

On the whole, the material presented in this chapter shows that a positive development may be traced when examining the committee system. The one-party committee system was of both lower quality and function than the current system. Under multipartyism, the committee system has been revised and it has become more specialized and elaborate. In combination with an overall increase in the MPs' skills the Bunge's ability to influence the legislative process has been enhanced and a slight improvement in the Bunge's accountability function has taken place. Despite considerable obstacles like lack of enforcement mechanisms, the MPs expressed relative contentment with the workings of the committee system. Notwithstanding this apparent change to the better, there is especially one core weakness to point to, which largely contributes to dampen down the potential benefits of the perked up committee arrangement and its workings—the functioning of the CCM party caucus.

The relative strengthening of the committees in the Bunge has been paralleled by an increase in the ruling party discipline. In particular, party discipline has been restrained after the first general multiparty elections in 1995. The CCM party group organization is well institutionalized with a well-functioning party whip. This, in combination with the ban on crossing the floor in the Bunge, and the possibility the parties have to expel members, effectively discipline the MPs into adhering to the party line. The executive is able to control and influence the behavior of its backbenchers significantly. In the present Bunge, the party delegate role is dominant in as good as all matters of any importance, while the role of the locally oriented patron is habitually played on other occasions. In accordance with the rule stipulating that party discipline and legislative viscosity are opposites, this tightened party discipline clearly hampers the degree of accountability exercised, and considerably limits the effect of the strengthened committee system.

Notes

1. Representative assemblies are designated by various names. The most common are parliament, legislature and national assembly. Here, these concepts will be used interchangeably without drawing a sharp distinction between them. They will all be used as synonyms with the legislative branch of government.
2. Schedler 1999: 14–16.
3. This chapter is mainly based on data collected during fieldwork in Tanzania (Dar es Salaam and Dodoma) in the period from 1 July to mid-September 2002. Altogether, 35 personal interviews were carried out with MPs, government representatives, members of civil society, the judiciary, academics, and bureaucrats.
4. Strøm 1995: 67.
5. Olson 1980; Shaw 1979.
6. Döring 1995: 15.
7. Authors like Norton (1998), Norton and Ahmed (1999), and Norton and Olson (1996) hypothesize that external conditions (e.g. legal framework, party and electoral system, external agents, political culture, legitimacy, and the judiciary) determine the basic relationship of the legislature to the executive, while internal variables can reinforce this capacity but not determine it. Variables in the internal environment, in other words, determine whether the legislature is strong or weak within the confines set by the external environment. While it is impossible to draw a clear-cut divide between external and internal variables, this distinction serves as a tentative guideline and a useful means of comparison.
8. Tripp 2000: 197; Baregu 1994: 165.
9. Hyden 1994: 94; Okema 1990: 37–38.
10. Okema 1990: 51; 1997 Constitution, Section 54.

11. Msekwa 1997: 16.
12. Mihyo 1994: 47.
13. Pinkney 1997: 24.
14. In the 2000–2003 parliamentary period, there were 22 vacant seats (Tanzania Parliament 2002: 11), most of them belonging to Zanzibar-elected Civic United Front (CUF) members who boycotted parliament due to the election irregularities in Zanzibar. By-elections took place in May 2003, and CUF won all 15 seats contested for the union parliament. These numbers are based on the actual parliamentary composition in 2000, and are therefore slightly misleading, especially with respect to CUF.
15. Van Cranenburgh 1996: 545.
16. Ewald 2002: 10; Mmuya 1998: 11–40.
17. See Ewald 2002.
18. Tripp 2000: 193, 198; Hyden 1999: 146–147.
19. Ewald 2002: 5; Tripp 2000: 198.
20. Shaw 1998: 247.
21. Strøm 1998: 47; Mattson and Strøm 1995: 250.
22. Kjekshus 1974a: 29.
23. Kelsall 2003.
24. The OIC issue involved a motion to establish a parliamentary constitutional committee to probe into a potential violation of the 1977 Union Constitution when the Zanzibar government decided to join the OIC (Msekwa 1995: 23; Mwakyembe 1995: 189).
25. In 1983, the minister of home affairs, Abdallah Natepe, resigned after being called on by parliament to bear responsibility for the escape from prison of two people involved in an attempted coup (Van Donge and Livigia 1986: 624).
26. EIU 1993: 10.
27. Kabakama 1997: 24; Mmuya 1998: 77.
28. EIU 1996: 10.
29. Kelsall 2002: 606.
30. EIU 2001: 17.
31. Ibid., 18.
32. Interviews Tanzania 2002.
33. Van Donge and Liviga 1986: 633; Kjekshus 1972; 353.
34. Kjekshus 1974a: 21.
35. Kelsall 2002: 599; Harrison 2001: 662; Therkildsen 2000: 62.
36. Bunge News 1999.
37. Janguo 1999: 18; Biddle et al. 2002: 22.
38. Janguo 1999: 18; Subilaga 2001: 23.
39. Mmuya 1998: 80.
40. Hopkins 1971: 148; Interviews Tanzania 2002.
41. Subilaga 2001: 19–20.
42. Damgaard 1995: 314.
43. Mihyo 1994: 54; Hopkins 1971: 165.
44. Hopkins 1971: 165.
45. Cited in Mukandala 1994: 12.

46. Mgaywa 1990: 130.
47. Interview Tanzania.
48. Hopkins 1971: 191.
49. Ibid., 148–149.
50. Mgaywa 1990: 116.
51. Subilaga 2001: 25.
52. Msekwa 2000: 95.
53. Interview Tanzania.
54. Ibid.
55. Mmuya 1998: 118.
56. Interview Tanzania.
57. The concept of "viscosity" was developed by Blondel and his associates (1969–1970) and refers to the capacity of the legislature to resist legislation initiated by the executive.
58. Hopkins 1971: 154.
59. Msekwa 1977: 38.
60. See Biddle et al. 2002: 22.
61. Interview Tanzania.
62. Rutashobya 2004.
63. Biddle et al. 2002.
64. Msekwa 2000b: 6.
65. Cited in Hopkins 1970: 769.
66. Mwakyembe 1995: 22.
67. Mgaywa 1990: 96.
68. *The Guardian* Feb. 14, 2003.
69. Interview Tazania.
70. *Daliy News* Aug. 2, 2002; *EastAfrican* Aug. 5, 2002.
71. Interview Tanzania 2002.
72. Pinkney 1997: 124.
73. See Okema 1990.
74. See also Kjekshus 1974b: 81; Barkan 1979: 75.
75. Hopkins 1971: 162.
76. Citation from the Nationalist in Msekwa 1995: 14.
77. Mgaywa 1990: 114.
78. Pinkney 1997: 123.
79. Tordoff 1997: 238, 243.
80. Observers have argued that with the retreat of the state the spoils character of the Tanzanian political elite has escalated. Economic liberalization has increased the elite's incentive for self-enrichment (Kelsall 2002: 608) and has accelerated a formalization of politics and a de-classing of the elite (Gibbon 2001: 842; 1998: 49; Kelsall 2002: 610–611; 2000: 549). Those members of the elite who did not manage to position themselves strategically with the advent of economic liberalization were retrenched and often ended up in their old villages where they started various businesses or retired. This has also led to political patronage asserting itself in various ways. Kelsall (2000: 550) maintains that the search for new sources of wealth is discernible in struggles for control of

local non-state institutions, which provides access to considerable resources. Alongside the increased flow of donor resources at this level, the districts have emerged as the crucial centers in which the MPs need to seek support.
81. See Kiondo 1994: 77; Kelsall 2000: 550; 2002: 611; Gibbon 1998: 49.
82. Biddle et al. 2002: 19.
83. Mmuya 1998: 119.
84. Msekwa 2000: 117.
85. Interview Tanzania.
86. Ibid.
87. Mtei 2000: 7.
88. Mmuya 1998: 41–63, 131.
89. Interview Tanzania.
90. Ibid.
91. Subilaga 2001: 41.
92. Mmuya 1998: 131.
93. Interview Makwetta July 22, 2002.

11

A Decade of Legislature–Executive Squabble in Malawi, 1994–2004

Boniface Dulani

Political and Administrative Studies, University of Malawi, Zomba, Malawi

Jan Kees van Donge

Institute of Social Studies, The Hague (Netherlands)

Introduction

Malawian case gives reason to qualify common beliefs that multipartyism and democratization have toughened the surface of African politics. Contrary to common views which portray African politics as consisting of not more than patron–client relations[1] or that whatever the outward form, the roots of the system remain the same and these will flow in new environments,[2] our account of parliament in Malawi after the democratization process shows that the form of state is relevant. The opportunity to resist arbitrary extension of presidential power was exploited by parliament, judiciary, and civil society. Arguably, in this case, politics cannot be reduced to a cynical game for state resources embedded in patron–client relationships.

Parliament and Presidency Relationship in Multiparty Malawi

The introduction of multiparty rule in 1994 marked an important watershed in Malawi's political development. The adoption of a new Constitution in 1994 sought to redefine the way the three branches of government operated. The new Constitution in 1994 redefined the relations between executive, legislative, and the judiciary in sections 7, 8, and 9 as separate, followed officially by a constitutional conference in 1995 that did not result in a new constitution. The most contentious issue at this conference was, however, the power of the president. The president is defined as head of state and commander in chief of the defense forces. However, at the constitutional conference it was strongly argued that the president should have only residual powers: that which is left over after legislative and judicial functions have been taken care of by the other branches.[3] In practice, the model of the American constitution was followed: checks and balances is the main concern.

Despite many pleas for an upper chamber, Malawi has retained a single-chamber parliament. According to section 48(1) of the Malawi Constitution that came into force in 1994, all legislative powers of the republic are vested in a parliament, which consists of a national assembly of 193 parliamentarians, representing 193 constituencies. Members of Parliament are elected for a period of five years. They represent geographical constituencies and are elected by a simple majority using the first-past-the-post electoral system. Section 8 of the 1994 Constitution implores parliament to "reflect in its deliberations the interests of all the people of Malawi" and thus to rise above party political considerations.

Parliamentary sessions are presided over by a speaker, who is elected by a majority vote of the chamber at the first sitting of parliament. Otherwise, parliament is empowered by the Constitution to regulate its own business, which is done through parliamentary standing orders. Decisions of the house are decided by a simple majority of the "votes of the members present at the time of voting." Constitutional amendment bills, however, require the support of at least two-thirds support to be effected.

Functions and powers of the national assembly are specified in section 66 of the Constitution. Besides the power to pass laws that have primacy over other forms of law, other functions of parliament include:

- receiving, amending, accepting, or rejecting government bills and private bills;
- initiating private members' bills on the motion of any member and amend, accept, or reject all private member's bills;
- conducting investigations and exercising the power to subpoena the attendance of any person or office holder required in connection with the exercise of parliamentary business.
- debating and voting on motions in relation to any matter, including motions to indict and convict the President or Vice-President by impeachment.

The Malawian national assembly has also the power of the purse: government needs to pass the budget as a law through parliament in order to be allowed to spend.

The mandate of parliament in Malawi comprises also of an oversight on administrative action and the day-to-day running of government. Parliamentary committees composed of members drawn from all the political parties represented in the national assembly are the main instruments for this. In all, there are a total of thirteen parliamentary committees, namely:

- public appointments committee
- budget and finance committee
- legal affairs
- defence and security
- public accounts
- agriculture and natural resources
- education, science, and human resources
- health and population
- commerce, industry, and tourism
- social and community services
- media and communications
- transport and public works
- international relations.

The two democratic parliaments have not distinguished themselves in legislative initiatives or penetrating oversight of the executive. It is only the public accounts committee that has developed a profile in this respect. However, resistance against encroaching presidential power has been a persistent theme in the past ten years. During the second parliament, this crystallized in the resistance to a constitutional amendment that would allow the president to stand for a third term. That resistance, in conjunction with the judiciary and public opinion, demonstrates a clear break in Malawi's political culture, which is the main theme of this chapter.

The 1994–1999 Parliament[4]

The Malawian transition to democracy in the period 1992–1994 was a success. Despite the fact that Malawi had been a very authoritarian regime for 30 years, the president for life, Kamuzu Banda, the MCP, accepted the referendum results rejecting the continuation of single party rule in 1993. The run up to the first multiparty elections in 1994 was without incident.

However, the vote was primarily determined by regional affiliation. The northern region of Malawi was loyal to the Alliance for Democracy (AforD) and their presidential candidate, Chakufwa Chihana. The central region supported Kamuzu Banda and the MCP, while the southern region backed the victorious president, Bakili Muluzi and the United Democratic Front (UDF). The reason for the victory of the UDF was in their regional allegiance: the southern region has a much bigger population than the other regions. However, that did not translate into absolute majority of seats: UDF had 85 seats compared to 56 for MCP and 36 for AforD.

Coalitions

There was a pressing need for Muluzi to form a coalition government, but this was thwarted. Toward the end of the election campaign, there was a rapprochement between MCP and AforD. Immediately after the election in June 1994, this was cemented into an alliance between the two parties. This did not, however, last long and AforD switched to a governmental coalition with UDF in September 1994. This necessitated the first extra-legal move, because Chakufwa Chihana insisted on the post of vice-president, which was not provided for in the Constitution. Chihana's appointment required an amendment to the Constitution to provide for a new post of second vice-president. Aided by support from the AforD MPs, the government was able to acquire the necessary majority in parliament to get the amendment.

However, AforD's decision to enter into a coalition with the UDF proved very unpopular with its supporters, who had not been consulted. As a result, a number of AforD parliamentarians insisted on their independence and refused to follow a UDF/AforD party whip. However, it came as a shock that AforD lost to the MCP in a by-election in Mzimba East in December 1995 where the party had won with 88.5 percent of the vote in 1994. AforD's hold on the North seemed, until then, unbreakable. Chihana reacted with a speech in Karonga at Christmas where he accused the UDF of monopolizing positions and resources in the southern region. More generally, Chihana argued that UDF rule had resulted in a situation where the rich were enriching themselves while life for the ordinary masses became unbearable. Despite many attempts at reconciliation, the relations between the two parties deteriorated further. Contrary to agreements made, AforD fielded their own candidates in areas where UDF was strong during by-elections. In April 1996, Chihana left the coalition officially.

However, the AforD members who had accepted cabinet seats in the UDF/AforD cabinet refused to follow their leader out of the coalition. This proved to be the beginning of a long legal battle. The Constitution stipulated that parliamentarians who changed party affiliation had to face a by-election. They could only switch parties if they renewed their mandates in by-elections. The rationale for that was to prevent opposition parliamentarians being bought by the ruling party. The simple solution was for the AforD ministers to face a series of by-elections, but this risk was never taken during the cabinet period. Instead, government faced protracted litigation on this issue in court. This litigation was fought along two lines. First, Chihana and the AforD backbenchers challenged the ministers' AforD membership. The party argued that the ministers were expelled because they had not followed the party whip. The ministers, on their part, argued that they had never left the party and therefore did not have to face a by-election. They were made independents by the party, but they had not crossed the floor, in their opinion. Second, the authority of the speaker of parliament was challenged. The speaker had to rule that the ministers had changed parties and needed to stand for a by-election. The speaker, Rodwell Munyenyembe, was chairman of AforD and sided with the ministers. Apart from the speaker who does not cast a vote, eight AforD parliamentarians, including the ministers, continued in the coalition. Therefore, Muluzi relied on a majority made up of UDF MPs and the AforD rebels.[5]

Boycott

The majority that Muluzi could count on fluctuated due to frequent deaths among Malawian parliamentarians.[6] They could not muster the quorum of two-thirds that the Constitution required for parliament to transact business. This gave the opposition the possibility to paralyze parliamentary proceedings. When the coalition broke and the AforD rebels were allowed to continue in their seats and ministerial positions, the official AforD decided to boycott parliament. MCP followed it in protest against the passage of a law that gave the government control over press trust. This trust was the owner of Press Corporation, a conglomerate of enterprises that were in the name of Kamuzu Banda as principal trustee.[7] It was therefore a main source of party finance for MCP.

The UDF government and especially its minister of finance Aleke Banda tried to get control over this business, arguing that Press Corporation could only grow to its present size because of government support. It seemed at first possible that it would fall into the hands of government through bypassing the checks and balances of the separation of powers. The director of public prosecutions, at the behest of the attorney general, prosecuted, among others, Kamuzu Banda for the murder of four of their colleagues near Mwanza in 1983 in order to have Kamuzu declared no longer in control of his faculties. That would have made government the guardian of his possessions. This attempt failed, as medical experts did not conclude that Kamuzu Banda was not of sound mind. The press case lasted through 1995 and it became increasingly clear that the prosecution would lose. That is the background against which Aleke Banda announced, in December 1995, that there had been massive fraud in Press Corporation and asked the police to prosecute. The police found, however, no reason to prepare a charge for committed crimes. Thereafter, Aleke Banda rushed through parliament a bill to nationalize Press without compensation. He did not observe the prescribed minimum 21 days' notice between tabling and discussing a bill. The bill could also not be tabled, as there had been no quorum at the beginning of the session because of the boycott. UDF had at that moment 84 seats and could count on eight votes from AforD rebels. It needed 118 members of parliament for a quorum.

It is significant that MCP took recourse to the courts and not Kamuzu Banda as owner of Press Corporation. The ownership of press trust was important, but not the essence of the case. Because of its political nature, the court cases surrounding Press Corporation had a direct bearing on constitutional law. MCP challenged the bill on two grounds: the prescribed period of notification was not adhered to and there was no quorum. Government argued in its defense that the speaker as guardian of parliamentary rules had allowed the bill to proceed. They argued as well that the constitution provided for a quorum at the beginning of a parliamentary session, but not at a normal sitting as the one in which the press bill was presented. The judgment of the high court, Judge Dunstain Mwaungulu, in July 1995, came as a surprise as he found in favor of MCP. He interpreted the spirit more than the text of the law and concluded that it cannot have been the purpose of the framers of the constitution to let bills pass without a quorum being present: "It could not have been in the mind of the framers of the constitution that any number of parliamentarians could bind the nation." If one insists that only a quorum is needed at the beginning of a session, then it is a provision without force: the loopholes are obvious. He also judged the bill unconstitutional as the right to property is enshrined in it. Expropriation of property is only possible for public utility and only when there is adequate compensation as well as provision for the owners to appeal to a court of law. The purpose of that was to prevent confiscation of property on political grounds, as had been common under one-party rule. The constitution takes precedence over any ruling of parliament. The speaker's decisions are therefore invalid if in conflict with the constitution. Mwaungulu was able to establish clearly the prerogative of the judiciary over parliament. The judiciary also enforced its decision when government did not want to follow the ruling. Mwaungulu ordered the government to return the property of press trust.

Government appealed to the supreme court. It was not a surprise that they found in favor of the government since Muluzi had appointed a number of new judges. They interpreted the constitution narrowly and considered a quorum at the beginning of each session sufficient. They also found that government could overrule the constitution following a doctrine of necessity in the national interest. They found cases in support from Cyprus, Pakistan, Canada, the United States (during the Second World War), and Rhodesia (during UDI). These governments found themselves faced with hostile and chaotic situations that necessitated such powers. This was of course reasoning that could have momentous consequences as it gave a free hand to the executive. Of direct constitutional relevance was their finding that parliament makes its own rules and elects its own speaker. Parliament was in their view the supreme law-making body and its internal rules are not subject to judicial review.

There were some cases initiated challenging the ruling on procedural grounds, but the case petered out. The boycott in parliament also ended in April 1996 through mediation of a catholic bishop. The president promised a review of the Constitution that would prevent situations as with the AforD ministers from emerging. In the words of MCP's Hetherwick Ntaba, "A constitutional amendment [will end] political horse-trading and chicanery in parliament." An important additional reason was that the boycotting parliamentarians were cut off from funding for sitting allowances, etc. Lastly, the boycott never had much popular appeal. On the contrary, there was a widespread feeling that parliamentarians were not doing the job they were supposed to do. The boycott also ended before the new financial year and paralysis of government was avoided. Parliament has in Malawi the power of the purse and without parliamentary approval there is no valid budget.

Parliamentarians Crossing the Floor

When the UDF/AforD coalition broke up, eight AforD MPs, among whom were ministers, stayed in the coalition. The UDF government was dependent upon the AforD rebels and it was attractive to break this dependency and have an absolute UDF majority. Government enticed MCP parliamentarians to cross the floor and was sometimes successful. One example was Chakakala Chaziya. He was MP in the MCP heartland, Lilongwe West, and spent considerable amounts of money on his campaign. Nevertheless, the area remained solid MCP. Another case was in Nsanje South in the lower shire where Gwanda Chakuamba, then vice chairman of MCP, comes from. There were many accusations of irregularities there. These resulted in complaints to the electoral commission. They saw no reason to postpone the election. MCP then turned to the courts who ordered a delay on a purely procedural ground: the electoral commission had not communicated promptly. The electoral commission had also heard only one person, Chief Tengani, and he is reputed to be pro UDF. The parliamentarian in question, Simeon Khamfula, retained his seat as a UDF candidate when the election was finally held in May 1997. Between 1994 and 1998, for example, 23 by-elections were held. These did not result in any major changes in party allegiance; only in three cases—one in the north, one in the center, and one in the south, was there a change in party allegiance.

Violence at By-Elections

The role of the electoral commission has been mentioned several times thus far. There were many complaints surrounding the by-elections and the electoral commission was seldom receptive to them. Only in one case did they order a new election. Cassim Chilumpha campaigned in Nkhotakota central for a seat that had fallen vacant because of the death of an MCP member of parliament. He had been seen distributing soft drinks and buns to voters waiting in line. The puzzling aspect of the case was that he won with a great majority in both instances. There seemed to be no need for irregularities. Later in the parliamentary term, the conflicts became more serious. During an MCP campaign meeting in Chiradzulu in 1997, troublemakers came running on the scene setting fire to a Land Rover and the public address system. The troublemakers wore patches with the portrait of Kamuzu Banda and identified themselves as MCP. No prosecution by police or any action of the Electoral Commission followed.

The most serious case was the by-election in Blantyre central in the Ndirande area in early 1997. The Ndirande area is a volatile political arena that had also been important at the onset of the campaign for multipartyism in 1992. It was seen as a kind of referendum on the performance of the UDF government. All three parties fielded candidates. The first instance of violence was during an AforD rally. Again, troublemakers claiming to be young AforD disturbed the meeting. This was followed by arson: the house of the MCP candidate was burnt down. The MCP candidate withdrew. A new MCP candidate was found, but this one again withdrew a few days before the election. The constituency leadership of MCP went into conclave to find another candidate. There they were arrested and locked up on the charge of meeting to disturb the peace. UDF won the seat with a large majority: 4,002 votes against 135 votes for the other candidates. MCP did not field a candidate. The arrested MCP leadership was later acquitted before the magistrate's court. A taxi driver testified later that he had brought the last MCP candidate who withdrew to the house of the chairman of the electoral commission, Justice Msosa.

In many of these instances, aggrieved parties sought recourse against the Electoral Commission to the judiciary. The courts gave some opinions in the beginning, but later the judiciary refused to have anything to do with these cases.

Legal Election Rigging!

In elections of 1999, the government resorted again to heavy-handed manipulation in order to guarantee victory at the polls. The electoral commission proposed to increase the number of constituencies by 70. Under the proposal, the number of seats in the north was to be increased from 33 to 46, in the center from 68 to 85, and in the south from 76 to 118. The southern region had, proportionally to its population, the lowest number of seats and therefore would get the biggest increase. This rationale of the increase was to balance better the population in the various constituencies. The ruling party's stronghold was in the southern region. In an acrimonious parliamentary debate, the increase was scaled down from 70 to 17 seats. Pressure from within the donor community, who financed the elections to a large extent, may have played a major role in that. In the end, a compromise was reached which increased the number of constituencies by 17 (1 for the north, 5 for the center, and 11 for the south). This effectively meant an increase in the number of parliamentary seats from the original 177 to 194. This attempt at gerrymandering did not lead to a change in the ratios between party victories: UDF gained in the south five of the new seats, three went to independents, and three to MCP.

The 1999–2004 Parliament

The 1999 elections seemed to bring a small but decisive shift in the political constellation of president and parliament. Bakili Muluzi retained the presidency against a combined ticket of MCP and AforD. His UDF party won 93 out of the 192 parliamentary seats that had been contested. The MCP increased the number of its MPs from 56 to 66, whilst the number of AforD MPs went down from 36 in the 1994 parliament to 29. For the first time, four candidates were elected on an independent ticket.[8] There was, however, little change in the regional distribution of support. Muluzi got 75.5 percent of his votes from the most populous southern region, from where 78 of the UDF's MPs came. Nevertheless, Muluzi obtained an absolute majority (51.4 percent) in the presidential elections. The UDF also had a very slim absolute majority if the four independents are added to it (97 out of 192 seats).[9] The way was open for a harmonious relationship where the president could rely on a parliamentary majority.

That did not happen and the relations between executive and parliament were often acrimonious in the period 1999–2004. As during the first parliament, this did not center on development policies or substantial legislation, but on constitutional issues. One issue was more important than any other: the presidency itself. A Constitutional provision[10] limits the presidential tenure of office to a maximum of two consecutive terms. The term 1999–2004 was therefore the last one allowed for Muluzi. Political life in that period was dominated by proposals to parliament to make it possible for Muluzi to stand again. The first proposed constitutional amendment was for a removal of the restriction to allow for unlimited tenure while a second proposal sought to increase the minimum presidential tenure of office from a maximum of two to three terms.

The Struggle for a Majority within UDF

The call for Muluzi's third term was first heard at UDF party rallies a few months before the 1999 general elections. Muluzi himself, during his swearing-in ceremony after the 1999 elections, made a passing reference to his desire for an extension to his tenure, when he said that he has "another 26 years to rule the country." [11](This call was later echoed by other UDF leaders, including Dumbo Lemani, one of the UDF's most influential members, who stated that "two-thirds or no two-thirds, the Constitution will be amended to pave the way to a third term for Muluzi."[12]) From then on, UDF factionaries went out to campaign for the extension of Muluzi's tenure of Office. They were given wide platforms to make their case at presidential rallies. In one such rally in August 2001, UDF southern regional governor, Davis Kapito, indicated that "all the country's 27 districts had agreed that Muluzi would have to stand again in the 2004 presidential elections and that the UDF would push for a Constitutional amendment in Parliament to make this possible."[13]

The last announcement came in the wake of an official denial by UDF of an allegation by one of its leaders, Brown Mpinganjira, that UDF was looking for an extension of Muluzi's term of office. Muluzi himself never formally acknowledged the campaign. It was portrayed as a spontaneous movement from below. The official UDF line became that the party had made no decision on Muluzi's tenure.[14]

The first bill proposing a constitutional amendment was a private member's bill proposed by an AforD MP. Only the second one was proposed by UDF as a party. This ambiguity is understandable, as potential successors to Muluzi would not have liked the bid for a third term. It is not surprising that three of the candidates within the UDF that were perceived as potential successors came into conflict with him. These were Brown Mpinganjira and Cassim Chilumpha, both founder members of the UDF, and Professor Matthews Chikaonda, who had been brought into the Cabinet in 1999 as finance minister. All three were dropped from Muluzi's Cabinet in early 2000. Whilst Chilumpha's and Chikaonda's dismissals did not necessarily cause major upheavals within the UDF ranks, Mpinganjira's did. He immediately went ahead to form a pressure group, the National Democratic Alliance (NDA) to fight against the extension to Muluzi's tenure of office. Six UDF MPs [15] joined Mpinganjira in the NDA. NDA was presented as a group campaigning within UDF, but it is not surprising that the UDF leadership did not accept that and Mpinganjira and his NDA colleagues were expelled.

Wooing of Opposition to Create a Majority

Muluzi needed to win the struggle for a third term within UDF, but that was not sufficient. A Constitutional amendment needs a two-thirds majority, 128 votes, to pass parliament. If all UDF parliamentarians including the independents (97 votes) would support Muluzi, then the amendment would need an additional 31 votes from the opposition.

The internal dissent within MCP offered an opportunity to woo support. MCP vice-president John Tembo had bitterly lost the leadership contest to Gwanda Chakuamba. The feeling of humiliation was reinforced in the campaign for the state presidency during which Tembo had to take a backseat in Chakuamba's campaign in comparison to the AforD's president, Chihana.

It is not surprising that Muluzi started courting John Tembo's support in the run-up to the 1999 elections. The informal alliance of the UDF and the Tembo faction of the MCP became manifest in Tembo's selection as leader of the opposition in parliament in mid-2000. This came after the UDF had successfully moved a motion to have Tembo's main rival, Gwanda Chakuamba, suspended from parliament for a year. In return for government support in his elevation to leader of opposition in parliament,

John Tembo was expected to boost government's support to give it the necessary two-thirds majority to amend the constitution.[16]

It seemed as if the other main opposition party—AforD—would willingly support the government in a bid for influence. The Alliance between AforD and MCP was formally dissolved on February 8, 2002 after the legal challenge to the election results proved unsuccessful.[17] Immediately after this formal dissolution, AforD leaders resolved to work with the UDF a second time. The UDF alliance with AforD climaxed on April 9, 2003, when Muluzi brought AforD president, Chakufwa Chihana and four other AforD MPs into his cabinet. In addition to his ministerial post, Chihana was given back the post of second vice-president, which he had previously dumped in 1996.

Chakufwa Chihana became one of the most vocal supporters of the Constitutional amendment bid. This led to a split in the party. An AforD party convention in early 2002 had urged its MPs not to support any amendments aimed at extending Muluzi's tenure of office. This led to a split within the AforD parliamentary faction. Some MPs followed Chihana. As mentioned above, the first bid to change the Constitution regarding the open term's motion was actually moved in parliament by an AforD parliamentarian, Khwauli Msiska. Another prominent AforD MP, Green Mwamondwe, accused his leader of accepting money as an inducement to support the bill.[18] About half of AforD's MPs openly broke ranks with their party leadership and voted against both the open terms and third term bills.

Seeking Majority through Legal Changes

The second prong of the UDF campaign involved legal changes that sought to weaken opposition to the third-term bid. The first of such strategies is the unsuccessful attempt to increase the number of parliamentary seats that was already referred to earlier in this chapter. Following the failure of this strategy, the UDF made a proposal in early 2001 that sought to empower the president to appoint up to 20 Members of Parliament. This would have strengthened the president's hand, as the loyalty of these nominated members would most likely have been to the president who appointed them. Thus, on crucial issues such as the amendment to extend the presidential tenure of office, there was a higher probability that these 20 MPs would side with the government.

However, when the proposal was discussed in parliament, it did not garner the necessary support from MPs. With a higher likelihood of defeat, the ruling party was forced to shelve the idea before it was voted on.[19]

Creating Majorities by Changing the Rules of the Game

Reduction of Quorum

In the first parliamentary period, it appeared that a boycott by the opposition was an effective way to paralyze parliament, as it did not allow the necessary quorum to be there to start proceedings. Section 50 of the Constitution provides that a two-thirds majority of the Members of Parliament be required to form a quorum. It allowed an opportunity to block the Constitutional amendment allowing Muluzi a third term. It is not surprising that the UDF moved for a motion in May 2001 for an amendment. The government proposed that the quorum be reduced to one-third of the members. A section of the opposition saw this clearly as part of the strategy to get a third term: "as a way of trying to clear the way for Muluzi to stand again."[20]

The proposal was later modified and passed on November 6, 2001 to provide for 50 percent +1 as the required quorum.[21] This received almost total support of the members in the house (146 out of 148 present). It nevertheless effectively blocked this path of opposition.

Amendment of Section 65 (1) of the Constitution

During the first parliament, government had exercised influence in parliament particularly through the speaker. It was backed by the supreme court judgment in the press trust case. The speaker used his influence to instill party discipline in the ruling party and to safeguard the parliamentary majority in the case of AforD. The Constitution could be interpreted much more narrowly as it mentioned only defection to parties already represented in parliament.

This issue became salient when a number of UDF MPs who had broken ranks with their party to oppose the third-term bid had formed the National Democratic Alliance (NDA). NDA was considered a pressure group and not a political party. Officially, they still claimed allegiance to UDF. Although dismissed from the UDF, these MPs were still able to remain in the house as independent MPs on the opposition benches.

The powers of the speaker were laid down in section 65(1) of the Constitution and it remained possible that either the speaker or the judiciary would interpret this section narrowly. Government therefore tabled a bill to amend section 65(1) on June 13, 2001. This was subsequently passed as the Constitution (Amendment) (No.2) Act of 2001 and sought to widen the powers of the speaker to read as follows:

> The Speaker shall declare vacant the seat of any Member of the National Assembly who was, at the time of his or her election, a member of a political party represented in the National Assembly, other than by that member alone but who has voluntarily ceased to be a member of that party or has joined another political party or association or organization whose objectives or activities are political in nature.

The obvious danger for freedom of speech was in the last sentence. In effect, it gave a whip to the speaker to decide whether oppositional activity was allowed or not.

The Amendment Bill was presented for a vote on June 19, 2001. From 192 MPs that were entitled to vote, 131 MPs—all UDF legislators, plus MPs that were loyal to John Tembo[22] faction, voted yes. Thirty-nine MPs—AforD and MCP Chakuamba faction, voted against the bill, while a further four abstained. Aided by Tembo's support, the voting gave the bill the required two-thirds majority and was enacted into law.[23]

The bill was opposed by those MPs from MCP and AforD who did not support the alliance with UDF. They argued that the amendment was deliberately designed to enable government to get rid of dissenting voices in parliament. Immediately after the bill's passage, the UDF wrote to the speaker to declare vacant the seats of seven MPs—NDA's Brown Mpinganjira and his wife Lizzie, James Makhumula, Peter Tchupa, Greshan Naura, and MCPs Gwanda Chakuamba and Hetherwick Ntaba. After a lengthy debate, the seven were expelled on November 7, 2001. Other MPs to fall victim to the amended section 65 included former UDF MPs, Jan Jaap Sonke and Joe Manduwa, who were expelled in October 2001. These two were expelled for having joined the forum for the defense of the Constitution, an umbrella grouping of civil society, religious leaders, and politicians, which opposed the attempts to amend the Constitution to allow for an open and third-term presidential tenure of office. Other victims of the section were former AforD MPs who had broken ranks with their party to form the breakaway Movement for Genuine Democratic Change (MGODE).

Resistance from Civil Society and the Courts against Muluzi's Hegemony

It was obvious that the amendment was selectively targeted at those in opposition and UDF MPs who fall out of grace with their party. The speaker had more reason to rule against those following Tembo and Chihana. They were voted in on a ticket of opposition to UDF and changed to support the government. This prompted the public affairs committee (PAC) to seek a judicial interpretation and have the amended section declared contrary to the human rights guaranteed in the constitution for violating the freedom of association.[24] PAC is a non-governmental organization for civic affairs sponsored by the catholic and protestant churches. PAC argued that the amended section 65 (1) was unconstitutional, and therefore invalid, by virtue of the fact that it curtails freedom of association as provided under section 32 of the Constitution and political rights in section 40.

In his ruling on the matter, the High Court observed that restricting a Member of Parliament in the performance of his or her duties as section 65 had done, would have negative consequences on the expectations of his or her constituents. The court justice went further to argue that:

> the amendment effected is so wide. Whereas in its original form the proverbial floor capable of being crossed by a Member of Parliament was only available in the National Assembly and then only between members belonging to political parties represented in that Assembly, the amended section 65(1) almost makes that floor magically available for crossing whenever and wherever a Member of Parliament joins, *inter alia*, some organization or association with objectives or activities that are political in nature. . . . Stretching the floor so much out of the National Assembly amounts to a gross interference with the enjoyment of the freedom of association and of the exercise of political rights guaranteed under Sections 32 and 40. . . .

The effect of this ruling was to clarify the usage of section 65 in parliament and meant that all MPs who had been expelled from the national assembly on the basis of the amended section 65 were reinstated.

Attempt to Break Judiciary Resistance

Muluzi had already encountered resistance from the judiciary in the first parliamentary term. Judge Dunstain Mwaungulu had ruled against the government in the case of press trust. A supreme court bench filled with recent appointments by the president overruled Mwaungulu's decision. The judiciary was also reluctant to take on the role of broker between judiciary and parliament.

That changed around the elections of 1999 when the judiciary ruled several times against the government. However, they did not rule consistently and the opposition lost, for example, the petition of the election results. Nevertheless, the relationship between government and the judiciary turned bitter when legal rulings blocked Muluzi's attempts to forge a two-third parliamentary majority in support of this bid. In this game, Muluzi sought a free hand to expel parliamentarians and the courts blocked this. The courts also consistently ruled against Muluzi's decrees banning public demonstrations against attempts to amend the constitution to extend his tenure of office.

The speaker of parliament responded furiously that the public appointments committee of the national assembly "will not hesitate to dismiss any judge who appears to be unfamiliar with the Malawi Constitution either because of plain professional incompetence or just political activism."[25] This threat was followed up by the presentation of a motion by the UDF during the November 2001 sitting of the parliament aiming to remove three high court judges on the pretext that they were political in their judgments. The motion targeted Justices Anaclet Chipeta, Dunstain Mwaungulu, and Chimasula Phiri.[26] Following a heated debate, the motion, which was largely supported by the ruling party, was passed to dismiss the three high court judges.

However, the dismissal of the three judges was widely criticized by the opposition, parties, the churches, non-governmental organizations, and Malawi's major donors as being indicative of government's meddling in the independence of the judiciary. The decision by parliament was also questioned because of the fact that it did not respect the concept of separation of powers, by making the judiciary responsive to the national assembly, contrary to the spirit of the Constitution. President Muluzi himself hesitated to assent to the bill and he was eventually forced to clear the judges in May 2002.[27]

Civil Society Influence and Repression Threats

The role of parliament was pivotal in the struggle around the amendment allowing an extra term to Muluzi. However, the influence of parliament could possibly have been broken if the NGO community had not been there. UDF seemed successfully to perpetuate and take advantage of fragmentation among the opposition. Government appeared to be able to pass amendments on the quorum and section 65, paving the way to a third term for Muluzi. It was, as already pointed out above, the public affairs committee who took recourse to the court when the speaker of parliament threatened to become all-powerful. Given the fragmentation of the opposition, the churches were particularly united and strong in their opposition. They were then voicing widely and strongly felt concerns as was evident in the demonstrations against the possibility of a third term for Muluzi. This led to an increasingly repressive stance of Muluzi and the UDF.

Threats of the Young Democrats

Another aspect of the UDF strategy involved the use of force, especially by the party's youth wing, Young Democrats, to silence critics. Among the victims of this violence included Members of Parliament that were against the motion, especially those on the opposition benches. Other victims of this violence included members from the independent media houses, civil society, university students, and church leaders, as well as members of the public who joined in the demonstrations against the third-term bid. Reminiscent of the notorious youth wing of the MCP regime, the Young Democrats in the majority of cases victimized opponents to the third-term bid in the presence of the police, who were unable to take any action.[28]

The NGOs Act

Government tried to obtain control over the NGO sector by proposing a bill in January 2001 to monitor and control them. Under the act, all NGOs are required to register with an NGO Board, which is also empowered to act as a regulator of all NGO activity. The act also prohibits NGOs from "engaging in partisan politics, electioneering and politicking."[29]

Both the bill and the act were roundly criticized by civil society for "undermining the democratic principles outlined in the Constitution, and also the trust which was established between NGOs and government during the consultative process." In particular, the compulsory requirement for NGOs to register with both CONGOMA and the NGO Board, with government having tight control over the composition of the NGO board's membership, was criticized as an attempt to bring NGOs under closer government control.[30] In a bid to stop government from passing the bill, civil society organizations sought a high court injunction to stop parliament from debating the bill and passing it. However, before the injunction could be granted, the bill was rushed through parliament, passed on January 12, 2001, and enacted into law before the court had delivered its ruling.

Bills to Ensure Muluzi's Third Term and their Fate

The Open Terms Bill

The climax of the second democratic parliament was the presentation in parliament of the bill that proposed to get rid of the restrictions on the presidential tenure of office to two terms of five years each.

The Open Terms bill was first presented on May 24, 2002, as a private member's bill with the purpose of removing the limitation on the number of terms a president may serve.[31] The rationale for the bill was that "Section 83(3) of the Constitution, which sets the limits on the presidential tenure of office, is considered to infringe upon people's power to elect into office of the President the person of their choice and to renew his mandate for as many times as they may wish him or her to serve them."

The Open Terms bill was tabled in parliament on July 4, 2002, and was moved by an AforD MP, Khwauli Msiska. Among those who spoke in support of the motion were UDF parliamentarians, the John Tembo faction of the MCP, and AforD MPs loyal to the party president, Chakufwa Chihana. Outside parliament, UDF party members led the campaigns in support of the third-term bill. Traditional leaders, especially the provisional leadership of the chief's council, also lobbied parliamentarians to vote in favor of the bill.

Leading the criticism of the proposal were MCP MPs loyal to Gwanda Chakuamba, AforD MPs who had broken ranks with Chihana and Brown Mpinganjira's NDA. Criticisms also came from civil society organizations, religious leaders, NGOs, professional associations, including the Malawi Law Society, and the sections of the opposition MCP and AforD.

When Parliament voted on the bill on July 4, 2002, it failed to muster the necessary two-thirds majority to be effected into law. In order to pass, the bill had needed 128 votes of the 193 MPs. However, 125 MPs (all from the UDF and those from the MCP and AforD factions loyal to John Tembo and Chakufwa Chihana respectively) supported the bill. Fifty-nine MPs from the MCP and AforD voted against the bill. A further three abstained while another five were absent. This meant that the bill fell short by three votes and was defeated.

Following the failure of the passage of the Open Terms bill, President Muluzi conceded defeat and called for conciliation between those that had supported the bid and those that were against it.

The Third Term Bill

Despite Muluzi's concession of defeat, the failure of the Open Terms bill did not put the issue of Muluzi's candidacy to final rest. At a meeting of UDF regional and district executives on July 20, 2002, delegates once again "endorsed Muluzi's candidature for the 2004 Presidential Elections." The meeting further agreed that a modified version of the bill seeking an extension to Muluzi's candidature be presented in parliament as a government bill, this time seeking for a third term, rather than unlimited tenure, of office for the presidency.[32]

The new bill, which was presented on September 8, 2002, proposed to extend to three terms the presidential tenure of office. Specifically, the bill proposed changing section 83(3) to state that, "Any President of Malawi may serve a maximum of three consecutive terms."

The UDF, with their newfound allies in AforD, campaigned vigorously for the new bill at every opportunity. The main gist of the argument in favor of the proposal was that two terms was not sufficient to realize all the development plans that President Muluzi and any other future president would have embarked on.

However, as with the failed Open Terms bill, the third-term bid also received widespread criticism from the opposition and civil society, including the churches. The civil society organizations came together and formed the Forum for the Defense of the Constitution (FDC) with the aim of campaigning and lobbying MPs to vote against the third term. In a statement, the FDC rejected the Third Term bill and called upon women, men, and the youth to close ranks and resist ever again from being used and abused in any political process for selfish political ends.[33]

The bill also saw the emergence of further cracks within the UDF party itself and loss of support from their former allies in the MCP. Whilst nearly all UDF MPs had supported the open-terms bid, a number of UDF parliamentarians openly broke ranks with their party and joined the opposition to criticize the bill. Notable among the signatories to the FDC statement quoted above were UDF MPs, Cassim Chilumpha, Jan Sonke, and Joe Manduwa. Commerce and industry minister, Peter Kaleso, also came out openly against the third term bid and was immediately dismissed from cabinet on the eve of the vote on the bill. At the same time, John Tembo's MCP faction, which had supported the Open Terms bill, made a sudden u-turn and united with his estranged president, Gwanda Chakuamba to lobby their supporters to vote against the bill.[34]

Although the new bill was supported by a section of AforD, it became clear that John Tembo's decision to align himself with Gwanda Chakuamba, and the decision by a number of UDF and AforD parliamentarians to break ranks openly with their leadership, would deprive the bill of the necessary two-thirds majority to turn it into law. Sensing defeat, Muluzi, in a national address on the eve of the October 2002 Parliamentary sitting, called upon the national assembly not to treat the Third Term bill as a priority, but, instead, to focus on starvation, which was a pressing national concern at the time.[35]

However, although the bill was not presented in the October 2002 sitting of parliament, the UDF continued to lobby MPs from the opposition side to support it. Whilst the ruling party attempted to induce a number of opposition parliamentarians with money to support the Bill, there was at the same time a systematic campaign of violence, spearheaded by the UDF's youth wing, the Young Democrats, against law-makers and members of civil society who were critical of the third-term bid.[36]

The shelving of the bill was, however, only temporary. It would appear that the UDF was working on securing the necessary numbers to amend the Constitution. An emergency session of parliament was called on January 27, 2003 and the Third Term bill was at last tabled for debate. Apart from UDF support, a number of opposition MCP legislators are also said to have been induced with monetary rewards to support the bill.[37] In the ensuing debate, however, it became clear that the bill would not garner the necessary two-thirds support to turn it into law. The government was subsequently forced to retreat by referring the bill to the legal affairs committee of parliament two days later.[38]

Two weeks following this second shelving of the Third Term bill, President Muluzi declared that he would not be standing for a third term of office, saying the Constitution was "very clear on that and that nobody needed to ask him if he would stand again."[39] However, given that the bill had not been formerly withdrawn, and that Muluzi had made similar statements following the defeat of the open-terms bid in July 2002, there was still uncertainty on whether the bill had been shelved for good or whether it would again resurface once the government was convinced it had enough numbers in parliament to support it. Reinforcing these fears of the bill's resurrection was the continued campaign by UDF supporters to ask Muluzi to call for a referendum to decide on the matter rather than entrusting it to parliament alone.[40]

The UDF was faced with little option but to withdraw efforts to get an extension to Muluzi's tenure of Office. However, it was only in the second half of 2003, and following the endorsement by the UDF of Bingu wa Mutharika as the party's presidential candidate in the 2004 presidential and general elections that the Third Term bill was formally withdrawn. However, instead of acknowledging that this decision was based on internal resistance to the bill, the attorney general, Peter Fachi, argued that the decision was based on government's desire "to follow the trend of change in Africa by limiting the term of any serving president as is provided in the Constitution. The trend in Africa is against us and we have to bow down to it."[41]

Conclusion

Instead of patrimonialism and politics of the belly, the Malawian case illustrates that the success of Muluzi's political engineering has only been partial. This has largely been due to the pivotal role that the Malawi parliament played since the introduction of multiparty politics in 1994. This significance did not stem from differences over particular policies; it was more of a struggle to contain the power of the president and the ruling party. Whereas in the first five-year parliamentary period, this seemed to be decided in favor of the presidency, parliament appeared in the second period an effective check against the enlargement of presidential power.

This particular role of parliament was partly possible because of the Malawian political environment.

First, the ruling party, UDF, did not have an absolute majority in the first period and a slim absolute majority in the second period. Therefore, President Muluzi and his UDF could not exercise substantial control and direction over parliament during this period. This is very unlike other African parliaments where the victorious parties had absolute majorities in parliament in the founding elections.[42]

Second, the judiciary took upon itself the role to guard the Constitution. Although the judiciary itself has seen its independence and authority challenged by the presidency, it made a number of decisions that helped to buttress the authority of parliament and allowed it to undertake its oversight role on the executive.

Third, parliament enjoyed a significant amount of support from civil society organizations. The decisive court case establishing the precedence of the freedoms enshrined in the Constitution was engaged by a church-sponsored NGO. At a time when the executive seemed to have established dominance by profiting from engineering splits in parties, parliament gained its autonomy to resist presidential domination.

Fourth, the resistance of parliament cannot be seen as separate from grass-roots resistance. Politicians who supported the bid for the extension of presidential powers would face a difficult re-election.

Fifth, this grass roots mobilization only occurred in the second parliamentary period around the proposal for a constitutional amendment giving the president the possibility to serve more than two terms. In the first parliamentary period, the struggle between parliament and presidency was not a significant issue of grass roots policy and it did not galvanize the judiciary to the extent it did in the second term.

Last, Malawi's major donor nations have weighed in on a number of occasions to make the case for the observance of the separation of powers principle. The intervention of the donors when the third-term bid appeared to be dominating the government agenda was also particularly influential in forcing government to put the bill on hold and concentrate on more pressing issues of national concern.

The elections of 2005 led to a further fragmentation of power among parties. Nine parties and thirty-eight independents are now represented in parliament. Bungu wa Mutharika was handpicked by Muluzi to become the presidential candidate for UDF. Mutharika got 36 percent of the vote and won the presidency. UDF gained however only 49 of the 187 seats in parliament. It was no longer the largest party in parliament: MCP gained 58 seats. Coalition government was thus unavoidable. As soon as Mutharika was in power, he commenced a campaign against corruption under the previous government. This occurred concurrently with vigorous work on the same issues by the public accounts committee of parliament. This brought Muthurika naturally on a collision course with Muluzi and UDF. Mutharika has now declared the presidency as above party politics and therefore cut himself loose from UDF. There is obviously no return to the old pattern of politics being dominated by one powerful patron, albeit that the political debate continues to center on the use of power and not on a policy vision on Malawi's future.

Notes

1. Bratton and van de Walle 1997: 61–97.
2. Bayart 1993.
3. Banda 1998.
4. Newspaper reporting is a major source throughout this chapter. However, in the part on the first parliament, we do not have exact references. They are based on overviews that one of the authors, Jan Kees van Donge, made for the Royal Netherlands embassy in Lusaka that mention a particular time period but not specific dates of events. We use newspapers crucially as resources. We read them as cultural documents and our judgement is informed on the experience of day-to-day life as well as checking with key informants.
5. It was of course obvious that in a situation where people continue to vote along regional lines some coalitions between MCP and AforD were necessary and that materialized in the 1999 election. In that election, Gwanda Chakuamba ran for president with Chakufwa Chihana (AforD) as a running mate.
6. In the first four years of multiparty democratic regime, 19 MPs (11 UDF, 4 MCP, and 4 AforD) died in office (source: Malawi Electoral Commission).
7. On the role of Press Trust in the Malawian political economy see van Donge 2002.
8. One seat in Mchinji district was not contested for following the death of the MCP candidate.
9. The independents were candidates who had lost in the primary elections for the UDF ticket and then stood without a party affiliation. They all joined the UDF immediately after regaining their seat.
10. Section 83(3) of the Constitution provides that "The President, the First Vice president and the Second Vice president may serve in their respective capacities a maximum of two consecutive terms, but when a person is elected or

appointed to fill a vacancy in the office of President or Vice-President, the period between that election or appointment and the next election of a President shall not be regarded as a term."
11. *The Nation*, June 22, 1999 "Muluzi Goes into Second Term."
12. *Daily Times*, Oct.14, 1999 "UDF Agrees on Bakili's Third Term.'
13. Ibid. Oct. 8, 2001 "Districts Declare that Muluzi Stands."
14. *The Nation*, Jan. 25, 2002 "No Third Term for Muluzi."
15. These included MPs Lizzie Mpinganjira, Gresham Naura, James Makhumula, and Peter Tchupa. They were later joined by Joe Manduwa and one of UDF's founder members, Harry Thomson.
16. *Daily Times*, July 25, 2000 "UDF Endorses Muluzi." It has to be kept in mind that losing elections means a big financial drain in African politics without the chance to recoup it. That may have played a role in the strange switches of allegiance by Tembo and Chihana. John Tembo and his relative Cecilia Kadzamira, the official hostess during Kamuzu Banda's reign, were also involved in a conflict over the estate of Kamuzu Banda. After this switch of support, nothing more of this conflict had been heard.
17. The opposition parties had challenged the 1999 election results for both the presidential and parliamentary elections in court. The main points of their arguments were that the UDF had rigged the parliamentary elections and that Muluzi had failed to secure a majority of the votes of the electorate, and that this required a re-run of the presidential race. For a fuller discussion of the court challenge, see Patel 2000: 42–45.
18. *Daily Times*, July 5, 2002.
19. The government did not admit to any wrongful or deplorable action. Ibid. April 30, 2003, "Response by the Malawi Government to the Issues Raised in the Pastoral Letter of the General Synod of the CCAP."
20. *The Nation*, May 16, 2001.
21. Ibid. July 7, 2001, "Parliament Passes Quorum Bill."
22. *Weekend Nation* Oct. 11–12/2003, "My Diary." When the Bill was tabled in Parliament on June 14, 2001, the then Opposition Leader, John Tembo, summoned all MCP MPs to his Area 10 House where he asked them to support the Bill.
23. *Daily Times*, June 20, 2001, "Bill Passed Amid Protests."
24. Civil Cause No. 1861 of 2003.
25. *Daily Times*, Sept. 27, 2000, "Speaker to Summon Judge over Gwanda."
26. Ibid. Sept. 30, 2001, "UDF Plots against Judges."
27. Ibid. Sept. 8, 2002, "Muluzi Clears Judges."
28. *Nation*, Sept. 11, 2002, "Public Affairs Committee (PAC), Statement Against the Third Term."
29. Section 20 of the NGO Act.
30. *Nation*, Jan. 11, 2001, "Press Release by Civil Society Organizations."
31. *Malawi Government Gazette Supplement*, May 24, 2002.
32. *Daily Times*, July 22, 2002, "Third Term Refuses to Die."
33. *Lamp*, Nov.–Dec. 2002, FDC Declaration and Resolutions on the Proposed 3rd Term Amendment to the Constitution, Oct. 8, 2002.

34. *Daily Times*, Jan. 16, 2003, "Gwanda, Tembo Warn MPs."
35. *Nation*, Oct. 1, 2002, "Prioritize Hunger, Not Third Term Bill."
36. Public Affairs Committee Statement, Oct. 22, 2002.
37. *Nation*, Jan. 28, 2003 reported that Gwanda Chakuamba hinted in parliament that a number of MCP's MPs had been offered money. They were kept in a secret house away from the MCP leadership and would only be brought to parliament during the crucial vote.
38. *Daily Times*, Jan. 29, 2003, "Third Term Deferred."
39. I wish to thank my Director of Studies, Elizabeth Sidiropoulos for her invaluable input into the chapter. Thanks are also expressed to Dr. Gavin Woods MP, Mr. Douglas Gibson MP, unnamed MPs and parliamentary officials as well as Mr. Ken Andrew, former MP and Chair of the Parliament's Standing Committee on Public Accounts, for interviews granted during research for this chapter.
40. *Daily Times*, Feb. 10, 2003, "Referendum for Third Term."
41. Ibid., June 13, 2003, "Government to Pull Out Third Term Bill."
42. Bratton 1999: 20.

12

The South African Parliament's Failed Moment

Tim Hughes[1]

South African Institute of International Affairs, Johannesburg, South Africa

Introduction

The nature of the relationship between the executive and legislative branches of government is only laid bare when tested. This is particularly so in a country growing into a new constitutional dispensation such as contemporary South Africa. This chapter examines a seminal test case in this relationship, namely the role of parliament[2] and particularly that of its standing committee on public accounts (SCOPA) in examining the risks involving the strategic defense packages for the acquisition of armaments at the department of defense (hereafter "the arms deal"). The national assembly's treatment of the investigation into the arms deal provides a lens through which the complex and convoluted relationship between the executive and legislative branches of government is likely better understood. It also raises important questions about the nature of constitutional democracy in South Africa, now and in the future.

Grappling with the Past

Even under the 1910 Union of South Africa Constitution, the country was an unusual case of form rather than substance in the operation of the separation of powers. Not only were the *trias politicas* formal separate political entities, their physical location nominally re-enforced this separation, with the executive branch residing in Pretoria, the legislature in Cape Town, and the judicial branch housed in Bloemfontein. Whilst prior to 1984, South Africa had nominally adopted a Westminster (prime-ministerial) system of government, power had been increasingly fused and concentrated within the executive branch. A series of constitutional and legal reversals had seen the ideology and policies of apartheid trump the constitutional provisions of justice and representativeness. Only on rare occasions did the judiciary hold its own against restrictive legislation and only on two occasions did the government directly seek a public mandate for constitutional changes via a whites' only referendum.[3]

Prior to the adoption of the 1996 founding law,[4] all Constitution-making and amendments had tended to entrench the supremacy of the executive branch of government, particularly the 1984 presidential constitution. Furthermore, two related trends had operated in pre-1990 South African governance. The first was the progressive exclusion and then limited re-admission of people of color from the formal constitutional representation in government. The second and related trend was the marginalization of parliament and, to some degree, the cabinet, under the final years of the P. W. Botha presidency during the 1980s.

Partially in response to the threat of popular uprising and the successive imposition of states of emergency and partially by dint of personality and persuasion, P. W. Botha established an inner circle of securocratic advisers known as the national security council. This was effectively handed and assumed *de facto* control of the formulation and implementation of national policy in the late 1980s. This development was an extreme case of what had gone before. South Africa had never been a liberal democracy nor had it ever embraced a bill of rights. Both of these would have rendered apartheid impossible, or both would have been expunged under a ruling apartheid ideology and government. Furthermore, the dominant ideology of twentieth-century South Africa had been (and remains) that of nationalism (Afrikaner and black variants). Such ideological dominance challenged only by socialism and to a lesser degree liberalism, made the provision of a bill of individual rights an anachronism. Thus, in addition to the effective exclusion of the majority of citizens from the formal political process of government prior to 1994, South Africa had no experience operating as a constitutional state, nor had it enjoyed the formal mechanisms of effective checks and balances between the respective branches of government.

Whilst the legacy of apartheid's social and economic precepts may never be expunged and indeed the structural conditions of racial capitalism persist, in the early years of the final decade of the twentieth century, political negotiators and constitutional lawyers were able to craft a progressive constitutional law for a democratic South Africa. The law simultaneously attempted to recognize and ameliorate past inequities and promote democratic governance in the future. The challenge confronting the constitutional committee of the convention for a democratic South Africa (CODESA) and its successor, the constitutional assembly, was profound. In addition to the guiding precepts of justice and equality, the constitution drafters were keen to prevent a repeat of the pattern of centralization and abuse of governmental power. This imperative had two dimensions: the first was a philosophical genuflection to a pluralist democracy, and the second was the need to provide assurances to minority groups in South Africa's heterogeneous society.

Institutional Bricks and Mortar[5]

The 1996 Constitution provided for a bi-cameral system, in contrast with its tri-cameral predecessor.[6] The national assembly requires a minimum 350 and a maximum 400 members to be fully constituted.[7] These are elected through a proportional representation party-list system. Two hundred members are elected from national candidate lists and the other half from the nine provincial party lists. The decision to introduce a PR/party-list system in 1994 was largely driven by a desire to assure broad-based representation in parliament and a converse fear of exclusion, or under-representation, of minorities that a plurality system may produce. Whilst this electoral system has assured minority ethnic and minority party representation in parliament, it is not without its detractors, particularly those arguing that the disconnection between a party-list system and constituencies is fundamental.[8]

The three democratic national general elections in 1994, 1999, and 2004 produced the results illustrated in table 12.1.

A number of electoral features have salience for the South African parliament. The first is the overwhelming and increasing majority of the African National Congress (ANC). The 1994 result was a remarkable

Table 12.1 South Africa Election Results, 1994, 1999, and 2004

	African National Congress (%)	Inkatha Freedom Party (%)	New National Party (%)	Democratic Party/Democratic Alliance (%)	Others (%)
1994	62.65	10.54	20.39	1.73	4.69
1999	66.36	8.59	6.87	9.55	8.63
2004	69.69	6.97	1.65	12.37	9.32
% gain/loss	+7.04	−3.57	−18.75	+10.64	+4.63

achievement for a party that had been banned for 30 years. Whilst the party did not achieve a two-thirds majority (required to amend the constitution unilaterally) in either the 1994 or 1999 elections, the support of the single representative of the Minority Front Party after the 1999 election, effectively gave the ruling party sufficient numbers to amend the constitution. The introduction during the second parliament of a constitutional amendment allowing members to "cross the floor" without losing their seats during a presidentially determined window period, has resulted in more fluidity within the national assembly. The second feature is the collapse and demise of the former ruling National Party, which has shed support to the Democratic Alliance, the ANC, and the Independent Democrats. Its catastrophic performance as an electoral alliance partner of the ANC in the 2004 election has resulted in the rump of the party effectively disbanding and being subsumed by the ANC. The third trend is the decline of the largely Zulu and Kwa-Zulu Natal-based Inkatha Freedom Party (IFP). The final trend is the growth and consolidation of the Democratic Alliance as the official opposition party in parliament, although it failed to win even a combined 20 percent of the popular vote in its electoral alliance with the IFP, let alone the 30 percent it had claimed was achievable. Thus, the ANC is not only by far the dominant political force in parliament; it has increased its majority in successive elections and faces no external political threat to speak of. Finally, the 2004 election saw the ANC sweep to power in all nine provincial legislatures, whereas before it had ruled outright in seven, excluding the Western Cape and Kwa-Zulu Natal.

The national assembly carries out the three cardinal roles of deliberation, passing legislation, and conducting oversight of the executive branch. Furthermore, every five years, the national assembly serves as an electoral college choosing the executive president during a special sitting after the official results of the general election. In turn, the president appoints his (currently 28-member) cabinet. In its first sitting, the national assembly chooses its presiding officers such as the speaker and her deputy.[9]

For purposes of this chapter, a number of other features of the Constitution finally adopted in May 1996 have particular bearing. Most importantly, unlike all its antecedents, the 1996 Constitution provided for the establishment of a constitutional state that is the Constitution, rather than parliament or the presidency, is supreme. In a profound break with the past, the final constitution of 1996 also contains strong provisions for the protection and promotion of individual rights, but also sets out clear provisions for checks and balances between arms of government. The constitution provides for a co-operative form of governance, which must operate in a manner that is effective, transparent, accountable, and coherent for the republic as a whole. However, the constitution also delineates specific powers to the legislature in the furtherance of executive oversight. Chapter Four (section 55) of the South African Constitution states that the national assembly must provide for mechanisms to ensure that all executive organs of state in the national sphere of government are accountable to it. Furthermore, it must maintain oversight of the exercise of national executive authority, including the implementation of legislation and any organ of state.[10] The national assembly may impeach/remove the state president on the grounds of serious misconduct or incapacity. Furthermore, it may pass a motion of no confidence in the cabinet, in which case it must resign and be re-constituted by the state president.

Additionally, the national assembly may summon any person to appear before it to give evidence on oath or affirmation, or to produce documents; require any person or institution to report to it; compel, in terms of national legislation or the rules and orders, any person or institution to comply with a summons and receive petitions, representations or submissions from any interested persons or institutions.[11]

The second house of parliament changed its name from that of the senate, to the national council of provinces (NCOP) in 1997. As the name suggests, this house is constituted to strengthen the links of governance and representation between the first (national), second (provincial), and third (local) tiers of government. The NCOP houses 90 members comprising ten members from each of the nine provinces. Members of the NCOP are nominated by provincial legislatures and a delegation from the South African local government association. Four special delegates are drawn from the provincial legislatures, including the provincial premier and may alter from time to time. The remaining six delegates are permanent. Members are voted in proportion to their party's respective representation in the provincial legislature. The NCOP shadows the deliberative and legislative role of the national assembly, but, importantly, it may also initiate or prepare bills in which provincial legislatures have joint law-making power with the national assembly. These schedule 4 (of the Constitution) laws pertain to areas such as agriculture, education, health, environment, and housing.

Key to the functioning of the post-1994 parliament has been an extensive committee system. Committees are designed with a number of functions in mind, to improve the efficiency of the legislative process, to deepen and enhance the deliberative function of parliament, and to maximize public participation in the legislative process through hearings and submissions. Crucially, however, committees are constituted to strengthen parliament's capacity to conduct effective oversight of the executive. Currently, the following genres of parliamentary committee are in operation: national assembly portfolio committees (discussed in more detail below), ad hoc committees, which dissolve after dealing with the specific matter for which they were constituted; constitutionally prescribed joint committees (human rights, public protector, defense, and finance), statutory committees (intelligence); joint committees with the national assembly (NA) and NCOP (joint committee on members' interests and the standing committee on public accounts); standing committees; joint ad hoc committees; and joint standing committees.

In accordance with Rule 199 of the rules of the national assembly, the speaker, in conjunction with the rules committee, established "a range of portfolio committees and assigned a portfolio of government affairs to each committee." Each committee was tasked with maintaining oversight of:

- the exercise of national executive authority within its portfolio;
- the implementation of legislation pertaining to its portfolio;
- any executive organ of state within its portfolio; and
- any other body or institution in respect to which oversight was assigned to it.

A parliamentary committee may monitor, investigate, or enquire into and make any recommendations concerning any constitutional organ of state within its purview. A committee is granted these powers with regard to the legislative program, budget, rationalization, restructuring, functioning, structure, or staff and policies of such organs of state or institution. Furthermore, a committee is tasked with considering all bills and amendments to bills referred to it. Thus, its powers are considerable. None is more important than the standing committee on public accounts (SCOPA), which monitors all government expenditure and is the first line of oversight and protection for the South African taxpayer in relation to the government.

Moreover, a raft of other independent institutions designed *inter alia* to hold executive power in check, are provided for in chapter 9 of the Constitution. These are sometimes referred to as state institutions supporting constitutional democracy (SISCDs). Section 181 of the Constitution holds that these institutions must be impartial and must exercise their powers and perform their functions without fear, favor, or prejudice. Furthermore, other organs of state, through legislative and other measures, must assist and protect these institutions to ensure the independence, impartiality, dignity, and effectiveness of these institutions. No person or organ of state may interfere with the functioning of these institutions. These institutions are accountable to the NA, and must report on their activities and the performance of their functions to the assembly at least once a year. Of most relevance to this case study are the offices of the public protector and that of the auditor-general.

Functions of the Public Protector

The public protector has the power, as regulated by national legislation, to investigate any conduct in state affairs, or in the public administration in any sphere of government that is alleged or suspected to be improper or to result in any impropriety or prejudice; report on that conduct; and to take appropriate remedial action.[12] The public protector has the additional powers and functions prescribed by national legislation. However, the public protector may not investigate court decisions. The public protector must be accessible to all persons and communities. Any report issued by the public protector must be open to the public unless exceptional circumstances, to be determined in terms of national legislation, require that a report be kept confidential. The public protector is appointed for a non-renewable period of seven years.

Functions of the Auditor-General

Section 188 (1) of the Constitution holds that the auditor-general must audit and report on the accounts, financial statements and financial management of all national and provincial state departments and administrations; all municipalities; and any other institution or accounting entity required by national or provincial legislation to be audited by the auditor-general. In addition to the duties prescribed in subsection (1), and subject to any legislation, the auditor-general may audit and report on the accounts, financial statements, and financial management of any institution funded from the national revenue fund or a provincial revenue fund or by a municipality; or any institution that is authorized in terms of any law to receive money for a public purpose. The auditor-general must submit audit reports to any legislature that has a direct interest in the audit, and to any other authority prescribed by national legislation. All reports must be made public. The auditor-general has the additional powers and functions prescribed by national legislation. The auditor-general must be appointed for a fixed, non-renewable term of between five and ten years. The president, on the recommendation of the national assembly, appoints the auditor-general. The independence and autonomy of the auditor-general is entrenched in rule 66 of the rules of the national assembly.

Skilled Tailor, Bad Fit?

Whilst the 1994 Parliament was in the unique position of re-inventing the historically exclusive institution as a "people's parliament," it was also confronted with a host of operational and procedural challenges.

The first was simply for the majority of newly elected MPs to understand and become experienced in the ways of parliament. New MPs by definition had no experience of, or exposure to, the inner workings and disciplines of parliament as an institution. Many had spent years in exile, in prison, engaged in guerrilla warfare, as civic leaders or as trade unionists. No newly elected African MP had ever served in parliament, although a number had held office in black local authority and bantustan administrations. Part of the challenge was to retain what was functional under the previous parliamentary system and meld this with new rules, new committees, and a new open and transparent *modus operandi*, given that the new constitution obliges parliament to facilitate public engagement in all its activities.

The second challenge was to commence with the arduous task of repealing and removing from the statute books all lingering discriminatory legislation and the drafting of new, democratic, and progressive/transformative legislation. This has been a considerable task and has seen some 800 new pieces of legislation enacted since 1994.

The third and most nebulous challenge was to give substance to the constitutional powers granted to parliament and in particular the committees of parliament in respect of the consideration, examination, and review of government policy, bills and departmental operations. Here, the performance of committees has been mixed. Some, such as the justice and finance committees, have been extraordinarily diligent and have thoroughly interrogated and indeed re-written legislation. Others have been less distinguished. The comparative performance of respective committees has in part been due to the nature of leadership shown by committee chairs, as well as by their composition and sphere of operations. The committee on foreign affairs, for example, has considered very little legislation since 1994 and has concerned itself with protocols, issues of departmental transformation, and department briefings on foreign policy.

The fourth and related challenge was the development, understanding, and implementation of parliament's oversight and accountability role. This has been the most vexatious challenge. Whilst the principle of parliament's oversight role is enunciated clearly within the constitution, its practical operation is wracked with difficulty. The first difficulty is at once constitutional, procedural, and political in that there is no complete separation of powers between the executive and legislative branches of government. Indeed the executive branch is drawn exclusively from parliament and in large part from the majority party. With the exception of the president who, after his election by parliament, departs the legislature, all cabinet members and their deputies are members of the national assembly. Furthermore, South Africa's proportional representation party list electoral system ensures tight caucus loyalty, rather than to a given electoral constituency and serves to militate against MPs' adopting independent positions. Questioning or critically engaging a minister or deputy does not achieve promotion from the back to the front benches of parliament. Arguably, too, the pervasive ideology and ethos of African nationalism within the majority party, the African National Congress, encourages solidarity, rather than critical engagement or public debate. Prior to the SCOPA arms deal hearings (and certainly not since), there has been no example of any ANC MP critically questioning a member of cabinet in parliament, even on matters of conscience such as HIV/AIDS and the death penalty.

A final peculiarity of the post-1994 parliamentary system that has further militated against its conducting effective oversight of the executive was the operation of a government of national unity (GNU) in which a deputy presidency and a number of cabinet positions were held by opposition parties. This transitional arrangement drew the National Party (until 1997), the Inkatha Freedom Party, and the Azanian People's Organization into government. Only the Democratic Party (now Democratic Alliance) declined the offer of a position in cabinet. Whilst the forging of a GNU held considerable merit given the centripetal forces at play in South Africa during the 1990s, its operation undoubtedly served to mute robust opposition and in turn government accountability to parliament.

Yet, to its credit, parliament commissioned an external team of legal experts in January 1999 to interpret, report on and make recommendations regarding its oversight and accountability role as provided for in the Constitution. Reporting back in July 1999, the expert report took its terms of reference as that of outlining and explaining the nature of the obligation that section 55 (2) of the Constitution places on the national assembly to hold "organs of state" and the "national executive authority" to account. The report questioned the practicality of parliament playing an effective oversight role of all organs of state, but strongly asserted the need for parliament to concretize and protect its role through new and specific legislation. The report also urged the protection of the independence of the chapter nine SISCDs. In this regard, it recommended the separation of the funding base of these institutions from the executive in order to remove potential political leverage over them and ensure credible operational independence. Moreover, the report noted a decline in the quantum of committee briefings received from departments,[13] and implied the marginalization of parliament by the executive.

Some three years later, the parliamentary ad hoc sub-committee on oversight and accountability produced its final report in response to the independent consultancy.[14] In summary, the ad hoc sub-committee castigated the consultancy for its omissions, inadequacies, and lack of practical recommendations. It concluded that parliament had already commenced strengthening its oversight and accountability roles and took issue with a number of the central contentions of the consultant's report. Finally, it recommended further examination by the parliamentary joint rules committee before coming to a decision on the modalities of future parliamentary oversight. Although the ad hoc sub-committee final report makes a number of specific recommendations, the most substantive of which was the acceptance of an Accountability Standards Act to provide form and substance to parliament's role vis-à-vis executive oversight. To date, however, it is difficult to establish evidence of new initiatives or developments emerging in practice from the "oversight and accountability," consultancy, or indeed from the ad hoc sub-committee's work.

In addition to this declining trend in oversight, the substantial dominance of the majority party and the fractured nature of the opposition ensure that all committees are numerically dominated by the ANC. Conversely, members of small opposition parties are forced to attempt to sit on a handful of committees simultaneously.[15] Clearly, such a situation is highly problematic for effective oversight. Moreover, the panoply of structural constraints has resulted in committees working less than optimally and failing to conduct thorough and robust oversights of the executive. The first difficulty has been that of establishing a clear and cooperative understanding between government departments and parliamentary committees about the nature and obligations of the relationship. Even where ministers, deputy ministers, and directors-general have not sought to avoid scrutiny and oversight, and where a transparent and cooperative relationship has been established, the modalities for ensuring oversight have not always been effective.

Two practical problems exist. The first is the format and extent of departmental briefings given to parliament. Information provided has not always been what committees want or need to know. Certainly, in the earliest days of the new parliament this may have been attributed to committee members not clearly understanding what it was they were supposed to be soliciting from departments. Given the legacy of opaqueness that characterized the previous apartheid administration, "old guard" officials were unused and perhaps uncomfortable with the new light of transparency scrutinizing their operations. More specifically, written departmental submissions to committees have often been voluminous and technical in nature, sometimes running to hundreds of pages. This problem is exacerbated when inadequate time is provided for committees to read, reflect and discuss written submissions prior to the departmental presentation being given. In certain committees, it is common for written submissions to be provided the day before, or, worse still, handed out at the time of the departmental briefing.

The second structural constraint is the lack of committee capacity. Although party whips attempt to ensure a fit between relevant experience and committee position, the relationship between committee MPs and departmental officials is by definition one of amateur to professional. This is not peculiar to South Africa, but certainly in the first parliament of the new democracy, the relevant skill levels of many committee MPs were found wanting. Furthermore, committees have lacked adequate research resources to interrogate ministers, deputy ministers, and their senior officials effectively. Departmental briefings are characterized by the attendance of a battery of senior officials with years of relevant experience and qualifications in support of a minister. Furthermore, argumentation by departments is often of a legalistic nature, frequently leaving committee members at a disadvantage. To some degree, this has been ameliorated by the allocation of a researcher dedicated to each Committee. However, on a purely technical basis, committees continue to struggle to carry out oversight of the executive effectively.

A further and related weakness is that there are few formal channels or requirements for executive to committee feedback and vice versa. Once the parliamentary committee has received the annual departmental briefing, there is no formal requirement to effect, and little evidence of, significant policy adjustment.

Before discussing the sharp face of parliament's oversight role in the shape of SCOPA, it is also worth noting the diminution of the quality of debate and questions in the chamber of the national assembly. The physical shape of the national assembly does not permit government/opposition exchanges across the dispatch box. Rather, ruling party members and the opposition occupy a podium and invariably read (often badly and monotonously) from a prepared text. Whilst motions are common, snap debates are rare. Furthermore, since being elected to office in 1999, President Mbeki has reduced the number of presidential question times to once every three months. This is far too infrequent for parliament to hold the president to account and contrasts markedly with the British prime-ministerial weekly question time.

Parliament and the Arms Deal: A Test of Oversight and Accountability

Like all matters in contemporary South Africa, the corrosive legacy of apartheid protruded into the origins of the debacle. The substantive basis for the arms deal was the threadbare state of the equipment of the South African National Defense Force, largely as a result of decades-long arms embargo and the financial limitations placed on the national party government through the dual impact of biting international banking sanctions and the country's involvement in a host of costly wars in the region, most notably in support of UNITA in Angola. The cutting of international lines of credit in 1985 forced the South African finance ministry and the reserve bank to attempt to run an overall balance of payments surplus and to protect the capital and current accounts. In practical terms, this translated into expensive (and irreplaceable) military equipment, such as jet fighters and naval warships, rapidly becoming both obsolete and unsustainable.

Yet whilst the case for the replacement of old and high-maintenance equipment was easy to make, the scope, content, and timing of any such replacement and procurement process were areas for considerable debate and disagreement. Disagreement centered on four areas. First, the identification of a national threat (or otherwise) necessitating the procurement package. Second, the identification and sourcing of appropriate hardware to meet such a real or potential threat. Third, the timing and structure of payment for such equipment, either as a package deal, or piecemeal. Fourth, questions of affordability and national priority—a classic guns or butter debate.

The former chair of the parliamentary committee on defense has claimed that it was the committee's rejection of the proposal by the defense minister at the time, Joe Modise, to make use of second-hand military equipment. The intension was to replace South Africa National Defense Force's (SANDF) aging and obsolete equipment that led to the drafting of the 1996 defense white paper and subsequent defense review.[16] If so, it was also parliament's somewhat superficial treatment and acceptance of the defense review in April 1998 that ultimately led to its own nadir with respect to the arms deal. Whilst the defense committee concerned itself with overseeing transformation and a shift in the ethos away from over-secrecy of SANDF operations, it was technically ill-equipped to make sense of and critically examine the massive and complex arms deal. In addition to its direct financial and macro-economic implications, the package included provision for the generation of counter-trade, or offsets, amounting to South African Rand (ZAR) 104 billion, while generating some 65,000 jobs.[17]

Numerous aspects of the arms deal are worthy of examination, but the sheer magnitude of the total procurement package, which was originally stated as ZAR29.8 billion, but when signed amounted to ZAR33 billion (equivalent to some US$5 billion at the time of signature at an exchange rate of ZAR6.25/US$) makes it South Africa's largest single public procurement package. Political and strategic arguments aside, the magnitude of the deal elevated it to a position of significant material importance for the South African taxpayer and indeed non-taxpayer. Furthermore, its sheer scope and complexity confronted parliament and a number of its committees (SCOPA, defense, and trade and industry) with the task of making sense of the deal in all its guises, as well as exercising adequate oversight and holding the executive to account for its actions, particularly given the deal's long-term implications.

Pursuant to the defense white paper of 1996, a cabinet subcommittee and thereafter the full cabinet approved the South African defense review, a comprehensive 15-chapter report of the entire operations and requirements of the South African National defense Force. Chapter 13 of the defense review laid out the equipment requirements and acquisition policy of the department of defense. In April 1998, parliament gave its approval of the Review, thus providing a mandate for the commencement of strategic defense packages for the acquisition of armaments at the department of defense. In November 1998, the first concerns were raised at the rapidity with which, in just seven months, the cabinet announced the names of the preferred bidders for supplying the new equipment. Then deputy-president Thabo Mbeki appointed Jayendra Naidoo to examine the affordability of the proposed arms package, taking into account the country's socio-economic priorities. In this regard, the attractiveness of the domestic investment and job-creation potential of the proposed counter-trade and offset programs within the arms deal became a highly significant dimension. Less than a year later, in September 1999, the cabinet announced that it was satisfied with all aspects of the proposed arms deal including that of offsets and counter trade and that it was approving the expenditure of ZAR21.3 billion over eight years (possibly rising to ZAR29.9 billion over 12 years). Given the weight of importance accorded to the offsets and counter trade, the ministries of defense and finance, and the department of trade and industry formed part of the government negotiating team. Also in September 1999, the first accusations of graft, bribery, and corruption became public when then Pan-Africanist Congress MP Patricia de Lille announced in parliament that she had received documentation from concerned ANC MPs of substantial malpractice in the granting of Arms Deal contracts.

Since there is a constitutional requirement that the auditor general examine all government expenditure and, in particular, the arms deal, given its magnitude, the attorney general (AG) commenced a review of the selection process for granting contracts to the primary contractors.[18] Consistent with the requirements and ethos of the constitution, the auditor-general reported his findings to parliament's standing committee on public accounts. The auditor general established and reported on a number of key areas of concern, including the choice of more expensive contractors within the tendering process, but added, "[A]spects of independence, fairness and impartiality could have been addressed more significantly . . . the potential conflict of interests that could have existed was not adequately addressed by this process." Additionally, the auditor-general found there to have been "material deviations from the originally adopted value system." Furthermore, the report noted,

> I am of the opinion that the guarantees, in the case of non-performance, may be inadequate to ensure delivery of National Industrial Participation (NIP) commitments. This could undermine one of the major objectives of the strategic defense packages which were the counter-trade element of the armaments package deal.

The auditor-general's review went on to note that elements of the process were not in line with ministry of defense requirements for dealing with international offers nor compliant with procedures laid down for armaments acquisition policy. State owned Armament Corporation of South Africa (ARMSCOR) procedures were not fully adhered to, budgets were inadequate, and accounting errors were found. The auditor-general's review concluded, "Many allegations regarding possible irregularities in contracts awarded to sub-contractors exist . . . I recommend that a forensic audit of or special investigation into these areas be initiated." Upon receipt of the auditor-general's report and recommendations, the national assembly referred it to SCOPA for consideration.

Enter SCOPA, Exit Left

Consistent with the convention practiced amongst parliaments of Commonwealth countries, the South African parliamentary public accounts committee has been chaired by a member of an opposition party since 1994. In the first term of the new parliament, the Chair was Ken Andrew, a member of the Democratic Party and in the second parliament, Dr Gavin Woods, a member of the Inkatha Freedom Party (who continued to serve in the cabinet until the 2004 elections). This continued practice ran against the trend of electing ANC chairs to all portfolio committees after the 1999 election.

It would be misleading to characterize SCOPA's treatment of the auditor general's review as flexing its constitutional muscles. Yet SCOPA's engagement with the arms deal enquiry became an important litmus test for it and, by extension, parliament's *locus standi*, not simply with respect to the Constitution, but also with respect to the executive and the chapter nine institutions of the auditor-general and public protector. SCOPA's hearing into the report of the auditor-general on October 11, 2000 established a number of important pegs in the ground. In addition to SCOPA members and the chair of the parliament's defense committee, the 11 October hearing saw present the head of the special investigative unit, Judge Edward Heath, the auditor-general, the ministry of finance, the head of the government arms acquisitions, the negotiator of the arms deal counter-trade packages, the chief executive and chairman of ARMSCOR, the secretary of defense and senior members of SANDF. Significantly, the chair of SCOPA refused SANDF the opportunity to conduct a presentation to the committee, but rather asserted that the DoD had been called to the hearing to answer questions raised by SCOPA. This set an important precedent.

Besides the inadequacy of certain responses provided by some of those questioned by SCOPA, what is of particular significance is the tenacity of the questioning by committee members belonging to the ruling party. ANC committee member, Laloo Chiba, is recorded as expressing the following during questioning of ANC stalwart and director of acquisitions, Chippy Shaik,

> Your response is not acceptable. The answer of statutory costs is not correct . . . I want total calculations to be resubmitted to this Committee within seven days . . . What will be the total outlay—ZAR50, ZAR60, or ZAR70 billion? Without such calculations, how could you motivate such purchases? . . . Submit copies of these agreements to this Committee within three-to-four days with the contracts and figure work.

The head of the ANC on SCOPA, Andrew Feinstein, although less aggressive in tone, asked the following questions of his fellow party member, Shaik,

> Why don't we spend most of our budget on arms in order to leverage economic development? It doesn't make sense to me as an economist. International literature suggests these offsets are subsequently diluted or disappeared, or the suppliers factor the penalties into the costs. Why should South Africa be different from the international experience? We need the legally binding contracts . . . was Cabinet misled? On what basis was the cabinet decision made? The Auditor General has noted that the packages were negotiated before the Budget was provided. Did the tail wag the dog? When did conflicts of interest occur? . . . Was the Minister advised of the conflicts of interest? . . . Did you declare your conflict of interest?[19]

This form of questioning illustrates the serious and non-partisan approach adopted by SCOPA in its hearings and was the guiding ethos underpinning its report into the arms deal. On October 30, 2000, SCOPA presented its findings to parliament in the form of its strategic arms purchases review: final report on standing committee on public accounts. The report concluded that given the evidence before it, the seriousness of the issues under investigation, the range and nature of the questions left unanswered, as well as the recommendations of the auditor-general, SCOPA recommended the establishment of an independent and expert forensic investigation. Most significantly, however, SCOPA argued that given the complex and crosscutting nature of the issues under investigation, a multisector investigative team ought to be assembled to carry out the investigation. SCOPA's recommendation was that the team be comprised of the chapter nine offices of the auditor general and public protector, the investigating directorate of the Serious economic offenses office and the (Judge) Heath special investigative unit and "any other appropriate investigative bodies." SCOPA proposed that it would prepare a written brief for such an independent investigative body and that it would report to parliament at regular intervals. Concurrently, SCOPA would continue with its own examination of the arms deal that would include the questioning of cabinet ministers. Crucially, the national assembly adopted SCOPA's report without debate on November 2, 2000. Whether parliament was aware of the political and constitutional implications of SCOPA's report and recommendations must remain speculative. Assuming it applied itself fully to the content and recommendations of the report, this may be interpreted as a strong mandate from parliament to the committee to push the boundaries of its activities and authority with respect to chapter nine institutions and indeed, the executive branch. If, on the other hand, parliament failed to apply itself fully to the consequences of the report without debate, this would reflect as an indictment on the institution.

Despite SCOPA's parliamentary mandate, the entities it corralled into the investigating team were less unquestioning of their role and mandate. Cognizant of the uncharted and potentially stormy seas they were about to sail into, the SCOPA meeting of November 13, 2000, debated the respective areas of expertise and overlap between the institutions involved.[20] Emerging from the November 13, meeting, however, was a clear objective for the investigation, the sourcing of finance, the resources required, administrative arrangements, processes to be followed, the contracting of expertise, the broad framework of the investigation as well as the identification and management of departmental documentation required. The team, coordinated under the aegis of the auditor-general, undertook to report back in July 2001.

It was at this time that the executive began to recognize that a tipping point had been reached in which parliament in the guise of SCOPA had successfully galvanized four powerful, professional investigative bodies to examine what was root and stock an executive initiative and program.

It was then that it mobilized in response to these rapid developments. The first line of attack from the executive was to remove Judge Heath and the special investigative unit from the team. Heath and his unit had developed considerable expertise in governmental corruption. The justice minister, Penuel Maduna, sought to have Heath removed from the SCOPA investigating team on the grounds that a sitting judge could not head the special investigative unit. On November 28, 2000, the constitutional court held that Heath's role in the SIU was unconstitutional. Woods responded by writing to President Mbeki requesting a presidential proclamation allowing the SIU to rejoin the investigation. Justice Minister Maduna recommended against such a proclamation, advice that the president took and announced that he would not issue such an enabling proclamation. Not content with blocking Heath's participation, Mbeki went on television to berate Heath for withholding important information. Mbeki displayed diagrams purporting to illustrate the fallacious basis of Heath's understanding of the arms deal. These drawings were later identified as the working drafts of an investigative journalist, not Heath's.

A further executive salvo was collectively fired by trade and industry minister Erwin, finance minister Manuel, defense minister Lekota, and public enterprises minister Radebe who put the case for the government to the South African public on January 12, 2001.[21] Preempting the SCOPA/Auditor General's Report, the thrust of the ministers' contention was that there had been no wrong-doing whatsoever and that even the figures of the ballooning cost of the Arms Deal where both an exaggeration and misreading of the financing calculations of the deal. Most significantly, however, the ministers took aim at both the auditor-general and SCOPA. According to the ministers, the auditor-general,

> [M]ay not have been adequately exposed to the high-level decision-making process.... Accordingly, the (AG's) inferences are based on incomplete information.... The Auditor General is entitled to his opinion as to the adequacy of the performance guarantees.... We believe that we are entirely within international practice and ... that the Auditor General is incorrect when he sees the counter-trade aspects of the deal as a major objective of the deal.... The Auditor General has not correctly dealt with the matter of the first order values.... and he will need to hold further discussions with the Ministry of Defense to clarify this matter.

SCOPA came off no less lightly. The ministers accused the committee of not understanding the immense complexity of the arms procurement process and arriving at false and erroneous assumptions. The irony of SCOPA not fully understanding the arms deal is not lost on the ministers who accused SCOPA of failing to take up the offer of ministerial assistance or even requesting ministerial assistance in explaining the details of the deal. More powerfully, however, the ministers signaled their strategic line of attack by asserting that SCOPA had acted *ultra vires* by involving investigative agencies other than the auditor-general. A further nail in the coffin of SCOPA's investigation was driven home by a letter issued in January 2001 to Woods by the leader of government business in the house, Deputy President Jacob Zuma,[22] who challenged the basis and approach of SCOPA's investigation.

Ironically, the *coup de grace* in the assault on SCOPA came not from the executive, but from within parliament itself. On December 27, 2000, the speaker of the national assembly, Frene Ginwala, issued a statement in which she questioned the association of the Heath SIU and the office for serious economic offenses in the SCOPA investigative team. Furthermore, she adjudicated that SCOPA had gone beyond its mandated powers in subcontracting outside units to conduct work on its behalf. She asserted further that the chair of a committee might not commit the committee to a course of action, hearing, or investigation, without the full consultation and support of the particular committee. As such, Ginwala implied that Woods had acted *ultra vires*.

On January 22, 2001, the ANC members of SCOPA fell into party line and publicly announced that their interpretation of SCOPA's 14th Report differed from Woods', in that they rejected the insistence that specific investigative units had to serve in the investigative team. This cleared the way for the Heath special investigative unit to be excluded. On the same day, the guillotine fell on Andrew Feinstein, head of the ANC study group on public accounts.[23] He was replaced by Geoff Doidge, deputy chief whip of the ANC. Justifying the tightening of party control in SCOPA, ANC Chief Whip, Tony Yengeni[24] commented,

> There was no objection to these changes, as it was the ANC government that was under attack, it was imperative that the lines of accountability between the ANC members in the committee (SCOPA) and the ANC leadership be strengthened. I don't want to cast aspersions. We really wanted to improve our capacity, but also wanted people who are going to be the political link with ANC structures so that the ANC from the president down could exercise political control.[25]

These developments signed the death warrant of bipartisanship in SCOPA, but also cast grave doubts about the ruling party's commitment to the cardinal principles of openness, accountability, and transparency. Moreover, it signaled the moment in which SCOPA's raison d'être was compromised for the sake of party solidarity and the protection of the executive rather than holding it to account. The die had been cast and hereafter, whilst the joint investigative team (JIT) continued its brief under the auspices of the auditor-general,[26] sans the particular skills and experience of Heath, the credibility of the investigation would always be in doubt. By the time of its second committee report on the arms deal in May 2001, SCOPA had become a divided and divisive entity unable to agree even on procedural matters. ANC members accused the chair of hijacking the committee and the official opposition, Democratic Alliance, unable to associate itself with the second report of the committee. The DA tabled eight substantive amendments to the report, some of which were profound and went to the heart of the constitutional mandate, authority, and obligation of the committee. All were rejected.

On November 15, 2001, the joint investigative team released its report to parliament and cleared the government of any wrongdoing in the arms deal. Whilst the report highlighted inadequacies and shortcomings within the tendering process, these were of a technical nature. Prosecutions pursuant to the findings of the report and the work of the directorate of public prosecutions were aimed at private individuals, who although strongly connected to cabinet ministers and the ANC, did not pose a threat to the integrity and reputation of the government. However, widespread public criticism of the JIT report resulted in the auditor-general taking the unusual step of drafting a special report on the JIT Report to refute and rebut allegations of a "whitewash" and of executive pressure to expunge potentially damaging details and evidence.

With the JIT Report completed and presiding over an irreconcilably divided committee, SCOPA chair Gavin Woods resigned his position on February 25, 2002. Minutes of the committee meeting of February 26, 2002 record the intensity of the debate as to whether part of the meeting ought to be held in camera and whether transcripts ought to be released to the public. The threatened or potential abrogation of core principles of openness, transparency, and accessibility provided for in the Constitution, parliament and committee work bears testimony to the depths to which the committee had sunk in the maelstrom of the Arms Deal.[27]

Conclusion

South Africa is a country politically unrecognizable from the crucible of conflict from which it emerged. By all standard criteria, it is a country moving rapidly from that of a transitional democracy to one of consolidation. It has undergone three increasingly peaceful, democratic, free, and fair elections. Its Constitution is universally regarded as enlightened and progressive. Moreover, respect for the Constitution has been demonstrated by heads of state, parliament, and indeed all political parties. Parliament today stands in vivid contrast to the exclusive and stolid institution that served to rubber stamp the racist, at times unconstitutional, and illegal policies of successive apartheid governments. Today, parliament is open, vital, and welcoming of all the South African public. Problems of experience and capacity besetting parliament are time-bound and are likely to be overcome with application and resources. However, parliament has been endowed by the Constitution and its own rules committee with considerable powers of oversight of the executive branch. The problem is less one of formal powers, but rather process and substance. To be sure, these problems are, in part, constitutional. The current proportional representation party-list system militates against constituency representation and responsiveness, while encouraging party loyalty. Given the relative fusion of powers between the legislative and executive branches, with all cabinet members drawn from parliament, party loyalty also parlays into a reverence and professional fear of the executive. A further problem is the skewed party representation in parliament in which the majority party occupies 70 percent of the seats in parliament and the official opposition little more than 12 percent. This is no fault of parliament, but has a direct bearing on its ability and indeed willingness to carry out effective oversight of the executive.

This chapter has argued that even where the magnitude of the issue is of acute national importance, the expenditure of tens of billions of Rands on arms in a country suffering from an HIV/AIDS pandemic, more than 34 percent unemployment, an acute housing and land shortage, and persistent structural poverty, parliament and its chief watchdog committee SCOPA have been found wanting. In being confronted with the arms deal, parliament attempted to exercise its constitutional and procedural powers to their fullest. In the final analysis, party loyalty, executive pressure, and parliament's own ineffectiveness arguably left it a weaker institution. SCOPA's work on the arms deal was not an exercise in futility, however. The executive branch, related ministries, individual MPs, and key individuals have been called to account and prosecutions are ongoing. The South African public has been made aware of crucial issues affecting their political, social, and economic well-being. Whilst, perhaps, tiring of the story or, worse still, capitulating, the South African media have provided a forum for the dissemination of key information and have served to ventilate pubic opinion and debate. Yet, the materiality of the massive arms deal notwithstanding, the greatest cost to South Africa may yet prove to be to its young, constitutional democracy.

Notes

1. I wish to thank my Director of Studies, Elizabeth Sidiropoulos, for her invaluable input into the chapter. Thanks are also expressed to Dr. Gavin Woods MP, Mr. Douglas Gibson MP, unnamed MPs and parliamentary officials, as well as Mr. Ken Andrew, former MP and Chair of the Parliament's Standing Committee on Public Accounts, for interviews granted during research for this chapter.
2. Whilst the South African parliament is bi-cameral with a 400-seat National Assembly and a 90-member National Council of Provinces, the use of parliament throughout this chapter denotes the National Assembly.
3. The first to introduce a tri-cameral legislature was in 1983, creating two new chambers (apart from the white one) for so-called colored people and Indians. The second referendum was held in 1992 to obtain approval for the negotiations the government of President F.W. De Klerk had embarked on with the African National Congress (ANC).
4. South Africa held its first democratic elections in 1994, but was governed by the provisions of a transitional constitution until May 1996. The parliament elected in 1994 also served as a Constitutional Assembly, which drew up and adopted the final constitution.
5. A useful handbook for understanding the governmental architecture of post-1994 South Africa is Venter 1998.
6. The 1983 constitution provided for a weak form of consociationalism, which established three ethnically and racially defined separate houses of parliament, a whites-only House of Assembly, a colored House of Representatives, and an Indian House of Delegates.
7. Since 1994, the National Assembly has always seated 400 MPs.
8. In 2002, President Mbeki instituted a task team to examine models of electoral reform for South Africa under the leadership of Dr. Frederick Van Zyl Slabbert. Although the Slabbert Report recommended the adoption of a mixed multi-member and national PR system, these proposals were not accepted for the 2004 election. For a useful discussion of the options considered, see Konrad Adenauer Foundation 2002.
9. Since 1994, the speaker and deputy speaker of the National Assembly have been women.
10. Constitution of the Republic of South Africa Act (108) 1996.
11. Ibid., section 56.
12. Ibid., section 182.
13. Corder, Jagwanth, and Soltau 1999.
14. South Africa, Parliament 2002.
15. There are cases where MPs of small opposition parties have sat on up to seven committees, some of which meet simultaneously.
16. Modise 2004.
17. Whilst much has been made of the offset, counter-trade, and job creating potential of the Arms Deal, the penalty clauses for non-delivery of the offset targets is a mere 10 percent of contract value, rather than the offset value. It is

contended by the government that this is twice as high as the international norm of 5 percent of contract value. Some of the offset elements of the deal have been met. For more information on the offset arrangements, see Wrigley 2003.
18. South Africa, Republic 2000.
19. South Africa, Parliament 2000. Note: Shaik's brother is and was a Director and material beneficiary of a company that won contracts in the arms deal.
20. SCOPA Chair Gavin Woods convened a meeting with the members of the JIT at which a working division of labor was thrashed out. Cognizant of the constitutional, legal, and political imperatives, in November 2000 Woods had sought independent legal counsel opinion. He additionally wrote to Fink Haysom, legal adviser to former President Mandela and retained by Speaker Dr. Frene Ginwala to request a legal opinion as to how SCOPA ought to interact with the four entities in the investigating team. Haysom forwarded a legal opinion that set out the distinctive constitutional and legal modalities required for the individual institutions in the JIT to report to SCOPA and parliament. He made the point, however, that SCOPA could not instruct the JIT with respect to its activities.
21. South Africa, Government 2001.
22. Head of the National Directorate of Public Prosecutions (the Scorpions) Bulelani Ngcuka subsequently announced publicly that the Unit had found prima facie evidence of corruption against Zuma as part of its investigation into the arms deal, but that the prospects of a conviction were too low to attempt to prosecute. The case against one of his associates is still ongoing and, depending on its outcome, it is not entirely impossible that he may still be prosecuted.
23. Feinstein subsequently resigned from Parliament and left the country to work in London.
24. Yengeni was subsequently charged with fraud and corruption by the Scorpions and found guilty of receiving a bribe from a successful contractor in the Arms Deal whilst Chair of Parliament's Defense Committee. He was convicted of a criminal offense.
25. As quoted in Paton 2001.
26. The JIT was finally constituted of the Public Protector, who was responsible for the public phase of the investigation and liaising with other investigating agencies, the Auditor-General, responsible for the overall investigation and reporting, with specific responsibility for examining the content and processes followed in the arms deal, (including areas of risk, conflict of interests, and cost to the State), and the National Directorate of Public Prosecutions, examining, inter alia, any criminal aspects of the arms deal.
27. All parliamentary committee minutes are available online at www.pmg.org.za

13

Conclusions

M.A. Mohamed Salih

Department of Political Science, University of Leiden, Leiden,
Institute of Social Studies, The Hague, The Netherlands

In this synoptic conclusion, I attempt to explore the salient features of African legislatures by responding to three substantive questions. 1) Are African legislatures unique by being more effective in responding to common public interest issues than playing a prudent governance role vis-à-vis the executive? 2) Why the executive predominates in single-party systems as well as multiparty democracy? 3) What are the constraints under which the African legislatures operate? Overall, the chapters presented in this volume illustrate that African legislatures cannot be dismissed as replicas of traditional assemblies not only because they are modern political institutions, but also because they operate in a dominantly modernist polity. In addition, they cannot be described as wholly unique vis-à-vis their Western counterparts because they are expected to perform similar functions. As such, African legislatures portray all the institutional formalities and procedures of modern Western parliaments, assemblies or legislatures and commonly struggle to discharge responsibilities as peoples' representatives. Nonetheless, because they are mirrors of the political cultures and societies they represent, African legislatures undoubtedly reflect the ethnic, regional, and cultural differences that exist within and between legislatures.

The chapters expose a number of factors which have contributed to parliamentary differences, including:

1. The level of socio-economic development, as demonstrated in other studies, have a direct bearing on muting out patronage, exclusion, vote-buying, and the issue of democracy as an instrument of

domination. Other political deficit practices are also very important considerations for democratic consolidation (Hout and Hughes in this volume);
2. The presence or absence of traditional (or pre-colonial) assemblies, states, and kingdoms (Ethiopia, Ghana, South Africa) is in constant contention vis-à-vis what they perceive as exclusionary African modern Western-style states. The values of such traditional assemblies (status role relationships, patronage) resonate in the functioning of African modern parliaments and, in the case of South Africa, became part of the modern political process. Olowu's chapter on local assemblies is a testimony to this blend between modern and traditional institutions in governance designed to be closer to the people than national assemblies or parliaments. However, as Olowu has succinctly demonstrated, the constraints confronting local assemblies cannot be overlooked;
3. The dominant type of postcolonial party system, whether predominantly single-party system (Malawi, Mali, Tanzania, and Zambia) or dominant-racist-party system (South Africa) and how the transition to democracy has been managed by the emergent modern African political elite;
4. The strength or weakness of civil society and the degrees of freedoms it enjoys to protect the interests of its constituency, make demands on government, political parties, and parliament and also uphold the high moral ground in its conduct vis-à-vis the social forces whose interests it seeks to protect;
5. The influence of chiefs in politics, particularly the manner in which the elite use traditional institutions to bolster their electoral chances, thus creating patron–client relationships at best and dependency relationships between the two at worst. As mentioned above, in most cases, traditional institutions have been mediated by modern social forces such as civil society organizations that cut across traditional political, ethnic, cultural, and regional divides.

The cumulative effect of these differences, has culminated in the emergence of a vibrant, complex, and at times turbulent political milieu overcharged with dynamism and unpredictability. In a sense, African legislatures often find themselves pulled in different directions to fulfill traditional chiefly functions as well as modern legislature roles. Thanks to the democratization process that commenced about two decades ago, parliaments have become the focus of public attention, and the social forces that democracy has produced in the form of vocal political voices, and interests kept in limbo during the dark decades of authoritarianism.

An important feature of the transition to democracy is the emergence of proactive civil society organizations, interest groups, and associations. These political organizations have become increasingly interested in the outcomes of parliamentary debates, laws legislated, and major policies passed because of their direct impact on their constituencies and the public at large. As the chapters on Zambia, South Africa, and Mali in this volume illustrate, these political organizations have taken sides with their parliaments in their struggle to exercise its oversight role in relation to the executive. Popular trust in parliament is important in that it supports and prevents executive pressure on parliamentarians to exhibit party loyalty misconstrued as loyalty to the executive (if their political party is in government). Practices reminiscent of one-party system regimes still haunt African legislature and the executive and members of parliament are still expected to support the government in power. Such tendencies magnify the importance of civil society organizations and their struggle to support parliament in the bid to be responsive to citizens' demands and agitation for genuine oversight over the executive.

In answering the question whether African parliaments were able to discharge democratic governance responsibilities, I use the recently published Economic Commission for Africa's (ECA) report entitled Striving for Good Governance in Africa to shed light on this issue. The Report purports that,

> The African Legislature now provides some parliamentary oversight of public institutions, makes laws in the interests of people, exercises power over the budget and promotes public accountability. People in South Africa, Namibia, Mauritius, Ghana, Benin, Botswana, Lesotho, Morocco, Senegal, Mozambique and The Gambia generally consider legislature free from external control of the executive... More than 50% of the expert respondents in 12 countries judged their legislatures to be free from the control of external agencies in all or most major areas of legislation—fewer than 50% in the other 15.[1]

Evidently, popular support for legislature (as also indicated in the chapters on South Africa, Mali, and Malawi in this volume) is a clear indication that some African legislatures have been able to engender solidarities at the local and national levels as well as develop political capacities adapted to serve the generic form of parliamentary oversight.

Invariably, the chapters question whether all African parliaments have been equally able to deliver the whole range of functions responsible for political account and the rebirth of democratic governance. It is, however, safe to argue that the struggle for exercising legislative oversight and ensuring the executive's accountability have proven most difficult under one-party systems as well as the initial period of transition to multiparty democracy. This was particularly so when legislature, executive, and judiciary powers were not sufficiently separated or hardly put to the test of competitive democracy. African legislatures have endured mounting pressures exerted upon them by the executive not withstanding the fact that the executive comprises the very government that they created through the electoral process and parliamentary majority. Legislatures' governance responsibility regarding their role as representatives of the people has been moderately discharged, given the constraints under which they operate. These constraints are narrated in the closing section of this chapter.

Parliaments, Democracy, and Governance in Context

African experience with parliamentary democracy is tied up with the experiences they gained during the transition to multiparty democracy. However, these experiences were nourished by a backdrop of historical experiments with multiparty democracy that dates back to the colonial legacy. The evolution from colonial to post colonial legislature is the subject of the first sub-theme of the volume. I introduced the reader to the historical developments that influenced the evolution of African legislature and parliamentary systems from colonial rule through independence. I attempted to explain the changing fortunes of African legislatures during one-party system, military, and authoritarian regimes as well as their contribution to Africa's current democratic experience. The peculiarity of African parliamentary systems vis-à-vis their universally assumed functions is alluded to in order to explain the discrepancy between theory and practice of parliamentary systems. I proposed that African parliaments are unique because they exhibit much of Africa's political culture albeit in a modern political setting and therefore oscillate between tradition and modernity. In this respect, I surmised that African parliaments have been more effective in responding to social problems and public interest issues than managing legislature—executive relations, assuming their full oversight responsibilities, or building political accounts in an efficient and effective manner.

The important linkage between parliament and democratic governance institutions is captured by Hout who provided a comparative analysis of the complex institutional relations and linkages in Africa, Asia, and Latin America and their effectiveness in delivering on the governance functions they are mandated to execute. He focuses on the relationship between features of national political systems, many of which relate to the functioning of national parliaments, and the quality of governance. Hout's chapter makes use of data from a number of recent data sets on political institutions and governance. At a larger synthesis, he concludes that the expectation that wealthier countries tend to have better governance is corroborated. African democracies tend to have, on average, a much lower quality of governance than democracies in Asia, Latin America, and the Caribbean. There is, however, a clear disparity in the quality of governance among African countries, with the poorest scoring least well. Moreover, the impact of international dependence and reliance on primary products appears to have a negative effect on governance quality in African democracies. A second set of analyses in Hout's chapter demonstrates that only few features related to African parliaments have a noticeable impact on the performance of democracies. In particular, the role of parliament vis-à-vis the executive, federalism, the degree of electoral competitiveness, and the length of democratic experiences tend to influence the performance of African democracies in a positive direction. In general, this conclusion ties well with the conclusions of the United Nations Economic Commission for Africa's (2004) report referred to earlier in this chapter.

The significance of local assemblies or democratization from below is addressed by Olowu's contribution. He reviews the evidence of the performance of local government assemblies in various African countries, identifies their weaknesses—comparing them with the national parliaments and then, based on a few cases of effective local governance, analyzes the way forward. He argues that during the last three decades African governments embarked on a fresh phase of democratic decentralization closely linked with the ambitious economic and political reform programs. There is the consensus that democratic decentralization is substantially different from earlier experiences implemented under authoritarian regimes.

However, even though substantial administrative and financial responsibilities, including oversight delegated and resources transferred to local assemblies and governments, local governance has not emerged as a strong force in exercising their oversight functions. Mirroring the difficulties confronting national assemblies and parliaments, local assemblies have not been able to advance the cause of accountability over the local government executive. Moreover, since the quality of vertical accountability leaves much to be desired, local government assemblies have only reproduced the weaknesses inherent in the national assemblies at the local level—and even amplified them further.

At the nexus between larger synthesis and country case study, Doorenspleet offers interesting analyses grappling with how Malians perceive and whether they are satisfied with the performance of their parliament. Although the chapter's focus is Mali, datasets covering a large number of African countries are used to offer a comparative view on African peoples' perceptions of democracy. Doorenspleet's contribution illustrates that Mali's parliament has gained mass support where people believed it has an important latent or symbolic function supportive of the creation and maintenance of a genuine democratic regime. Explaining why Malians take parliamentary functions for granted, Doorenspleet suggests that such a role is critical and problematic. It is critical because parliament seems to play its oversight function and problematic in part because parliament cannot deliver on tangible developmental aspiration. Uncommon in most African countries, Doorenspleet answers the question, what are the sources of Malian parliamentary legitimacy? She argues, partially because Malians legislative support tallies with "perceptions" of better economic performance under democratic rule. Thus, affecting the quality of information made available to the electorates and the extent of peoples' general support for democracy.

In Africa, the question whether there is a relationship between development or underdevelopment and democracy looms large. It is therefore imperative not to lose sight of consequences of underdevelopment on the democratic performance by questioning the extent to which the long-term sustainability of African democratic gains is contingent on its ability to generate economic development. Obviously, it is almost near impossible to have one without the other. The rest of the chapters directly or indirectly engage the association between democracy and the manifestations of under development in terms of the human and financial resources available to political institutions (parliament, party, etc.) in their struggle to improve the quality of Africa's emergent democratic governance.

Executive Struggle to Control Legislature

While legislatures strive to deliver on their constitutionally prescribed functions, the executive struggles tirelessly to control the legislature. Three chapters focused specifically on post-1990s democratic developments and the added significance of the governance role of the legislature during multiparty democracy. The democratic norm, which postulates that legislature should control the executive is, in some circumstances, reversed with the legislature under sustained pressure from an executive constantly striving to control the legislature's law-making capacity so that it can govern unhindered by democratic checks and balances. Although this was characteristic of one-party systems, the dominance of African executives[2] and its ambition to control legislature even during multiparty democracy, has not diminished—as the chapters have revealed.

Ghana's case is introduced by Boafo-Arthur who traces the evolution of current parliamentary practices as well as the changes that have taken place over the last decade such as during the rule of the National Democratic Congress (NDC) and the New Patriotic Party (NPP) governments. According to Boafo-Arthur, considering its turbulent recent political past, Ghana's democratic gains are commendable and probably irreversible. This is explained against the backdrop of the ability of parliament to exhibit signs of political maturity and vigilance vis-à-vis the political executive. However, the chapter raises questions about Ghana's parliamentarian ability to comprehend the expansive functions and expectations bestowed on parliament where the executive is bound by global development and processes that render it incapable of influencing the global power structures and that form its policies and expected developmental outcomes. Implicit in Boafo-Arthur's contribution is the sad reality that underdevelopment is the single most significant constraint to genuine democratic flourishing in Ghana and, by implication, developing countries.

Momba uses longitudinal analysis to explain the struggle of Zambia's executive to control the legislature during national rule: the First Republic (1964–1972), the Second Republic (1974–1990), and the Third Republic (1990 to date):

- parliaments under one-party system and the excessive powers of the president;
- one-party system's failure to capture power after the onset of multiparty democracy; and
- government by party coalition constituted of opposition parties under the movement for multiparty democracy (MMD).

Zambian legislatures lack maturity and have only a decade of experience with multiparty politics. Rash party coalitions to generate an instant "parliamentary majority" coupled with the overriding power of the president made Zambia's multiparty legislatures subservient to executive power. It is, however, only fair to argue that, in very few cases legislatures were able to play their oversight role effectively hence subverting the executive's attempt to amend the constitution in order to serve private interests. Such positive interventions occurred where rivalry within the political entities, represented in coalition government, could not be solved by the elite's interest aggregation. Apparently, competitive politics, rather than elite consensus over how to share the spoils of politics, is the critical factor in empowering the legislature to undertake its oversight responsibilities.

Berhanu offers detailed analysis of the performance of Ethiopia's legislature under three successive and distinctive political regimes: imperial under Emperor Haileselassie; military socialist under Dergue's military socialism; and "multiparty democracy" under the Ethiopian People's Revolutionary Democratic Front (EPRDF). He compares and contrasts these parliamentary systems with respect to the legislature's organization and mode of operation and relationship with the executive and asks whether they were successful in undertaking effectively their oversight and accountability functions. Berhanu argues that all three parliamentary systems were characterized by a suppressed legislature operating under the autocracy (a no-party imperial rule), the Dergue (one-party military socialist regime), and the current EPRDF coalition (a multiparty system in an overwhelming party dominance). The chapter illustrates that most common amongst Ethiopia's three different parliamentary systems is that, without exception, they have been under the control of the political executive.

Although the chapters have demonstrated varying degrees of the executive's ability to control legislatures, such anomalies are not unique to Africa. Considering its underdevelopment, evidently, the power of the purse seems to find more leverage over government in the African context than in mature democracies, as Hout's chapter illustrates.

If the executive strives to control the legislature, the following section shows that under the current democratic conditions, African legislatures too struggle to perform their governance role and hold the executive accountable to legislative supremacy, specifically through parliamentary committees (Tanzania) and public accounts oversight (South Africa)—albeit with mixed results.

Legislatures Struggle to Control Executives

A commonly generalized phrase in describing the African legislature is that it is a "rubber stamp" operating under executive wings. Such commentaries lose sight of the fact that multiparty democracy generates its own dynamics, which inform the competing interests with Members of Parliaments and the social forces they represent. Party coalitions (Malawi, Zambia, and Mali) reveal that the governing coalitions drive hard bargains in all issues that matter to their party's "ideological' orientation and supporters. Likewise, some case studies (Tanzania, Malawi, and South Africa) depict the legislature's struggle to control the executive. In these cases, the legislature is caught between the dual roles of making and breaking government while being responsible for bringing the political executive to account. Wang interrogated the capacity of Tanzanian parliament to discharge its oversight functions in conjuncture with other watchdog agencies such as supreme audit institutions, anti-corruption agencies, ombudsman and human rights institutions, as well as media, political parties, and civil society organizations in vertical accountability. Tanzania's experience illustrates that government has exhibited high or low levels of accountability because parliament's oversight functions are negatively affected by the inefficiency of parliamentary committees, including late reporting, inability to audit budgets or comprehend the audit's implications for government performance.

Malawi's recent political development since the election of Bakili Muluzi as president under the first multiparty elections in 1994 with a simple majority is illustrative of continued struggles between legislatures and executive. Malawi's first parliamentary election after the defunct regime of Dr. Banda was characterized by coalition formation, which proved hazardous, and the government resorted to other tactics such as inducing floor-crossing and using heavy-handed methods in by-elections. Conflicts, high court appearances, and attempts to introduce constitutional amendments characterized the relationship between government and parliament. Crucial in these conflicts was the role of civil society. For example, civil society organizations initiated the crucial court case establishing the superiority of constitutionally guaranteed human rights over any attempt to change the constitution. In the Malawi case, Dulani and van Donge illustrate that parliamentary coalitions were difficult to manage often resulting in conflicts between president and parliament. Interestingly, the authors provided near perfect prognosis of the election results with the ruling party's, United Democratic Front (UDF), presidential candidate, Bingu wa Mutharika, winning the 20 May 2004 Presidential and Parliamentary elections, defeating a divided opposition.

Hughes' chapter deals with the arms deal scandal in South Africa and how it was treated by the legislature. He argues that when confronted with the arms deal scandal, the South African parliament attempted to exercise its constitutional and procedural powers and governance role to their fullest. However, according to Hughes, party loyalty, executive pressure, and parliament's own ineffectiveness arguably left it a weaker institution. SCOPA's work on the Arms Deal was not an exercise in futility, however. The executive branch, related ministries, individual MPs and key individuals have been called to account and prosecutions are ongoing. The South African public has been made aware of crucial issues affecting their political, social, and economic well-being. Whilst perhaps tiring of the story or, worse still, capitulating, the South African media have provided a forum for the dissemination of key information and have served to ventilate pubic opinion and debate. The executive has in some ways been able to maximize its power vis-à-vis the legislature. However, according to Hughes, South Africa's parliament failed to hold the executive accountable. This case should not direct our attention away from South Africa's parliament to prevail in several other issues of sharp contrast with the political executive opinions such as in the case of HIV/AIDS activists' campaign for ensuring that free prescriptions for antiretroviral drugs are distributed for patients.

The chapters which make up this sub-theme show that legislature's power of the purse struggles to ensure that revenue and spending measures are implemented in order to serve the public good for which public resources have been allocated. African legislatures differ from their Western counterparts. Western national legislatures' role in budgeting has declined due the devolution of financial management and spending to the lower levels of government organs, including local assemblies and municipalities. African legislatures acting on their own or pressured by civil society organizations are increasingly active in financial scrutiny, agitating for the implementation of anti-corruption measures and demanding more financial transparency and accountability from the political executive and public institutions.

Legislature and Executive Vie to Control the Judiciary

Most of the country-specific chapters grappled with the tenuous relationship characteristic of the difficulty of ensuring the separation of power, particularly during one-party and dominant-party systems as are described by Kassahun (Ethiopia) and Melber (Namibia). Political party dominance according to these authors created a majoritarian tyranny where the legislature and the judiciary are under the whim of a strong executive supported by absolute parliamentary majority exercised through a semi-revolutionary "ruling party." Melber's chapter is instructive. He observes that the independence of the judiciary is openly questioned when it makes decisions not in favor of the government's political will. Party officials, including MPs and ministers, articulate repeatedly unconstitutional demands without being corrected by the leadership, even in African democracies with more competitive multiparty regimes such as introduced by Boafo-Arthur (Ghana), Momba (Zambia), Dulani and van Donge (Malawi), and Wang (Tanzania). Since the 1970s, the relationship between Ghana's judiciary and executive was uneasy. In the particular case of Ghana, the one-party executive has subordinated the judiciary to party control. This situation has changed considerably to the better with the transition to multiparty democracy, according to Boafo-Arthur. However, Saffu reports in the case of Ghana that legislature has been able to exercise oversight functions over the executive but its ability to perform the critical role of holding the executive to account on a continuous basis is weakened by the excessive partisan approach of MPs toward this assignment.[3] As between legislature and executive, the judiciary, according to the report, shows cases where litigation through the courts to assert or defend legal rights is frankly beyond the overwhelming majority and that the judiciary bracketed with the police remains a case for concern.

The case of Zambia, as discussed by Momba, portrays the same pattern, although here we see a situation where the Constitution Review Commission expressed its intention to increase the number of constitutional offices that would be accounted to the national assembly and to measures intended at increasing accountability. Among these was the creation of the position of parliamentary ombudsman in place of the current investigator-general. The commissioners recommended that this officer should come under and appointed by the national assembly in consultation with judiciary service commission. Because the investigator-general plays the role of ombudsman whose main function is to protect the citizens from maladministration, petitioners did not think that any officer appointed by the executive, and accountable to the executive, could be expected to check effectively and control the executive. It was a contradiction in terms as it violated the notion that one power ought to be balanced by a different power."[4] Malawi offers an interesting case where both presidency and the legislature attempt to use the judiciary to its advantage. Dulani and van Donge have observed that, historically, the two democratic parliaments following the transition to democracy have not distinguished themselves in legislative initiatives or penetrating oversight of the executive. However, resistance against encroaching presidential power has been a persistent theme in the past ten years. During the second parliament, this crystallized in the resistance to a constitutional amendment that would allow the president to stand for a third term. That resistance, in conjunction with the judiciary and public opinion, demonstrates a clear break in Malawi's political culture. The judgment of the high court on the matter came as a surprise as it concluded against granting the president a third term. The judgment established clearly the prerogative of the judiciary over parliament.

Hughes and Wang's chapters mainly discuss these thorny issues in South Africa and Tanzania, respectively. Despite their different historical experiences, they fall into the same pattern, even though it is safe to argue that South Africa probably exhibits more judiciary independence than most.

Parliamentary Accountability

Parliamentary accountability is at the heart of political governance, emphasizing the rule of law, accountability, transparency, and oversight. It is the instrument through which the legislature's role in holding government accountable to the representatives of the governed is discharged leading to greater efficiency in government performance and service delivery. The chapters dealing with Tanzania (Wang), Zambia (Van Donge and Dulani), and South Africa (Hughes) gave special attention to parliamentary accountability echoing World Bank characterization of parliament's place in the accountability cycle in terms of information, action, and response.[5] In particular, the five types of accountability and their relevance to the cases studies could be summarized here with examples provided from the case studies presented in this volume:

- *Political accountability* consists of the parliamentary role in making and unmaking governments, the ultimate accountability mechanism. This could be illustrated by Zambia's parliament, which pressed charges of graft, nepotism, and violation of the constitutions against President Levy Mwanawasa. Although the motion was defeated it damaged the president's reputation and stifled his efforts to engineer the constitution for a third term in office (Van Donge and Dulani);
- *Committee investigation* consists of the work of parliamentary committees in investigating and reporting publicly on the performance of government. Two case studies speak for the exercise of African parliaments of this type of accountability. The first is that of South Africa's arms scandal analyzed by Hughes in this volume. The second is Tanzanian parliaments, after a private motion by a Member of Parliament required the government to explain a purported bribe deal between the finance minister and oil importers. A parliamentary select committee was formed to look into the matter. In its report, the committee concluded that the finance minister should be held accountable for the granting of exemptions where they were not due. Hence, on November 3, the president's office announced that the president had accepted Minister Mbilinyi's resignation (Wang in this volume).
- *The power of the purse* describes the role of parliament in authorizing governments to raise and spend budgets. This is almost a routine activity, which almost all African parliaments perform. Compared with other parliaments (for example, Eastern and central European), very few African parliaments have rejected budgets, although the opposition often exercises its right to reject or seek amendments that are often not heeded by the majority that formed the government in power.

- *The MP as ombudsman* describes the role of parliamentarians in investigating and solving problems on behalf of citizens of the constituency. In the introduction, I alluded to the case of Kenyan parliamentarians solving ethnic clashes in the Rift Valley and the Malian war in 1999, which were solved through the engagement of local chiefs, religious and community leaders, civil society organizations supported by political parties, and parliamentarians. One can add to these cases the role of Nigeria's local assemblies in conflict management; particularly in the Niger Delta area and religious violence in the north.[6]
- *Parliament as the citizens' forum* describes the function parliaments perform in serving as a forum in which citizens and their groups and organizations can publicly air grievances, concerns and recommendations. For example, the South Africa report (Folsher, W. Krafchik and I. Shapiro 2000) on transparency and public participation in the budget process is commendable in calling on parliament and civil society to participate and monitor the budget.[7] However, even in South Africa, the lack of legislation on the publication of contingent liabilities and extra-budgetary activities remains a gap in the country's transparency requirement.[8]

The last point on parliament as a citizen forum also demonstrates the important dimension of representation of diverse social forces such as women, youth, and minorities. The only chapter dealing explicitly with this subject is Tripp's contribution, which is particularly important as it tackles one of the most important recent developments in the African legislatures and its increasing gender sensitivity. Women's representation in parliament came as a result of their struggle but was also supported by and part of the international women's movements. The factors giving rise to women quotas and better representation are diverse (domestic and international women's movements, diffusion factors, symbol appeal, and creating new lines of patronage) and have therefore been received differently by different actors (women's groups, political parties, and government) in the political spectrum, including the legislatures. The divide in accepting quotas critically or at its face value is still simmering and begging for more research and socio-political interrogation to attest to its impact on the behavior of the legislature vis-à-vis women's interests and concerns.

Despite the difficulties African legislatures have to endure, they have been able to develop budgetary authority, with the right—at least in theory—to request governments to modify draft budgets or to reject the budget entirely. The African executive is aware of legislatures' power to give or withhold permission to implement the budget.

In addition to this role in accountability, in 1999 African parliamentarians established the African Parliamentarian Network against Corruption (APNAC) based in Kampala, Uganda. APNAC's main objective is building the commitment and capacity to exercise parliamentary oversight, especially in relation to financial matters. Another important objective is to cooperate with civil society organizations to combat corruption.[9] APNAC National Chapters are established in Kenya, South Africa, Tanzania, and Uganda, which also forms an anti-corruption alliance expanding within southern and eastern Africa. APANC shares several characteristics with the national anti-corruption commissions and boards established in these countries: they are all under-funded, which stifles their efforts to operate as an effective anti-corruption liaison between civil society and the legislature's capacity to legislate new laws or plug the gaps that exist in current legislation.

African parliamentarians are still under immense executive pressure, at times forging parliamentary alliances to secure government favors or refraining from embarking in genuine oppositional politics in fear of de-selection at the next election. Regrettably, the executive's ability to starve public accounts committees of funds is real. It is a complaint that runs through most of African parliamentary and oversight committees, including anti-corruption committees and boards.

Are African Parliaments Different? Why the Executive Dominates? And What Constraints Confront Them?

Before closing, I will attempt to respond briefly to the three questions posed at the opening of this chapter. First, are African parliaments different from other parliaments? The contributors to this volume argue that the generic functions of African parliaments are not different from those of their Western counterparts. However, they differ markedly in terms of the political cultures within which they deliver these universal parliamentary functions. African parliaments operate as the pulse of society representing not only the modern forces (public, civil society, and party), they are also slaves of African ethnicity, regional interests, and patronage. African parliamentarians often undertake more burdensome functions, such as managing local conflicts and participating in social events, from marriage ceremonies to death celebrations.

However, unlike Western parliaments, most of the issues confronting African parliaments are under-development driven—a recipe for conflict of interests about resource allocation and management. Intermittently, the contributors attributed the presence of uneasy executive–legislature relations to this issue, as the control or enforcing oversight and accountability rules governing the resources and personnel of government become a major arena for the war of will between the two.

Second, why does the executive dominate both in one-party and multparty systems? The contributors to this volume argue that the long gestation of military regimes, one-party rule, and civil authoritarian governments following independence have produced state-centered governance, thus blurring state and public domains of authority. By extension, the subservient attitudes toward the executive in one-party governments tend to linger for quite some time before transition takes hold and the consolidation of democratic values blossom. Despite the existence of parliamentary committees, poor quality of representation, inadequate general awareness of parliamentary supremacy, and the non-hierarchical nature of parliamentarians also make legislators operate under immense party pressure to affirm rather than challenge the executive, even when they should do so. The absence of internal democracy in most African political parties questions Members of Parliament ability to be loyal to the nation rather than the patronage of the party in power. Under the circumstances, African parliamentarians find their loyalty divided between the party leader (who is often the president or prime minister) and the country under the watchful eye of party disciplinary committees.

Third, African legislatures are confronted with several constraints emanating from the gap between the political and civil liberties they enjoyed during the transition to democracy and the cynicism generated by the lack of improvement in peoples' standards of living. The failure of African democratically elected governments to prove true the association between democracy and development as perceived by the poor and underprivileged citizens meant that the legislatures have to work even harder to make a difference by showing their ability to hold the executive accountable to the governed. Coupled with an inherently short and at times skewed democratic experience, insufficient internalization of democratic norms and values has contributed to the prevalence of only virtual democracies or democracies without democrats. Such instances have contributed to people's questioning of the ability of democratic institutions to deliver better economic and livelihood gains.

Despite people's relative goodwill toward African legislatures, they operate under immense constraints and pressures. These include inadequate human and financial resources in support of parliament and parliamentary committees. This leads to an increasing dependence on external parliamentary support, which has become a common feature of most African parliaments. External support often takes the form of training, logistics (audio-visual, computer, and communication equipment, etc.), documentation centers, parliamentary committees, and attendance at transnational parliamentary conferences. Unfortunately, not only is donor support received with caution in fear that it could compromise parliamentary independence from foreign pressures, it is irregular, unreliable, unpredictable, or provided after the pressing need for it has passed.

A large number of African parliamentarians are socialized over a long period of one-party rule to non-democratic practices. The long gestation of one-party regimes and military governments suspended the true practice of parliamentary democracy for too long, and in most cases obscured the relationship between party, government, and parliament. Few Members of Parliament command the full range of knowledge pertaining to parliamentary procedures in a multiparty democracy. Some have no experience of modern legislative procedures and are inept at understanding their duties and powers as representatives of the people, let alone the working of parliamentary committees which deal with complex contemporary issues, from globalization, free trade to terrorism and international crimes.

Although African parliamentarians are better educated than those in the early independence parliaments, today Members of Parliament have to deal with a wide range of issues ranging from globalization to migration, refugees, genetically modified foods, information and communication technology (ICT), legal and administrative regulatory frameworks, and policies. Added to the conventional functions of parliament, which I have narrated in the introductory chapter, some Members of Parliament can hardly comprehend the complexity of issues with the global, regional, and national issues with which they must contend.

In most of rural Africa there is the general popular misconception that parliament is an extension of government, leading the electorate to ridicule the commonly held notion of separation of power. For many ordinary Africans, parliament's main role is to work with government and local councils to solve their immediate individual or local problems. Political culture aside (ethnicity, social obligations, patron–client relationship), Members of Parliament are often constrained by social obligations that require large spending sprees on funerals, marriages, contributions to public festivities, and at times school fees and medical prescription fees. These financial obligations put Members of Parliament under huge financial pressure and may even contribute to financial insecurity and vulnerability to the executive's manipulation.

Most African legislatures are poorly served by a weak civil society unable to engage the public, lobby government or political parties, or come to the aid of parliament to avoid succumbing to executive pressure. Although, there is no denying that there are exceptions (e.g. the cases of Mali, South Africa, and Malawi legislatures presented in this volume), overall, African civil society organizations have failed to become active watchdogs against both government's graft and parliament's inaction. There are few incidences where civil society has worked together with the legislature to amend or introduce new legislation in order to cleanse the executive from circumventing public interest for private gain. Legislature oscillation between government and government greatly harms the former's ability to exercise parliamentary accountability to the full. To this effect the linkages between civic governance (active participation of media, unions, professional and business associations) and political parliamentary governance are weak and require special attention if legislatures are to be strengthened.

In sum, because governance traverses socio-economic, political structures, and institutional boundaries, it requires the cooperation and coordination of efforts amongst multiple stakeholders and partnerships, including the national integrity system Legislature, executive, auditor general, public service, judiciary, media, civil society, ombudsman, anti-corruption commissions, watchdog agencies, private sector, international community, etc.) in its entirety. The role of parliamentary governance is complementary to those other actors play, but it could be rendered in-effective if others failed to execute their governance mandate or lend it their support. However, the significance of the role of parliamentary governance is derived from its centrality in public life as representative of people's sovereignty, straddling the ambiguous domain between government and governance.

Notes

1. ECA 2004: 4–5. The Report is a result of a survey conducted in 28 African countries (Benin, Botswana, Burkina Faso, Cameroon, Chad, Egypt, Ethiopia, Gabon, Gambia, Ghana, Kenya, Lesotho, Malawi, Mali, Mauritius, Morocco, Mozambique, Namibia, Niger, Nigeria, Rwanda, Senegal, South Africa, Swaziland, Tanzania, Uganda, Zambia, and Zimbabwe).
2. Van Cranenburg 2003; Doornspleet 2003.
3. Saffu 2004: 3.
4. Zambia, Government of 1995a.
5. World Bank 2000: 14–15.
6. See Salih 1999; 2001.
7. South Africa 2000.
8. Ibid., 13.
9. For more on the African Parliamentarian Network against Corruption (APNAC), see its proceedings of the Nairobi meeting (African Parlimentarian Network against corruption 2003).

Bibliography

Åfreds, Johanna. *History and Nation-Building: The Political Uses of History in Post-colonial Namibia* (Uppsala: Department of Economic History, Uppsala University, 2000).

African Parliamentarian Network Against Corruption. *Challenges to the Fight Against Corruption*, Conference proceedings (Nairobi, November 3–4, 2003).

Almond, G.A. and S. Verba. *The Civic Culture* (Princeton: Princeton University Press, 1963).

Apter E. David. *The Gold Coast in Transition* (Princeton: Princeton University Press, 1955).

Arsano, Y. "People's Choice and Political Power in Ethiopia: Elections and Representations Under Three Regimes" in Tafesse Olika and Kassahun Berhanu (eds.), *The May 1995 Elections in Ethiopia: The Quest for Democratic Governance in A Multiethnic Society* (unpublished manuscript, Addis Ababa: 1997).

Austin, Dennis (1970) *Politics in Ghana, 1946–1960.* (London and New York: Oxford University Press, 1970).

Ayee, J. "Ghana: A Top-Down Initiative" in D. Olowu and J. Wunsch (eds.), *Local Governance in Africa: The Challenges of Democratic Decentralization* (Boulder: Lynne Rienner, 2004), 125–154.

Ayensu, K.B. and S.N. Darkwa. *The Evolution of Parliament in Ghana* (Accra: Institute of Economic Affairs, 1999).

Banda, J.R. "The Constitutional Change Debate of 1993–1995" in K.M. Phiri and K.R. Ross (eds.), *Democratisation in Malawi: A Stocktaking* (Blantyre: 1998), 316–334.

Banfield, E.C. *The Moral Basis of a Backward Society* (New York: Free Press, 1958).

Baregu, M. "The Rise and Fall of the One-party State in Tanzania" in Jennifer A. Widner (ed.), *Economic Change and Liberalisation in Sub-Saharan Africa* (Baltimore: Johns Hopkins University Press, 1994), 129–157.

Barkan, J.D. "Legislators, Elections, and Political Linkage" in Joel D. Barkan and John J. Okumu (eds.), *Politics and Public Policy in Kenya and Tanzania* (London: Praeger Publishers, 1979), 64–92.

Barro, R.J. *Determinants of Economic Growth: A Cross-Country Empirical Study* (Cambridge: MIT Press, 1997).

Basta-Fleiner, L.R. "Can Ethnic Federalism Work?" Paper Presented at the Conference, Facing Ethnic Conflicts (Bonn: Center for Development Research, 2000).

Bauer, Gretchen. "Challenges to Democratic Consolidation in Namibia" in R. Joseph (ed.), *State, Conflict and Democracy in Africa* (Boulder and London: Lynne Rienner, 1999), 429–448.

———. "Namibia in the First Decade of Independence: How Democratic?" *Journal of Southern African Studies*, 27/1 (2001), 33–55.

———. *The Greenwood Encyclopedia of Women's Issues Worldwide: Sub-Saharan Africa* (Westport: Greenwood Press, 2003), 271–293.

Bayart, J.F. *The State in Africa: The Politics of the Belly* (London: Longman, 1993).

Baylies, C. and M. Szeftel. "The Rise of a Zambian Capitalist Class in the 1970s" *Journal of Southern African Studies*, 9/3 (1982), 201–202.

Bayme, von, K. *Parliamentary Democracy* (Basingstoke: Macmillan, 1999).

Beck, L.J. "Democratization and the Hidden Public: The Impact of Patronage Networks on Senegalese Women" *Comparative Politics*, 35/2 (2003), 156.

Beck, T. et al. "New Tools in Comparative Political Economy: The Database of Political Institutions" *World Bank Economic Review*, 15/1 (2001), 165–176.

Befekadu Degefe and Berhanu Nega (eds.), *Annual Report on the Ethiopian Economy*, Vol. 1. 1999/2000. (Addis Ababa: United Printers, 2000).

Berhanu, K. "Ethiopia Elects A Constituent Assembly" *Review of African Political Economy*, 22/63 (1995), 129–135.

Beyene, A. "Some Notes on the Evolution of Regional Administration in Ethiopia" *Ethiopian Journal of Development Research*, 9/1 (1987), 21–49.

Biddle, J., M. Cassidy and R. Mukandala. "Assessment of the Operations of the Union National Parliament of Tanzania." Report prepared for United States Agency for International Development/Tanzania (Dar es Salaam, Tanzania: Office of Democracy and Governance, 2002).

Blair, H. "Participation and Accountability in the Periphery: Democratic Local Governance in Six Countries" *World Development*, 28/1 (2000), 21–39.

Blondel, J. et al. "Legislative Behaviour: Some Steps toward a Cross-National Measurement" *Government and Opposition*, 5 (1969–1970), 67–85.

Boafo-Arthur, K. "Political Parties and Prospects for National Stability" in Kwame A. Ninsin and F.K. Drah (eds.), *Political Parties and Democracy in Ghana's Fourth Republic* (Accra: Woeli Publishing, 1993), 234.

Boateng, E.A. *Government and the People: Outlook for Democracy in Ghana* (Accra, Institute of Economic Affairs, 1996).

Boynton, G.R. and C.L. Kim (eds.), *Legislative Systems in Developing Countries* (Durham: Duke University Press, 1975).

Bratton, M. "Second Elections in Africa" in Larry Diamond and Marc F. Platter (eds.), *Democratization in Africa* (Baltimore: Johns Hopkins University Press, 1999), 18–34.

——— and N. van de Walle. *Democratic Experiment in Africa: Regime Transitions in Comparative Perspective* (Cambridge: Cambridge University Press, 1997).

——— and R. Mattes. "How People View Democracy: Africans' Surprising Universalism" *Journal of Democracy*, 12/1 (2001), 107–121.

——— et al. *Afrobarometer Round 2: Compendium of Comparative Results from a 15-Country Survey*. Afrobarometer Working Paper No. 34 (Cape Town: IDASA,

Legon-Accra. Ghana Centre for Democratic Development and East Lansing: Michigan State University, 2004).

Brynjúlfsdóttir, O.L. *Tolerance for Non-Conformity. A Study of the Namibian Political Elite* (Uppsala: Department of Government/Uppsala University, 1998).

Bukurura, S.H. "Promoting Accountability: Optimism and Unrealistic Aspirations" in S.H. Bukurura, *Essays on Constitutionalism and the Administration of Justice in Namibia 1990–2002* (Windhoek: Out of Africa, 2002), 57–88.

———. "Between Liberation Struggle and Constitutionalism. Namibia and Zimbabwe" in Henning Melber (ed.), *Re-examining Liberation in Namibia. Political Culture since Independence.* (Uppsala: Nordic Africa Institute, 2003), 34–46.

Burkhart, R. and M. Lewis-Beck. "Comparative Democracy: The Economic Development Thesis" *American Political Science Review*, 88/4 (1994), 903–910.

Burnell, P. "Parliament in Zambia after the 2001 Elections" (unpublished paper, 2001).

———. "Parliamentary Committees in Zambia's Third Republic: Partial Reforms, Unfinished Agenda" *Journal of Southern African Studies*, 28/2 (2002), 292–313.

———. "Legislative-Executive Relations in Zambia: Parliamentary Reform on the Agenda" *Journal of Contemporary African Studies*, 21/1 (2003), 47–68.

Chabal, P. and J.P. Daloz. *Africa Works: Disorder as a Political Instrument* (London: James Currey, 1999).

Chama Cha Mapundizi (CCM). *The CCM Constitution* (Dar es Salam: Tanganyika Standard Limited, 1977).

Chikulo, B. "The 1978 Elections" in Evolving Structure of the Zambian Society. Proceedings of a Seminar at the Center of African Studies, University of Edinburgh, Edinburgh, May 30–31, 1970.

Clapham, C. *Haile Selassie's Government* (London: Longman, 1969).

———. "The Politics of Failure, Cleintalism, Political Stability and National Integration in Sierra Leone" in C. Clapham (ed.), *Private Patronage and Political Power: Clientelism in the Modern State* (London: Frances Printers, 1982), 76–92.

———. "Preface" in S. Pausewang, et al. (eds.), *Ethiopia Since the Derg: A Decade of Democratic Pretension and Performance* (London: Zed Books, 2002), pp. xv–xviii.

Cliffe, Lionel et al. *The Transition to Independence in Namibia* (Boulder and London: Lynne Rienner, 1994).

Coleman, J. *Politics of Developing Countries* (Princeton: Princeton University Press, 1960).

Commonwealth Secretariat. *The Presidential and National Assembly Elections in Namibia, 7–8 December 1994. The Report of the Commonwealth Observer Group* (London: Commonwealth Secretariat, 1995).

Corder, H., S. Jagwanth and F. Soltau. "Report on Parliamentary Oversight and Accountability' Faculty of Law" (Cape Town: University of Cape Town, July 1999).

Dahl, R.A. *Polyarchy: Participation and Opposition* (New Haven: Yale University Press, 1971).

———. "A Democratic Dilemma: System Effectiveness versus Citizen Participation" *Political Science Quarterly*, 109/1 (1994), 23–34.
Dalton, R. *Citizen Politics*, 2nd edn. (Chatham: Chatham House, 1996).
Damgaard, E. "How Parties Control Committee Members" in Herbert Döring (ed.), *Parliaments and Majority Rule in Western Europe* (New York: St. Martin's Press, 1995). 308–325.
Delhey, J. and Verena Tobsch. *Understanding Regime support in New Democracies: Does Politics really Matter more than Economics?* (Berlin: Wiessenschftszentrum Berlin fur Socialforschung, 2002).
Di Palma, G. *To Craft Democracies: An Essay on Democratic Transitions* (Berkeley: University of California Press, 1990), 308–325.
Diamond, L. "Rethinking Civil Society: Toward Democratic Consolidation" *Journal of Democracy*, 5/3 (1994), 4–17.
———. *Developing Democracy: Toward Consolidation* (Baltimore: Johns Hopkins University Press, 1999).
Diop, A.S. "Senegalese Women Want to be Elected not Electors" (Addis Ababa: Panafrican News Agency, 2001).
Dobell, Lauren. *Swapo's Struggle for Namibia, 1960–1991: War by Other Means* (Basel: P. Schlettwein Publishing, 1998).
Doorenspleet, R. "The Fourth Wave of Democratization: Identification and Explanation." Ph.D. dissertation (Leiden: University of Leiden, 2001).
———. *Transitions to Democracy: Exploring the Structural Sources during the Fourth Wave* (Boulder: Lynne Rienner Publishers, 2005).
Döring, H. "Introduction" in Herbert Döring (ed.), *Parliaments and Majority Rule in Western Europe* (New York: St. Martin's Press, 1995), 13–20.
Du Pisani, Andre. "Liberation and Tolerance" in Henning Melber (ed.), *Re-examining Liberation in Namibia: Political Culture since Independence* (Uppsala: The Nordic Africa Institute, 2003), 129–136.
Duverger, M. *Political Parties: Their Organization and Activity in the Modern State* (London: Methuen, 1958).
Economic Commission for Africa. *Striving for Good Governance in Africa* (Addis Ababa: ECA, 2004).
Economist Intelligence Unit. 3rd quarter, "Country Report: Tanzania, Comoros" (London: EIU, 1993).
———. 4th quarter, "Country Report: Tanzania, Comoros" (London: EIU, 1996).
———. Nov., "Country Report: Tanzania, Comoros" (London: EIU, 2001).
Elliot, Aubxy. *Zulu: Heritage of a nation* (Cape Town: Struik, 1991).
Englebert, P. *State Legitimacy and Development in Africa* (Boulder: Lynne Rienner, 2000).
Erasmus, G. "The Constitution: Its Impact on Namibian Statehood and Politics" in Christiaan Keulder (ed.), *State, Society and Democracy: A Reader in Namibian Politics* (Windhoek: Gamsberg Macmillan, 2000), 77–104.
Erdheim, M. "Revolution, Totem und Tabu: Vom Verenden der Revolution im Wiederholungszwang" in *Herrschaft, Anpassung, Widerstand. Ethnopsychoanalyse*, 2 (Frankfurt/Main: Brandes and Apsel, 1991), 153–166.

Eriksen, Karen. "Zambia: Class Formation and Détente" in *Review of African Political Economy*, 9 (1978), 4–26.
Ethiopia, Federal Democratic Republic of "The Constitution of the Federal Democratic Republic of Ethiopia" *Federal Negarit Gazette*, 1st year, no. 1 (Addis Ababa: Government Printers, August 21, 1995).
Ethiopia, People's Democratic Republic of. *The Constitution of the PDRE* (Addis Ababa: Ministry of Information, 1987).
———. *A Leap Across Centuries* (Addis Ababa: Ministry of Information, 1987).
Ethiopia, Transitional Government of. "The Transitional Period Charter, 1991" (Addis Ababa: Government Printers, 1991).
———. "Proclamation No. 111/95, Proclamation to Make the Electoral Law of Ethiopia Conform with the Constitution of the Federal Democratic Republic of Ethiopia" (Addis Ababa: Government Printers, 1995).
Ethiopian Human Rights Council "The 2001 Ethiopian Local Elections: A Report on EHRCO's Monitoring Activities and Findings" (Addis Ababa: EHRCO, April 2001).
Evans-Pritchard, E.E. *The Azande: History and Political Institutions* (Oxford: Clarendon Press, 1971).
Ewald, J. "Economic Reforms and Democratisation in Tanzania: The Case of the Election 2000 and the Need to Go Beyond Electionalism" Paper to the conference on Democratization and Conflict Management in East Africa, March 2–3, 2002.
Ferree, K.E. and S. Singh. "Electoral Institutions and Economic Performance in Africa, 1970–92" in S. Chan and J.R. Scarritt (eds.), *Coping with Globalization: Cross-National Patterns in Domestic Governance and Policy Performance* (London: Frank Cass, 2002), 89–120.
Folsher, A. Warren Krafchik and Isaac Shapiro. *Transparency and Budget Participation in the Budget Process, South Africa: A Country Study* (Cape Town: Institute for Democracy in South Africa, Budget Information Service, October 2000).
Forrest, Joshua Bernard. *Namibia's Post-Apartheid Regional Institutions: The Founding Year* (Rochester: Rochester University Press, 1998).
Fortes, M. and E.E. Evans-Pritchard (eds.), *African Political Systems*, (London: Oxford University Press, 1940).
Forum for the Future. *Conference Report: Namibia after Nine Years—Past and Future* (Windhoek: Forum for the Future, 1999).
Freedom House. Freedom in the World Country Ratings 1972–1973 to 2001–2002 (2003). Downloaded from www.freedomhouse.org, Sept. 16, 2003.
Freund, B. *The Making of Contemporary Africa* (Basingstoke: Macmillan, 1984).
Gawaya-Tegulle, T. 2001. "Electoral College: A Shield for Non-Performing MPs" *The Other Voice* (Kampala, 2001), 2.
Geisler, G. " 'Parliament is Another Terrain of Struggle': Women, Men and Politics in South Africa" *Journal of Modern African Studies*, 38/4 (2000), 605–630.
Gertzel, Cherry. "Dissent and Authority in the Zambian One Party State, 1973–80" in Cherry Gertzel (ed.), *The Dynamics of One Party State in Zambia* (Manchester: Manchester University Press, 1984), 79–115.
Ghana, Government of. "The 1969 Constitution of the Republic of Ghana" (Accra: Government Printers, 1969).

Ghana, Parliament of. "A Guide to the Parliament of Ghana (mimeo.)" (Accra: Government Printers, n.d.).
———. "Standing Orders of the Parliament of Ghana" (Accra: Government Printers, Nov. 1, 2000).
———. "A Guide to the Parliament of Ghana" (Accra: Government Printers, Dec. 2004).
———. "First Report of the Appointments Committee on the President's Nominations for Ministerial Appointments" (Accra: Government Printers, Feb. 1, 2005), 3.
Gibbon, P. "Limping Towards a Ditch Without a Crutch: The Brave New World of Tanzanian Cotton Marketing Cooperatives" Working Paper Subseries, No. 3 (Copenhagen: Centre for Development Research, 1998).
———. "Civil Society, Locality and Globalization in Rural Tanzania: A Forty-Year Perspective" *Development and Change*, 32/2 (2001), 819–844.
Glover, Susan K. "Namibia's Recent Elections: Something New or Same Old Story?" *South African Journal of International Affairs*, 7/2 (2000), 141–148.
Goldworthy, D. "Ghana's Second Republic: A Post-Mortem" *African Affairs*, 72 (1973), 11.
Griffith, J.A.G. et al. *Parliament Functions, Practice and Procedures*, 2nd edn. (London: Sweet and Maxwell, 2003).
Gudina, M. "Authoritarian Populism and Democratization in Ethiopia" in K.K. Prah and Abdel Ghaffar Mohammed Ahmed (eds.), *Africa in Transformation: Political and Economic Transformation and Socio-Political Responses in Africa*, Vol. 2 (Addis Ababa: Organization for Social Science Research in Eastern Africa, 2000), 179–191.
Gump, J.O. *The Formation of the Zulu Kingdom in South Africa, 1750–1840* (San Francisco: Mellen Research University Press, 1990).
Gupta, A. "The Zambian National Assembly: Study of an African Legislature" in *Parliamentary Affairs*, 19/1 (1965–1966), 48–55.
Harrison, G. "Bringing Political Struggle Back in: African Politics, Power and Resistance" *Review of African Political Economy*, 89 (2001), 387–402.
———. "Post-Conditionality Politics and Administrative Reform: Reflections on the Cases of Uganda and Tanzania" *Development and Change*, 32 (2001), 657–679.
Heilman, B., N. Kamata and L. Ndumbaro. "Is Mkapa's Honeymoon over? Corruption, Politics, and Societal Values in Tanzania: An Overview of Benjamin Mkapa's First Five Year Term" (unpublished manuscript, 2001).
Heywood, A. *Politics* (Basingstoke: Palgrave, 2002).
Hindess, B. *Parliamentary Democracy and Socialist Politics* (London: Routledge and Kegan Paul, 1983).
Hinz, Manfred O. "To Achieve Freedom and Equality: Namibia's New Legal Order" in Ingolf Diener and Olivier Graefe (eds.), *Contemporary Namibia. The First Landmarks of a Post-Apartheid Society* (Windhoek: Gamsberg Macmillan, 2001), 75–91.
Hopkins, R.F. "The Role of the M.P. in Tanzania" *American Political Science Review*, 64 (1970), 754–771.

Hopkins, R.F. *Political Roles in a New State* (New Haven and London: Yale University Press, 1971).
Hopwood, Graham. "Caprivi—A Year After" *Namibian*, August 2, 2000.
Huntington, S.P. "How Countries Democratize" *Political Science Quarterly*, 106 (1992), 579–616.
Hyden, G. *No Shortcuts to Progress: African Development Management in Perspective* (London: Heinemann, 1983).
———. "Party, State, and Civil Society: Control Versus Openness" in Joel D. Barkan (ed.), *Beyond Capitalism vs. Socialism in Kenya and Tanzania* (Nairobi: East African Educational Publishers, 1994), 75–99.
———. "Top-Down Democratization in Tanzania" *Journal of Democracy*, 10 (1999), 142–155.
——— and Charles Okigbo, "The Media and the Two Waves of Democracy" in G. Hyden, Michael Leslie and Folu F. Ogundimu (eds.), *Media and Democracy in Africa* (Uppsala: Nordic Africa Institute, 2002), 29–53.
Ibrahim, S. *The Nupe and their Neighbours* (Ibadan: Heinemann Educational Books, 1992).
Imperial Ethiopian Government. "Administrative Regulations" *Federal Negarit Gazette*, 1st year, no. 6 (Addis Ababa: Government Printers, Aug. 27, 1942).
Inglehart, R. *Culture Shift in Advanced Industrial Society* (Princeton: Princeton University Press, 1990).
———. *Modernization and Postmodernization: Culture, Economic, and Political Change in 43 Societies* (Princeton: Princeton University Press, 1997).
———. *The Silent Revolution: Changing Values and Political Styles in Western Publics* (Princeton: Princeton University Press, 1977).
Institute for Democracy in Southern Africa. Afrobarometer. *Democracy and Electoral Alternation: Evolving African Attitudes*. Afrobarometer Briefing Paper, No. 9 (Apr. 2004).
Institute of Democracy and Electoral Assistance. *Democracy at the Local Level in Eastern and Southern Africa: Policy Summary* (Stockholm: IDEA, 2004).
Inter-Parliamentary Union. *Parliaments: a comparative study on the structure and functioning of representative institutions in forty-one countries.* (London and Paris: Inter-Parliamentary Union and Cassell and company, 1961).
Janguo, A. "The Need for Parliamentary Reform in CPA Countries" *Bunge News*, 11 (Oct. 1999).
Johnson, J.K. and R.T. Nakamura. "Concept Paper on Legislatures and Good Governance" (New York: United Nations Development Program, 1999). Downloaded from www.undp.org/governance/parldev/docs/concepaper.htm, Aug. 2005.
Johnson, R.W. "Six Countries in Search of Democracy" *Focus Newsletter,* 9 (Helen Suzman Foundation, 1998).
Judge, D. *The Parliamentary State* (London: Sage, 1993).
Kaakunga, R.A. (Othy), "Constitutional Development in Namibia from 1900 to 2000" in Manfred O. Hinz, Sam K. Amoo and Dawid van Wyk (eds.), *The Constitution at Work: 10 Years of Namibian Nationhood*. (Pretoria: VerLoren van Themaat Centre/University of Pretoria, 2002), 27–37.

Kabakama, J. "The Position and Role of Parliament in the Era of Multipartyism in Tanzania" (unpublished paper submitted in partial fulfilment of B degree, Dar es Salaam: University of Dar es Salaam, 1997).

Kaela, L.C.W. "The 1991 Constitution" in Laurent C.W. Kaela (ed.), *Zambia in Transition: Studies in Democratization and Institutional Reform* (Global Coalition for Africa and Africa Leadership Forum, 1994), 107–109.

Kaufmann, D., A. Kraay and M. Mastruzzi. Governance Matters III: Governance Indicators for 1996–2002 (Washington, D.C.: World Bank, 2003). Downloaded from www.worldbank.org/wbi/governance/govdata 2002, Sept. 24, 2003.

Kelsall, T. "Governance, Local Politics and Districtization in Tanzania" *African Affairs*, 99 (2000) 533–551.

———. "Shop Windows and Smoke-Filled Rooms: Governance and the Re-Politicization of Tanzania" *Journal of Modern African Studies*, 40 (2002) 597–619.

———. "Governance, Democracy and Recent Political Struggles in Tanzania" *Commonwealth and Comparative Politics*, 41 (2003), 55–82.

Kenworthy, L. and Malami, M. "Gender Inequality in Political Representation: A Worldwide Comparative Analysis" *Social Forces*, 78/1 (1999), 235–268.

Keulder, Christiaan, *Voting Behaviour in Namibia: Local Authority Elections, 1998* (Windhoek: Friedrich Ebert Stiftung, 1998).

———. *Voting Behaviour in Namibia II: Regional Council Elections, 1998* (Windhoek: Friedrich Ebert Stiftung, 1999).

———, Antonie Nord and Christoph Emminghaus. "Namibia's Emerging Political Culture" in Christiaan Keulder (ed.), *State, Society and Democracy: A Reader in Namibian Politics* (Windhoek: Gamsberg Macmillan, 2000) 237–263.

——— and Dirk Spilker, "In Search of Democrats in Namibia: Attitudes Among the Youth" in Henning Melber (comp.), *Measuring Democracy and Human Rights in Southern Africa*, Discussion Paper No. 18 (Uppsala: Nordic Africa Institute, 2002), 19–28.

Kick, E.L. et al. "World-System Position, National Political Characteristics and Economic Development Outcomes" *Journal of Political and Military Sociology*, 28/1 (2000), 131–155.

Kilimwiko, L. I. M. *The Fourth Estate in Tanzania* (Dar es Salaam: Colour Print, 2002).

Kiondo, A.S.Z. "The New Politics of Local Development in Tanzania" in Peter Gibbon (ed.), *The New Local Level Politics in East Africa*, Research Report No. 95 (Uppsala: Nordiska Afrikainstitutet, 1994).

Kjekshus, H. "The Question Hour in Tanzania's Bunge" *African Review*, 2 (1972), 351–379.

———. "Parliament in a One-Party State: the Bunge of Tanzania, 1965–70" *Journal of Modern African Studies*, 12 (1974a), 19–43.

———. "Perspectives on the Second Parliament, 1965–1970" in Election Study Committee, University of Dar es Salaam. *Socialism and Participation* (Dar es Salaam: Tanzania Publishing House, 1974b).

Klaus, von B. *Parliamentary Democracy: Democratization, Destabilization, Reconsolidation, 1789–1999* (Basingstoke: Macmillan, 2000).

Konrad Adenauer Foundation. "Electoral Models for South Africa: Electoral Task Team Review Roundtable" (Cape Town: Konrad Adenauer Foundation, 2002).

Kössler, Reinhart, *Towards Greater Participation and Equality? Some Findings on the 1992 Regional and Local Elections in Namibia* (Windhoek: The Namibian Economic Policy Research Unit, 1993).
——— and Henning Melber. "Political Culture and Civil Society: On the State of the Namibian State" in Ingolf Diener and Olivier Graefe (eds.), *Contemporary Namibia: The First Landmarks of a Post-Apartheid Society* (Windhoek: Gamsberg Macmillan, 2001), 147–160.
Krafchik, W. and J. Wehner. "The Role of Parliament in the Budgetary Process" *South African Journal of Economics*, 66/4 (1998), 512–541.
Kriger, Norma. "The Politics of Creating National Heroes: The Search for Political Legitimacy and National Identity" in N. Bhebe and T. Ranger (eds.), *Soldiers in Zimbabwe's Liberation War* (London: James Currey, Portsmouth: Heinemann, and Harare: University of Zimbabwe Publications, 1995), 139–162.
Lamb, Guy. "Putting Belligerents in Context: The Cases of Namibia and Angola" in Simon Chesterman (ed.), *Civilians in War* (Boulder and London: Lynne Rienner, 2001). 25–39.
———. "Debasing Democracy: Security Forces and Human Rights Abuses in Post-Liberation Namibia and South Africa" in Henning Melber (comp.), *Measuring Democracy and Human Rights in Southern Africa*, Discussion Paper No. 18 (Uppsala: Nordic Africa Institute, 2002), 30–49.
Lemarchand, R. "Africa's Troubled Transitions" *Journal of Democracy*, 3 (1992), 98–109.
Levine, D. *Wax and Gold: Tradition and Innovation in Ethiopian Culture* (Chicago: University of Chicago Press, 1965).
Leys, Colin et al. *Namibia's Liberation Struggle: The Two-Edged Sword* (London: James Currey and Athens: Ohio University Press, 1995).
Lijphart, A. *Patterns of Democracy: Government Forms and Performance in Thirty-Six Countries* (New Haven: Yale University Press, 1999).
Linz, J.J. "Crisis, Breakdown and Reequilibration" in Juan J. Linz and Alfred Stepan (eds.), *The Breakdown of Democratic Regimes* (Baltimore: John Hopkins University Press, 1978), 3–13.
——— "Transitions to Democracy" *Washington Quarterly*, 13/2 (1990), 143–164.
Lipset, S.M. "Some Social Requisites of Democracy: Economic Development and Political Legitimacy" *American Political Science Review*, 53/1 (1959), 69–105.
Lloyd, A.F. (ed.) *The King's Men: Leadership and Status in Buganda on the Eve of Independence* (London, Oxford University Press, 1964).
Lodge, Tom. "Report of Electoral Commissions Forum of SADC Countries, on the Namibian Elections Report December 1999" (Auckland Park: Electoral Institute of Southern Africa, 1999).
———. "Heavy Handed Democracy: SWAPO's Victory in Namibia" *Southern Africa Report*, 15/2 (2000), 26–29.
Lord Hailey Report, *Native Administration and Political Development in British Tropical Africa* (Nendeln, Liechtenstein: Kraus Reprint, 1979).
Mamdani, M. *Citizen and Subject: Contemporary Africa and the Legacy of Late Colonialism* (Princeton: Princeton University Press, 1996).

Mandelbaum, M. *The Ideas that Conquered the World: Peace, Democracy, and Free Markets in the Twenty-first Century* (Oxford: Public Affairs Ltd., 2002).

March, J.G. and J.P. Olsen. *Democratic Governance* (New York: The Free Press, 1995).

Markakis, J. and Asmelash Beyene. "Representative Institutions in Ethiopia" *Journal of Modern African Studies*, 5/2 (1967), 193–219.

———. *Ethiopia: Anatomy of A Traditional Polity* (London: Oxford University Press, 1974).

Matland, R.E. and D.T. Studlar. "The Contagion of Women Candidates in Single Member and Multimember District Systems: Canada and Norway" *Journal of Politics*, 58/3 (1996), 707–733.

Mattes, Robert et al. *Public Opinion and the Consolidation of Democracy in Southern Africa: An Initial Review of Key Findings of the Southern African Democracy Barometer* (Institute for Democracy in Southern Africa, 2000).

Mattson, I. and K. Strøm. "Parliamentary Committees" in Herbert Döring (ed.), *Parliaments and Majority Rule in Western Europe* (New York: St. Martin's, 1995).

Mazrui, A. and M. Tidy. *Nationalism and New States in Africa* (Nairobi: Heinemann, 1984).

Mbahuurua, V.H. "The Executive Power in the Namibian Constitution: Precept and Practice" in Manfred O. Hinz, Sam K. Amoo and Dawid van Wyk (eds.), *The Constitution at Work: 10 Years of Namibian Nationhood* (Pretoria: VerLoren van Themaat Centre/University of Pretoria, 2002), 38–61.

Melber, Henning. "The Culture of Politics" in Henning Melber (ed.), *Namibia: A Decade of Independence, 1990–2000* (Windhoek: The Namibian Economic Policy Research Unit, 2000), 165–190.

———. "Liberation and Democracy in Southern Africa: The Case of Namibia" in Henning Melber and Christopher Saunders (eds.), *Transition in Southern Africa; Comparative Aspects. Two Lectures* (Uppsala: The Nordic Africa Institute, 2001), 17–28.

———. "From Liberation Movements to Governments: On Political Culture in Southern Africa" *African Sociological Review*, 6/1 (2002), 161–172.

———. "Namibia, Land of the Brave: Selective Memories on War and Violence within Nation Building" in Jon Abbink, Mirjam de Bruijn and Klaas van Walraven (eds.), *Rethinking Resistance: Revolt and Violence in African History*, African Dynamics 2 (Leiden and Boston: Brill, 2003a), 305–327.

———. "Limits to Liberation. An Introduction to Namibia's Postcolonial Political Culture" in Henning Melber (ed.), *Re-examining Liberation in Namibia: Political Culture since Independence* (Uppsala: Nordic Africa Institute, 2003b), 9–24.

———. "Decolonization and Democratisation: The United Nations and Namibia's Transition to Democracy" in Edward Newman and Roland Rich (eds.), *United Nations Democracy Promotion: Ideals and Reality* (Tokyo: United Nations University Press, 2004), 233–257.

Mgaywa, R.M. "Parliamentary Control over the Executive through the Budgetary Process in Tanzania" (unpublished dissertation submitted in partial fulfillment MA political science degree. Dar es Salaam: University of Dar es Salaam, 1990).

Mishler, W. and R. Rose. *Legislatures and New Democracies: Public Support for Parliaments and Regimes in Eastern Europe.* Studies in Public Policy No. 217, Centre for the Study of Public Policy Publications (Glasgow: University of Strathclyde, 1993).

Mmuya, M. *Political Reform in Eclipse* (Dar es Salaam: Friedrich Ebert Stiftung, 1998).

——— and A. Chaliga. *Political Parties and Democracy in Tanzania* (Dar es Salaam: Dar es Salaam University Press, 1994).

Modise, T. "Parliamentary Oversight of the Department of Defense: 1994 to 2003" in L. Le Roux, M. Rupiya, and N. Ngoma (eds.), *Guarding the Guardians: Parliamentary Oversight and Civil-Military Relations. The Challenges for SADC* (Pretoria: Institute for Security Studies, 2004).

Momba, J.C. "Uneven Ribs in Zambia's March to Democracy" in P. Anyang' Nyongó (ed.), *Arms and Daggers in the Heart of Africa* (Nairobi: Academy Science Publishers, 1993), 201–203.

Moore, M. "Political Underdevelopment: What Causes 'Bad Governance'" *Public Management Review*, 3/3 (2001), 385–418.

Morris, A. *The Growth of Parliamentary Scrutiny by Committee* (Oxford: Pergamon Press, 1970).

Mozaffar, S. "Mali" in A. Reynolds and B. Reilly (eds.), *The International Institute for Democracy and Electoral Assistance Handbook on Electoral System Design* (Stockholm: IDEA, 1997), 45–55.

Msekwa, P. *Towards Party Supremacy* (Dar es Salaam: Eastern Publications Limited, 1977).

———. *The Transition to Multiparty Democracy* (Dar es Salaam: Tema Publishers Company Ltd and Tanzania Publishing House Limited, 1995).

———. *Reflections on Tanzania's First MultiParty Parliament: 1995–2000* (Dar es Salaam: Dar es Salaam University Press, 2000a).

———. "Public Hearings as Part of the Parliamentary Legislative Process" *Bunge News*, Apr. 4–6 2000b.

———. *Reflections on Tanzania's First MultiParty Parliament, 1995–2000* (Dar es Salaam: Dar es Salaam University Press, 2001).

Mtei, B. "The Tanzania Parliamentary Committees and SADC Parliamentary Forum" *Bunge News* Apr. 12, 2000.

Mubako, Simbi. "Presidential System in Zambian Constitution" M.Phil. dissertation (London: University of London, 1970).

Mukandala, R. "Civil Service Reforms, Capacity Building and Politics in Tanzania" Paper presented at the 2nd State of Politics Conference in Dar es Salaam, July 4–6, 1994.

Mushota, R. "The Voter, Intra and Inter-Party Relations and During the 1996 Elections: A Comparative Study of Southern, Lusaka and Copperbelt Provinces" Paper presented at the 1996 Elections Project, a workshop held at Pamodzi Hotel, Lusaka, Aug. 7, 1997.

Mwakyembe, H.G. "The Parliament and the Electoral Process" in Issa G. Shivji (ed.), *The State and the Working People in Tanzania* (Dakar: Committee of the Convention on Democratic South Africa, 1986), 16–57.

———. *Tanzania's Eighth Constitutional Amendment and its Implications on Constitutionalism, Democracy and the Union Question* (Hamburg: Literature, 1995).

Naschold, F. and A. Fozzard. "How, When and Why Does Poverty Get Budget Priority? Public Reduction Strategy and Public Expenditure in Tanzania" Working paper 165 (London: Overseas Development Institute, 2002).

Nathanael, Keshii. *A Journey to Exile: The Story of a Namibian Freedom Fighter* (Aberystwyth: Sosiumi Press, 2002).

National Advisory Committee. Establishment Proclamation. The Rebirth of Ghana: The End of Tyranny (Accra: NAC Document, Feb. 26, 1966).

National Democratic Institute for International Affairs. "Parliament Organizations: The Role of Committees and Party Whips" (NDIIA, Proceedings of a workshop held at Club Makokola, Mangochi, Malawi June 15–17, 1995).

National Election Board. *Mirchachin*, Report (Addis Ababa: NEB, June 1994).

———. Outcomes of the May 7, 1995 National and Regional Elections, (Addis Ababa: NEB, June 1995).

———. "Election Officers' Manual" (in Amharic) (Addis Ababa: NEB, 2000).

National Society for Human Rights. *Namibia Disputed Elections 2004: Monitoring National and Presidential Elections* (Windhoek: National Society for Human Rights, 2004).

Neubauer, D.E. "Some Conditions of Democracy" *American Political Science Review*, 61/4 (1967), 1002–1009.

New Patriotic Party. *The Stolen Verdict* (Accra: NPP document, n.d.).

Norris, P. and R. Inglehart. "Cultural Obstacles to Equal Representation" *Journal of Democracy*, 12/3 (2001), 126–140.

North, D.C. "Institutions, Transaction Costs and Economic Growth" *Economic Inquiry*, 25/3 (1987), 419–428.

———. "The New Institutional Economics and Third World Development" in J. Harriss, J. Hunter and C.M. Lewis (eds.), *The New Institutional Economics and Third World Development* (London: Routledge, 1995), 17–26.

Norton, P. (ed.) *Parliaments and Governments in Western Europe*, Vol. 1. (London: Frank Cass, 1998).

——— and D.M. Olson. *The New Parliaments of Central and Eastern Europe* (London: Frank Cass, 1996).

——— and N. Ahmed (eds.). *Parliaments in Asia* (London: Frank Cass, 1999).

Ntalasha, G. "The Search for an Acceptable Constitution" *Weekly Post*, Apr. 10–16, 1992.

Nujoma, Sam. *Where Others Wavered: The Autobiography of Sam Nujoma* (London: Panaf Books, 2001).

Nyukuri, B.K. "The Impact of Past and Potential Ethnic Conflicts on Kenyan's Stability and Development" A Report Prepared for United States Agency for International Development. (Nairobi: Department of History, University of Nairobi, 1997).

O'Brien, G. South Africa's New Upper Chamber, in *Canadian Parliamentary Review*, 20 (1997) www.parl.gc.ca/infoparl/english2on2_97_e.html.

Ojanen, J., Granstedt P. and J. Balch. *Parliament as an Instrument of Peace*. AWEPA, Occasional Paper Series, No. 8 (2001).

Okema, M. "Some Salient Changes in the Tanzania Parliamentary System" in Haroub Othman, Immanuel K. Bavu and Michael Okema (eds.), *Tanzania: Democracy in Transition* (Dar es Salaam: Dar es Salaam University Press, 1990), 37–57.

———. *Political Culture in Tanzania* (New York: Edwin Mellen Press, 1996).

Okoth-Ogendo. "The Quest for Constitutional Government" in G. Hyden, D. Olowu and H.W.O. Okoth Ogendo (eds.), *African Perspectives on Governance* (Trenton, NJ: African Word Press, 2000).

Olowu, D. "The African Governance Crisis: Cause or Consequence of Development Crisis?" Paper presented at the ISS 50th Anniversary Conference (The Hague: Institute of Social Studies, Oct. 9, 2002).

———. "Property Taxation and Democratic Decentralization in Developing Countries" Working paper series No. 401 (The Hague: Institute of Social Studies, 2004).

——— and J. Wunsch (eds.) *Local Governance in Africa: The Challenges of Democratic Decentralization* (Boulder: Lynne Rienner, 2004).

Olson, D. *The Legislative Process: A Comparative Approach* (Cambridge: Cambridge University Press, 1980).

———. *Legislative Institutions: Comparative View* (Amonk: M.E. Sharpe, 1994).

Olson, M. *The Rise and Decline of Nations: Economic Growth, Stagflation and Social Rigidities* (New Haven: Yale University Press, 1982).

Osei, A.P. *Ghana: Recurrence and Change in a Post-Independence African State* (New York: Peter Lang, 1999).

Ostrom, Elinor. *Governing the Commons: The Evolution of Institutions for Collective Action* (Cambridge: Cambridge University Press, 1990).

Ott, M. et al. (eds.) *Malawi's Second Democratic Election: Process, Problems and Prospects* (Blantyre: Christian Literature Association of Malawi, 2000), 13–22.

Ottaway, M. "Ethiopian Transition: Democratization or New Authoritarianism" *Northeast African Studies*, 2 (1995), 67–84.

Owusu-Ansah, R. "Parliament in the Fourth Republic: Lessons Learnt" Address delivered at the 55th annual New Year School organized by the Institute of Adult Education, University of Ghana, Legon, Dec. 29, 2003–Jan. 4, 2004.

Parliamentary Centre, World Bank Institute and the Canadian International Development Agency. "Handbook on Parliamentarians and Policies to Reduce Poverty" (2000). Available from www.parlcent.parl.gc.ca.

Patel, N. "The 1999 Elections: Challenges and Reforms" in M. Ott et al. (eds.) *Malawi's Second Democratic Election: Process, Problems and Prospects* (Blantyre: Christian Literature Association of Malawi, 2000), 22–52.

Paton, C. "Drowning in a Sea of Troubles" *Sunday Times* (South Africa), Feb. 4, 2001.

Patterson, S.C. and A. Mughan (eds.) *Senates: Bicameralism in the Contemporary World* (Columbus: Ohio State University Press, 1999).

Pausewang, S. *The 1994 Elections and Democracy in Ethiopia* (Oslo: Norwegian Institute for Human Rights, 1994).

———. "A Process of Democratization or Control?" in S. Pausewang et al. (eds.) *Ethiopia Since the Derg: A Decade of Democratic Pretension and Performance* (London: Zed Books, 2002), 26–45.

—— and Aalen Lovise, *Ethiopia 2001: Local Elections in the Southern Region*. Report No. 3 (Oslo: Norwegian Centre for Human Rights, 2002).

—— and K. Tronvoll. "The Elections in Context" in S. Pausewang and Kjetil Tronvoll (eds.), *The Ethiopian 2000 Elections: Democracy Advanced or Restricted*. Human Rights Report No. 3 (Oslo: Norwegian Institute for Human Rights, 2000).

Paxton, P. "Women in National Legislatures: A Cross-National Analysis" *Social Science Research*, 26 (1997), 442–464.

Perham, M. *The Government of Ethiopia* (New York: Oxford University Press, 1948).

Pettman, J. *Zambia: Security and Conflict* (Lewes: Julian Friedmann Publishers Ltd., 1974).

Pickering, Arthur, "Instilling Democracy and Human Rights Values in Namibian Society" in *Human Rights Education and Advocacy in Namibia in the 1990s: A Tapestry of Perspectives* (Windhoek: Gamsberg Macmillan, 1995), 101–107.

Pinkney, R. *Democracy and Dictatorship in Ghana and Tanzania* (Basingstoke: Macmillan, 1997).

Price, J.H. *Political Institutions in West Africa*, 2nd edn. (London: Hutchinson and Company 1975).

Przeworski, A. *Democracy and the Market* (Cambridge: Cambridge University Press, 1991).

—— et al. *Democracy and Development: Political Institutions and Well-being in the World, 1950–1990* (Cambridge: Cambridge University Press, 2000).

Putnam, R.D. *Making Democracy Work: Civic Traditions in Modern Italy* (Princeton: Princeton University Press, 1993).

Rakner, L. *Political and Economic Liberalization in Zambia, 1991–2001* (Uppsala: Nordic African Institute, 2003).

Rakodi, C. *The Urban Challenge in Africa: Growth and Management of its Large Cities* (Tokyo: United Nations University Press, 1998).

Reynolds, A. "Women in the Legislatures and Executives of the World: Knocking at the Highest Glass Ceiling" *World Politics*, 51/4 (1999), 547–572.

Riker, W.H. "The Justification of Bicameralism" *International Political Science Review*, 13/1 (1992), 101–116.

Robert, M. "The Voter Intra and Inter-party Relations during 1996 Elections" Paper presented at the Elections Project Workshop Evaluating the 1996 Elections, Held at Hotel Pamodzi Lusaka, Aug. 7, 1997.

Rose, R. *Survey Measures of Democracy* studies in Public Policy No. 294, Centre for the Study of Public Policy Publications (Glasgow: University of Strathclyde, 1997).

—— and D.C. Shin. *Democratization Backwards: The Problem of Third Wave Democracies*. Studies in Public Policy No. 314, Centre for the Study of Public Policy Publications (Glasgow: University of Strathclyde, 1999).

Rostow, W.W. *The Stages of Economic Growth: A Non-Communist Manifesto*. (Cambridge: Cambridge University Press, 1960).

Rustashobya, L. "Fiduciary Risk Assessment for the Provision of Direct Budgetary Support in Tanzania: Summary Focus on Areas of High Risk" Report submitted to Department for International Development (Dar es Salaam: DFID, 2004).

Saffu, Yaw. "Integrity Assessment" in *Global Integrity: An Investigative Report Tracking Corruption, Openness and Accountability in 25 Countries* (Washington DC: Centre for Public Integrity, 2004). www.publicintegrity.org/ga/ii.aspx.

Sagasii, J. "Contempt of Parliament" *Bunge News*, Jan. 7, 1998.

Salih, Mohamed M.A. (ed.) *Environmental Politics and Liberation in Contemporary Africa* (Dordrecht: Kluwer Academic Publishers, 1999).

Salih, Mohamed M.A. *Majoritarian Tyranny in a World of Minorities* (The Hague: Institute of Social Studies, 2000).

———. *African Democracies and African Politics* (London: Pluto, 2001).

———. "Introduction" in M.A. Mohamed Salih (ed.)*African Political Parties* (London: Pluto Press, 2003) 1–33.

Saul, John, "Liberation Without Democracy? Rethinking the Experiences of the Southern African Liberation Movements" in Jonathan Hyslop (ed.), *African Democracy in the Era of Globalisation* (Johannesburg: Witwatersrand University Press, 1999), 167–178.

——— and Colin Leys. "Truth, Reconciliation, Amnesia: The 'Ex-Detainees' Fight for Justice" in Henning Melber (ed.), *Re-examining Liberation in Namibia: Political Culture since Independence* (Uppsala: Nordic Africa Institute, 2003), 69–86.

Saunders, Christopher. "From Apartheid to Democracy in Namibia and South Africa: Some Comparisons" in Henning Melber and Christopher Saunders, *Transition in Southern Africa: Comparative Aspects. Two Lectures* (Uppsala: Nordic Africa Institute, 2001), 5–16.

———. "Liberation and Democracy. A Critical Reading of Sam Nujoma's 'Autobiography' " in Henning Melber (ed.), *Re-examining Liberation in Namibia. Political Culture since Independence* (Uppsala: Nordic Africa Institute, 2003), 87–98.

Schedler, A. "Conceptualizing Accountability" in Andreas Schedler, Larry Diamond and Marc F. Plattner (eds.), *The Self-Restraining State: Power and Accountability in New Democracies* (London: Lynne Rienner, 1999).

Schiavo-Campo, S. "Government and Pay: The Global and Regional Evidence" *Public Administration and Development*, 18/5 (1998), 457–478.

Shaw, M. "Conclusions" in J.D. Lees and M. Shaw (eds.) *Committees in Legislatures: A Comparative Analysis* (Oxford: Martin Robertson, 1979a).

———. "Committees in Legislatures" in Philip Norton (ed.) *Legislatures* (Oxford: Oxford University Press, 1979b).

———. "Parliamentary Committees: A Global Perspective" *Journal of Legislative Studies*, 4 (1998), 225–251.

Simon, David. "Namibian Elections: SWAPO Consolidates its Hold on Power" *Review of African Political Economy*, 27/83 (2000), 113–115.

Smith, B. *Decentralization: The Territorial Dimension of the State* (London: Allen and Unwin, 1985).

Smith, J. and L.D. Musolf (eds.), *Legislatures in Development: Dynamics of Change in New and Old States* (Durham: Duke University Press, 1979).

Soiri, Iina. "SWAPO Wins, Apathy Rules: The Namibian 1998 Local Authority Elections" in Michael Cowen and Liisa Laakso (eds.), *MultiParty Elections in Africa* (London: James Currey, 2001), 187–216.

Sondashi, L. "Human Security and Development: Zambia's Challenges at the Threshold of the Next Millennium" Paper presented at the 15th Pawpa Annual Conference, Aug. 27–30, 1998 at Ibis Gardens Country Hotel, Lusaka.

South Africa, Government of the Republic of. "Background Notes on the Strategic Defense Procurement Package for the Press Statement Issued by the Ministers of Defense, Finance, Public Enterprises and Trade and Industry" (Pretoria: Communication and Information Service, Jan. 12, 2001).

South Africa, Parliament of the Republic of. "Hearings of Standing Committee on Public Accounts Parliamentary: Selection Process of the Strategic Defense Packages; Stockholdings in Department of Defense" (Pretoria: Parliament of South Africa, Oct. 11, 2000).

———. "Final Report of the Ad Hoc Sub-Committee on Oversight and Accountability" (Cape Town: Parliament of South Africa, Sept. 3, 2002).

South Africa, Republic of. Constitution of the Republic of South Africa Act (108) (Pretoria: Government Printers, 1996).

———. "Auditor General's Special Review of the Selection Process of Strategic Defense Packages for the Acquisition of Armaments at the Department of Defense" Report No. 161–2000 (Pretoria: Government of South Africa, Sept. 15, 2000).

South West African People's Organization (SWAPO Party). *SWAPO: The Driving Force for Change* (Windhoek: SWAPO Department of Information and Publicity, 1999).

Steffensen, J. and S. Trollegaard. "Fiscal Decentralization and Sub-national Government Finance in Relation to Infrastructure and Service Provision" Synthesis Report of 6 African Country Cases (Washington DC: World Bank, 2000).

Strøm, K. "Parliamentary Government and Legislative Organisation" in Herbert Döring (ed.), *Parliaments and Majority Rule in Western Europe* (New York: St. Martin's Press, 1995), 51–82.

———. "Parliamentary Committees in European Democracies" in Lawrence D. Longley and Roger H. Davidson (eds.), *Journal of Legislative Studies*, 4 (1998), 21–59.

Subilaga, S. "The role of Parliamentarians in Law-making in Tanzania under Multipartyism: 1995 2000." (unpublished paper submitted in partial fulfillment of BL degree, Dar es Salaam: University of Dar es Salaam, 2001).

Ta'a, T. and Zekarias Kenea. "Constitutional Development in Ethiopia" in Tafesse Olika and Kassahun Berhanu (eds.), *The May 1995 Elections in Ethiopia: The Quest for Democratic Governance in a Multiethnic Society* (unpublished manuscript, Addis Ababa: 1997).

Tamale, S. *When Hens Begin to Crow: Gender and Parliamentary Politics in Uganda* (Boulder: Westview Press, 1999).

Tanzania, Parliament of. "Who is Who for Members of Parliament" Memo published by the Clerk of the National Assembly (Dar es Salaam: Tanzania National Assembly, 2002).

Tanzania, United Republic of. *The Constitution of the United Republic of Tanzania 1977* (Dar es Salaam: Government Printers, Apr. 30, 1998).

Tapscott, Chris, "War, Peace and Social Classes" in Colin Leys and John Saul (eds.), *Namibia's Liberation Struggle: The Two-Edged Sword* (London: James Currey and Athens: Ohio University Press, 1995), 153–170.

———. "Class Formation and Civil Society in Namibia" in Ingolf Diener and Olivier Graefe (eds.), *Contemporary Namibia. The First Landmarks of a Post-Apartheid Society* (Windhoek: Gamsberg Macmillan, 2001), 307–325.

Therkildsen, O. "Public Sector Reform in a Poor, Aid-dependent Country, Tanzania" *Public Administration and Development*, 20 (2000), 61–71.

Tordoff, W. *Government and Politics in Tanzania* (Nairobi: East African Publishing House, 1967).

———. "Residual Legislatures: The Cases of Tanzania and Zambia" *Journal of Commonwealth and Comparative Politics*, (1977), 235–249.

———. and Robert Molteno. "Parliament" in William Tordoff (ed.), *Politics in Zambia* (Manchester: Manchester University Press, 1974).

Tripp, A.M. "Political Reform in Tanzania. The Struggle for Associational Autonomy" *Comparative Politics*, 32 (2000), 191–214.

———. "The Changing Face of Africa's Legislatures: Women and Quotes" in J. Ballington (ed.), *The Implementtation of Quotas: African Experiences* (Stockholm: IDEA, 2004a).

———. "Women's Movements, Customary Law, and Land Rights in Africa: The Case of Uganda" *African Studies Quarterly*, 7/4 (2004b). web.africa.ufl.edu/asq/

Tsebelis, G. and J. Money. *Bicameralism* (Cambridge: Cambridge University Press, 1997).

United Nations Development Program. *Human Development Report 1993* (Oxford: Oxford University Press, 1993).

United States Agency for International Development (USAID) Conference on Conflict Resolution in the Greater Horn of Africa, 2–4 June (USAID: Nairobi, 1997), 45.

Van Cranenburgh, O. "Tanzania's 1995 MultiParty Elections: The Emerging Party System" *Party Politics*, 2 (1996), 535–547.

———. "Power and Competition: The Institutional Context of African MultiParty Politics" in M.A. Mohamed Salih (ed.), *African Political Parties: Evolution, Institutionalisation and Governance* (London: Pluto, 2003), 188–206.

Van de Walle, N. *African Economies and the Politics of Permanent Crisis, 1979–1999* (Cambridge: Cambridge University Press, 2001).

———. "Africa's Range of Regimes" *Journal of Democracy*, 13 (2002), 66–80.

Van Donge, J.K. "Kaunda and Chluba: Enduring Patterns of Political Culture" in J. Wiseman (ed.), *Democracy and Political Change in Sub-Saharan Africa* (London: Routledge 1995a), 193–219.

——— "Kamuzu's Legacy: The Democratization of Malawi"*African Affairs*, 94 (1995b), 227–259.

———. "The Fate of an African 'Chaebol' " *Journal of Modern African Studies*, 40/4 (2002), 651–683.

——— and A.J. Livigia. "Tanzanian Political Culture and the Cabinet," *Journal of Modern African Studies*, 24 (1986), 619–639.

Vaughan, S. "The Addis Ababa Transitional Conference of July 1991: Its Origins, History and Significance" Occasional papers No. 51 (Edinburgh: Centre of African Studies, University of Edinburgh, 1994).

Venter, A. (ed.) *Government and Politics in the New South Africa* (Pretoria: Van Schaik, 1998).

Wehner, J. "Parliament and the Power of the Purse: The Nigerian 1999 Elections in Comparative Perspectives" *Journal of South Africa Law*, 46/2 (2002), 216–231.

Weiland, Heribert, "Landslide Victory for Swapo in 1994: Many New Seats But Few New Votes" *Journal of Modern African Studies*, 32/2 (1995), 349–357.

———. "Namibias Demokratie auf dem Prüfstand: Ist das Experiment gescheitert?" *Aus Politik und Zeitgeschichte*, 27/99 (1999), 21–29.

——— and Matthew Braham (eds.), *The Namibian Peace Process: Implications and Lessons for the Future* (Freiburg: Arnold Bergstraesser Institut, 1994).

Werbner, Richard. "Smoke from the Barrel of a Gun: Postwars of the Dead, Memory and Reinscription in Zimbabwe" in Richard Werbner (ed.), *Memory and the Postcolony: African Anthropology and the Critique of Power* (London and New York: Zed Books, 1998), 71–102.

Wiese, T. "Bringing Down the House: Bicameralism in the Namibian Legislature" *Briefing Paper* No. 23 (Windhoek: Institute for Public Policy Research, 2003), 12.

Woldemeskel, M. *Zikra Nagar* (in Amheric) (Addis Ababa: Berhanena Selam Printing Press, 1946).

World Bank, *Governance and Development* (Washington, DC: World Bank, 1992).

———. *Parliamentary Accountability Handbook* (Washington DC: World Bank Institute, 2000).

———. *World Development Indicators CD-ROM* (Washington, DC: World Bank, 2002).

———. *World Development Report* 2004 (Oxford: Oxford University Press, 2004).

World Health Organization. *Local Government Health Systems: Opportunities and Challenges for Developing Countries. Lessons of Experience* (WHO: Geneva, 1990).

Wrigley, C. *The South African Deal: A Case Study in the Arms Trade* (London: Campaign Against Arms, June 2003) www.caat.org.uk/information/publications/countries/southafrica-0603.pdf.

Wunsch, J. and D. Olowu (eds.), *The Failure of the Centralized State* (Boulder: Westview Press, 1990).

Young, T. "Introduction" in T. Toung (ed.), *Readings in African Politics* (Oxford: James Currey, 2003), 1–18.

Zambia, Government of the Republic of. "Report of the National Commission on the Establishment of a One Party Participatory Democracy" (Lusaka: Government Printer, 1967).

———. *Laws of Zambia* (Lusaka: Government Printers, 1972).

———. *The "Watershed Speech" by His Excellency the President, Dr. K.D. Kaunda* (Lusaka: Government Printers: June 30–July 3, 1975), 23.

———. "Report of the National Commission on the Establishment of a One Party Participatory Democracy" (Lusaka: Government Printer, 1992), 10–4.

Zambia, Government of the Republic of. "Report of the Constitutional Review Commission" (Lusaka, Government Printers, 1995a).
———. "Summary of the Recommendations" (Lusaka: Government Printers, 1995b).
Zielonka, J. "New Institutions in the Old East Bloc" *Journal of Democracy*, 5/2 (1994), 87–104.

Newspapers

BBC News, August 8, 2002 (Tanzania).
Bunge News, October 1999, vol. 11. (Tanzania).
Bunge News, July 2000, vol. 13. (Tanzania).
Daily News, February 8, 2002 (Tanzania).
Debates 13, February 14, 1968 (Zambia).
Debates 113, August 24–31, 1999 (Zambia).
East African, May 5, 2002 (Tanzania).
East African, May 8, 2002 (Tanzania).
Guardian, February 14, 2003 (Tanzania).
Guardian, April 2, 2003 (Tanzania).
Post Newspaper, October 7, 1994. (Zambia).
Post Newspaper, November 8, 1994. (Zambia).
Times of Zambia, March 22, 1969.
Times of Zambia, March 1, 1992.
Times of Zambia, November 16, 1992.
Times of Zambia, July 9, 1993.
Times of Zambia, November 18, 1994.
Times of Zambia, March 18, 1995.
Times of Zambia, June 16, 1995.
Times of Zambia, September 9, 1996.
Times of Zambia, February 12, 1998.
Times of Zambia, February 13, 1999.

Websites

Afrobarometer www.afrobarometer.org/round1c.html
BBC News www.news.bbc.co.uk/1/hi/business/1478244.stm
East Africa www.nationaudio.com/News/EastAfrican/12082002/Opinion/Editorial24.html
Freedom House www.freedomhouse.org
Guardian www.ippmedia.com/guardian/2003/02/14/guardian1.asp
Parliamentary Monitoring Group www.pmg.org.za
Polity IV Country Reports www.cidcm.umd.edu/inscr/polity/Mli1.htm

Interviews

National Assembly staff and bureaucrats

T. D. Kashililah, Dar es Salaam, Aug. 1, 2002, Budget, Project and ICT Coordinator, Parliament Office.
E. Manyesha, Dar es Salaam, Aug. 12, 2002, Parliamentary Draftsman, Ministry of Justice and Constitutional Affairs.
B.F. Mtei, Dodoma, July 27, 2002, Director of Parliamentary Committees.
J.M. Sagasii, Dodoma, July 22, 2002, Director, Legislation and Table Matters, Speakers Office.

Academia, NGOs, media, business

Mr. Bomani, Dar es Salaam, Aug. 12, 2002, lawyer, Attorney General, 1965–1976.
L. Kilimwiko, Dar es Salaam, July 16, 2002, Chai, Association of Journalists and Media Workers.
Prof. Max Mmuya, Dar es Salaam, July 9, 2002, Department of Political Science, UDSM.

Index

Accountability, 183, 258, 259
   Parliamentary, 258–260
ACDR, 135
ADEMA, 81–83
AforD, 204, 207–209, 211, 218–220
Afrobarometre, 85, 89
ANC, 105, 227, 229, 233
APNAC, 260
Apter, E. David, 122
ARMSCOR, 238
ARPS, 122
Auditor General, 231, 237–238

Banda, Kamuzu, 203
Banifield, E.C., 88
Bi-cameral, 16–20, 48
Bond, 121–122
British Military Administration, 164

CDC, 168
Chama Cha Mapinduzi, 184–185, 189, 195, 197
Chamber of Deputies (Ethiopia), 164
Chiefdoms, 4
Chikulo, B., 109
Chiluba, F., 113–116
Chona Commission, 107
City manager, 64
Civil society, 214–215, 216–217
Civil Society, 262–263
Civil war, 53,
Clapham, C., 167
Coalitions, 204–205
CoD, 145
CODESA, 227

Cognitive (mobilization theory), 90
Commission plan, 64
Conflict management, 14
Constituent Assemblies (colonial), 5
Constitution
   Amendment, 213, 214
   Ethiopia, 163
   FDRE, 177–179
   Forum for the Defence of, 219
   Malawi, 202,
COR, 173

DAS (Ghana), 70–72
Democracy (support for), 91
Democratic
   consolidation, 79
   decentralization, 72–73
   transition, 80
Diamond, L., 85
DTA, 144, 149
DUDO, 147

ECA, 249
Economic perceptions, 87
ECOWAS, 49
Election (boycott) 2005, 205–207
Electoral system, 82
Emminghaus, C., 154
Emperor on revised Constitution, 165–166,
EPA, 172
EPRDF, 162, 173, 176, 179
Eriksen, K., 110
ETA, 172
Executive (oversight), 254–256